Praise for the Book

Having led transformational efforts both as a management consultant and as a corporate executive, I found *Rao's* insightful, step-by-step approach on executing a business transformation to be an essential tool for managers looking to build or maintain their company's leadership position. **– Paul Brown, President, Global Brands and Commercial, Hilton Worldwide**

Any business transformation has strategic and tactical components. To make them work in unison is an art and a science. *Mahesh,* in his *Front Runners,* offers an exceptional framework that pulls all the key elements together in a well-choreographed fashion. I highly recommend this book for all business leaders. **– Chakib Bouhdary, EVP and Chief Strategy & Customer Value Officer, SAP**

In Front Runners, *Mahesh* has created a pragmatic but comprehensive framework for driving transformation change. The framework has the necessary structure for the novice and enough flexibility that more mature practitioners can use it as well. **– Randy Pond, EVP, Cisco Systems**

In Front Runners, *Mahesh Rao* has written a smart, concise guide for business leaders looking to transform their company. This book provides valuable frameworks, approaches and tips on how companies can improve their performance. Try any number of ideas in this book and not only will your business grow, but so will you! **– David G. Thomson, Best-Selling Author, Blueprint to a Billion, Mastering the 7 Essentials of High-Growth Companies**

Front Runners is a must read for any executive when faced with the need to drive transformational change in their organization. The 10 step process is the perfect roadmap for the business transformation journey and can be applied at the department, business unit or broader organizational level. The book is easy to read, structured for quick learning and provides the tools and skills for immediate application. **– Kevin A. Peters, President, North America Retail Office Depot**

When *Mahesh Rao* talks about business strategy, he does so with the insight of a practitioner and corporate leader. His "10 game-changing strategies" offer readers fresh perspectives for transforming their enterprises—in good times and more challenging times. Those seeking new ideas for differentiating themselves and their organizations will find much value in this book. - **Prof. Dipak Jain, Dean at INSEAD Business School**

Front Runners is a practical and no-nonsense "how to" book for general managers charged with reviewing, developing and executing successful business strategies. Through a structured and disciplined approach, it teaches how to go from strategy development to results utilizing a number of effective tools and techniques. Front Runners is a thoughtful yet pragmatic book -- a must-read for any business leader. - **Ana Dutra, CEO, Korn/ Ferry Leadership and Talent Consulting**

Front Runners is a must-read for every company seeking a competitive edge. The new world economy forces corporations to transform themselves by making transformation part of every employee's DNA, and *Mahesh Rao* offers a blueprint for how to go about it. – **Joseph M. DePinto, President and CEO, 7-Eleven, Inc.**

The principles in *Mahesh Rao's* book not only help transform companies, but help transform leaders within companies. This book will help you and those around you acquire the kinds of skills you need, to be a true front runner. – **Bill Boltz, Senior VP, Home Depot**

I consider *Mahesh Rao's Front Runners* an action-packed transformational playbook—a must-read for every executive! I'll certainly be adding it to my reference material and to my suggested reading list. - **Alan Maxwell, Chief HR Technology Strategist, Lockheed Martin**

Mahesh Rao has written a guide that businesses large and small can use to orchestrate constant improvement. The book is high-level enough to appeal to management, and contains enough nuts-and-bolts detail that all people can apply its directions to what they need to do. Grab the book and become a leader who puts your organization on a path to robust change! – **Bob Bozeman, General Partner, East Lake Ventures**

We all know that change is inevitable. When the inevitable happens, will you be leading the pack or struggling to keep up? In his new book, Front Runners, *Mahesh Rao* provides a roadmap that will enable you to transform your business by embracing change. Going beyond simply making the case, Rao, offers a practical and systematic approach to the process, filled with real life examples from his many years of consulting with Fortune 100 companies. – **Katherine E. Simmons, President & CEO, NETSHARE, Inc.**

Front Runners provides the insight and mechanisms needed to transform companies from one generation of product to the next in the most effective way. Front Runners approach will allow leading companies to maintain their innovation edge, and will help companies that are stuck to move on to the next generation with compelling products. – **Nick Ilyadis, VP and CTO, Infrastructure and Networking Group, Broadcom**

Front Runner will give you insight into what makes a company great— what makes a small company seem big and what makes a big company stay nimble. The lessons on how to drive company performance are outstanding. – **Brad Cook, Global Vice President of Talent Acquisition, Informatica**

FRONT RUNNERS

Lap Your Competition
With 10 Game-Changing Strategies
For Total Business Transformation

FRONT RUNNERS

*Lap Your Competition
With 10 Game-Changing Strategies
For Total Business Transformation*

MAHESH RAO

Bascom Hill Publishing Group
Minneapolis, MN

Bascom Hill Publishing Group
212 3rd Avenue North, Suite 290
Minneapolis, MN 55401
612.455.2293
www.bascomhillpublishing.com

ISBN-13: 978-1-935098-62-1
LCCN: 2011904099

Distributed by Itasca Books

Cover Design by Alan Pranke
Typeset by Sophie Chi

Printed in the United States of America

**On your way to the front of the crowd,
take time to appreciate all that deserves appreciation.**

To sprint forward without looking back
    is to risk regret for having outrun our history.
The places we have been are central to the places we might go,
    and the people in our lives have helped make us who we are.

For me, my wife and two awesome kids are everything,
    and I have for them nothing but love and high praise.
To them I dedicate this work for their having endured
    a writer's passions—and frustrations.

And to my parents, my greatest heroes on the planet,
    for giving me life and continuing to shape me,
Dad here on earth in ways greatly appreciated
    and Mom from up above in ways indescribable.

Finally to my clients, who bring out the best in me,
    and who ask all the right questions.
You encourage me to explore my thoughts to their depths,
    and for that encouragement I will always be grateful.

To all leaders of training and those who must train,
    know that this is a book for winners.
Know that I am better for having written it,
    and that you, by deciding to read it, have already won!

Table of Contents

About this Book

For some companies, change is something to be avoided until it can no longer be avoided. These companies treat change like an event. Unfortunately, that "event" usually comes in the form of a crisis that wreaks havoc on the organizational structure because there are no ready protocols in place to deal with that change, let alone avoid it in the first place.

For other companies, change is a way of life; it is not just an event, but a part of their organizational DNA—a habit to be learned, coveted, and celebrated. Why do some companies welcome and even embrace change while other companies fear it? Because they understand that change is a regular event. Why not get used to it? Better yet, why not use it to your advantage?

Like it or not, change is here to stay. What's more, change is rapidly evolving—in the pace, the challenge, and the repetitiveness in which businesses experience it. Specifically, the vision, strategy, plans, and roadmaps you and your company developed before the economic "crisis" may no longer be applicable.

Today, customer needs have changed and so has the market landscape. As a result, priorities for companies have shifted. This calls for a game-changing (or transformational) approach—one that turns crisis into opportunity.

With some creative thinking, teamwork, and a systematic approach, you *can* transform a business and gain new ground. With this book, you not only learn how to turn crisis into opportunity but also how to leverage the opportunity to achieve success as *you* define it.

Front Runners: Lap Your Competition with these 10 Game-Changing Strategies for Total Business Transformation talks about change and how front-running companies such as Cisco, Coca-Cola, Apple, and Amazon.com don't run from change but instead embrace it and actually use it to their competitive advantage.

My name is Mahesh Rao, and I call such successful companies "front runners." As an executive consultant for Fortune 100 companies, I work daily with front-running individuals who in turn work for leading front runners in business today.

If your company is doing well, this approach will help you lead the pack. If your company is doing poorly, it will help you do better—maybe even your personal and professional best. This is what I like to call the "front runner approach to total business transformation."

Now more than ever, change is a constant in corporate America. Regardless of whether economic recovery comes tomorrow, next week, next month, or next year, the damage has already been done. Just ask the former executives at Circuit City, Bennigans, Linens 'n Things, Steve & Barry's, Steak & Ale, and countless smaller organizations that ceased operations.

Recessions come and go but change is a business constant. Indeed, recession or no recession, according to a Dun & Bradstreet survey, "The most common causes of business failure are 46% management incompetence and 30% lack of management experience." To be a front runner, either *as* an organization or *at* an organization, leadership must not only recognize the need for change but actively welcome change so that it becomes a part of their daily recipe for success.

This book introduces ten simple steps for business transformation that turn managers into leaders and leaders into front runners. Through a systematic process over a decade in the making, I have introduced these ten steps for companies who may be unaccustomed to dealing with change but who recognize that, without facing change on a daily basis, the crises they face will only get more plentiful—and more serious—over time.

Oftentimes various functions within companies work in silos as a result of employees not getting an opportunity to understand what goes on in other groups or departments. It is important that employees understand how the work they do and decisions they make impact other groups or departments. This book will give every employee a bird's eye view of how well-run businesses operate.

Many people keep asking me how different this methodology is from Six Sigma or Continuous Improvement. These best practices are certainly leveraged where they are appropriate in this book. As a Six Sigma practitioner, I feel that while they help you identify a problem and take it through a resolution process, they are not very effective in transforming an entire organization.

This book does not just recount the importance of transformation; it facilitates transformation through a simple ten-step process, which I liken to a long-distance race that has ten "laps."

These ten steps—or "laps," as I call them—result in a process of transformation that literally helps change the very DNA of your organization.

10 Steps to Business Transformation

Perhaps your product sales have been on a steady decline, or maybe the various divisions or functions in the company are not working in unison, causing efficiency to drop and directly impacting your bottom line. It could be that the sales and marketing teams do not see eye to eye on your go-to-market strategy. Maybe the product management and development team has over-engineered the product, robbing the company of its profits. Perhaps decisions do not get made in a timely and effective manner across the entire organization, causing the company to miss deadlines and even windows of opportunities.

Maybe the problem is the corner office, middle management, the frontline employees, or the back-of-the-store staff. Or maybe your company just doesn't know how to turn crises into opportunities; thus, making changing part of the company's DNA more difficult than it should be.

Whatever your company needs to transform, whichever department is the weakest link, whoever your competition is, these ten game-changing strategies for total business transformation can help you run laps around your competition:

> Lap 1: Draft Your Transformation Charter
> Lap 2: Gather Outside-In Data
> Lap 3: Gather Inside-Out Data

Lap 4: Analyze Data

Lap 5: Craft Your Future State

Lap 6: Design Your Organizational Structure

Lap 7: Assess the Competency of Leaders and Employees

Lap 8: Transform Product and Services

Lap 9: Transform Functions

Lap 10: Define Measures and Roadmaps

The Wheel of Progress—The 10 Steps Illustrated

In Illustration 1.1, you will find what I call the "ten steps to business transformation." This circle of business life, if you will, is literally a wheel of progress that begins and ends with change.

Fundamentally there are three phases that you will be taking your organization through—the ten steps mentioned above fall into these three phases. You begin assessing where you are currently ("As Is" State) relative to where you want to be ("To Be" State) before working on the transition. This is similar to a GPS in your car. The GPS in this case will find out where you are ("As Is" State) and, based on the destination address you type in ("To Be" State), it provides you with directions (the "transition plan" or "strategy").

You'll see that the wheel closely aligns itself to the ten steps listed in the book's Table of Contents. That's because this isn't just a happenstance circular motion but a cyclical process that begins with step one and moves through each step until reaching step ten, and then the process starts all over again at step one. The idea is to make this cycle part of your company's DNA.

If you follow the circle closely you can see the logic behind it. Simply put, you begin by defining the transformational scope and crafting a specific charter to help you achieve that change.

Next comes information gathering: first from the "outside in," observing what customers feel about your products/services followed immediately by gathering "inside out" data relating to your "quality" execution. This data is then analyzed with relations to the vision of the company you will build.

After crafting your vision, i.e., by the halfway point, you are ready to work your way around the rest of the "circle of business life" as you design the organization's structure and assess leadership and employee competency.

Illustration 1.1: 10 Steps to Business Transformation

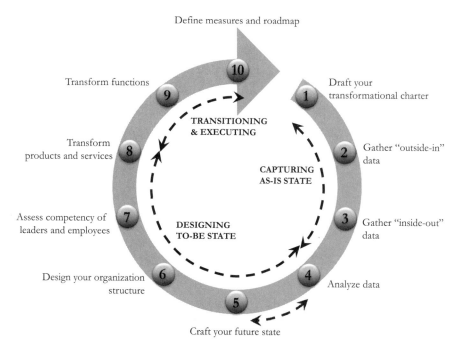

Copyright © Mahesh Rao, 2005-2011

Next you transform your products and services to fit the company's new mission and/or direction.

Finally, you begin the process of functional transformation by following the steps you've put in place for yourself. As the circle ties around and "closes the loop," you enter into an ongoing phase of measurements and roadmaps.

John Kotter is a Professor at Harvard University and widely regarded as an expert on business change. He introduced his eight-step change process in his 1995 book, *Leading Change*, which highlights the eight steps for leading change, namely: 1.) create urgency, 2.) form a powerful coalition, 3.) create a vision for change, 4.) communicate the vision, 5.) remove obstacles, 6.) create short-term wins, 7.) build on change, 8.) anchor the changes in corporate culture.

Having managed and consulted on large-scale "transformation" initiatives for global companies over the past couple of decades, I can say with confidence that these steps are logical. The ten-step business transformation process I am sharing in this book aligns quite well to Kotter's eight steps. The process will walk you through each step in order for you to be able to identify and remedy big gaps relative to your vision and develop innovative products that get the job done better than your competitors. It also clearly describes how all the functions in an organization can work in unison like a well-orchestrated symphony. In other words, it shows you in detail the steps to be a "front runner."

Ready to be a Front Runner?

At the end of the day, being a front runner is all about looking forward and has very, very little to do with looking back. Remember that front runners compete with themselves more than anyone else; that is how they're able to stay ahead regardless of how stiff, or how numerous, the competition is.

Front runners stay ahead because they refuse to slow down. In good times, they forge ahead; in bad times, they grow their lead over the competition. They turn obstacles into opportunities and they are relentless in finding such opportunities.

When the economy, globalization, technology, or a fickle buying public threatens to make them impotent, these companies embrace the challenge through change and find a solution that propels them forward double-time. In short, change is what makes them front runners to start with, not what helps them to catch up and take over.

This is not just another book about "go team," "your attitude determines your altitude," or a series of platitudes designed to make yourself feel better. Instead, this book is about how to systematically make your company better through change. Simply put, transformation is nothing to be afraid of. In fact, change is a necessary and vital part of success and the sooner you splice that "change gene" into your organizational DNA, the better equipped you'll be to lead and the faster you'll move to the front of the pack.

Introduction

The Case for Change

*Economies, markets, and customer needs change over time. This is not necessarily your fault. However, adapting to the change so as to achieve the desired outcome in the most effective way **is** your job.*

Wal-mart	Apple	SAP
McDonalds	Cisco Systems	Hilton Worldwide
Google	Nike	Tata Group
Amazon	Facebook	Ford
Target	Coca Cola Company	LinkedIn
Toyota Motor Company	Procter & Gamble	General Mills
Trader Joe's	Samsung Electronics	Kraft Foods
Netflix	Nissan	Twitter

In every industry and across every consumer need, in every size, shape, and stratosphere, there are front runners—and then there is everybody else running to keep up. The front runner knows what it's like to lead, is comfortable setting the pace (versus keeping it), and truly enjoys the challenges placed upon him or her by the competition.

Which will you be: front runner or pack follower?

Do you want to proactively identify opportunities, or wait for opportunities to come to you?

Will you kick toward the front, making decisions that impact not only your company but the industry you serve?

Could you possibly even lead? . . .

Front Runners

Front runners are a breed unto themselves. These are companies with great teams and leaders—that thrive on challenge, that see opportunity in failure and who never, ever avoid change. In fact, they welcome it! Remember, great teams make great companies not the other way around.

Everybody *wants* to lead the pack, but few know how to do so or, for that matter, realize what it genuinely feels like to be out front—and stay there. To be the front runner means ceaseless competition from established brands and new upstarts alike; both represent equal threats to the front runner's success.

No matter how new, ambitious, or young you are there is always someone newer, more ambitious, and even younger still who wants to lead the pack. No matter how distinguished, solid, and established you are there is always someone who's been around just a little longer and desperately wants to take the top slot away from you.

Think of how long a company like Coca-Cola has "led the pack" in customer service, quality control, cutting-edge technology (to meet voracious demand), and not just adequate marketing but game-changing print, media, and TV ads and social media campaigns. This worldwide dominance of market represents not just a commitment to succeed but a further commitment to face change every single day. You simply can't be a front runner on auto pilot; you can't be a game changer without change.

The Case for Change

Front runners are intimately familiar with change. Change is the reason why Coca-Cola continually produces newer, more entertaining, and more challenging ads than almost any other company on the planet. The same product—with the same exact formula, taste, and flavor that has been in existence for decades—is continually relevant to customers despite changes in market trends.

Change is the reason why Gatorade is continually introducing new flavors and other technologically-improved products. Change is why the iPod keeps evolving, why Amazon.com is continually beta-testing new features, and why Target adds A-list fashion designers to its budget-conscious and ever-evolving clothing lines.

Every company, at some time or another, faces a crisis in which they must literally transform their organization to stay relevant, to stay afloat, and to eventually lead. Front runners experience fewer and fewer major transformations and complete overhauls over time because they have learned the value of making change a part of their organizational DNA from the outset.

Change is Difficult

Change is difficult. If you don't believe me, just try . . .

- ❑ Sitting in a different chair at the dinner table this evening
- ❑ Writing with your left hand
- ❑ Sleeping on the other side of the bed tonight
- ❑ Taking a different route to work tomorrow morning
- ❑ Tying your left shoe before your right (or vice versa)

As I said, change is difficult; particularly when you try to change deeply ingrained habits that have been habitually present for years and years. Take tying your shoes, for instance. No doubt this is a deeply ingrained behavior you formed well before kindergarten.

So if you've been tying your right shoe before your left for years, likely decades, tying your shoes out of your regular order is going to take some time; it may even require a process to facilitate change. Now, if tying your shoe or sleeping on one side of the bed or even sitting in a different chair are challenging, just imagine changing elements of what your company has been doing for years!

Change is Not an Event

Many companies see change as an event; something to do when, and only when, a crisis arises. A product recall, a customer complaint, the loss of a big contract, an employee or patent infringement lawsuit—whatever the crisis may be, this rarity called "change" is brought down off its shelf, dusted off, and put into action only until the crisis has been averted and/or rectified. Then where does it go? Right back up on the shelf until the next crisis comes along and requires more change.

Front runners in every industry have learned to make change a part of their structural DNA. In fact, these companies see opportunities in crisis. This is what separates front runners from the rest of the crowd.

Take Cisco, for example. Even in an economic downturn such as what we are going through at the moment, they have invested more money into developing innovative solutions for target markets, improving customer service, and creating new marketing strategies in emerging markets than the competition.

As a result of these costly but necessary efforts, Cisco has leveraged the current financial crisis to build a lean, mean operation. They have prioritized their investments based on detailed analysis of the opportunities ahead of them. When the market comes back up eventually, they will not only have survived the crisis but also increased their lead as a front runner.

Central to being a front runner is the idea of company-wide "operational excellence" (OE). OE insists on continuous improvement throughout the organization to ensure that every department is working at peak efficiency and effectiveness.

Main drivers for change come from paying attention to the customer, continuously improving existing practices while adding/finessing new ones, and giving employees the power to not only perform their duties but succeed beyond their own expectations. Not surprisingly, OE is central to coming out on top—and out in front.

Here is the thing about leading the pack: every lap involves change. In other words, continuous improvement is not just the endgame but the primary goal necessary to achieve the endgame. There is no finish line for change, only constant and continuous improvement across all areas of the company—not just that "problem" department or "niche" that might need transforming right now.

Who is Your Competition?

Are you afraid of competition? Or do you welcome it? Do you see competition as a threat? Or an opportunity to test yourself in real time— to adapt and continuously improve in order to meet and then surpass your closest competitors?

The answers to these questions matter. How you respond to competition says a lot about how you respond to change because, after all, the more competition that exists the more the need for change on nearly every level of your company.

Here is a secret you may or may not know about front runners: they are in competition only with themselves. True change occurs because the organization recognizes that change must occur to make their products and services better for their customers.

Are front runners concerned with the competition? Absolutely. But are they *obsessed* with them? Hardly. It is merely important to know where the competition stands in order to perform better and serve customers more effectively. That is oftentimes the reason they are out front in the first place; rather than worrying about what everyone else is doing all the time they make a concerted and consistent effort to improve their own operations on a daily basis.

Transformation: A Call to Action

People are often intimidated when they hear worldwide brands like Cisco, Gatorade, Coca-Cola, and Nike, but having been on the inside and taken a good, long look around I can tell you that any success such companies have had is not due to huge budgets, endless staff, or top-notch recruiting. I argue that ALL of the success these companies have had is because of their ability to respond to change rapidly, effectively, and daily, in manners that are both continual and habitual.

Case Study: The 10-Step Process in Action

What can the ten-step process found in *Front Runners* do for *your* company? Well, that's up to you, of course (see illustration 1.1, page xi). But allow me to show you what the very same process you're about to learn did for a global Fortune 100 company I worked with recently.

In 2006 the revenue generated by this company's major division was about five to six billion dollars. (Needless to say, this is one of the most profitable divisions within the company, with several thousand employees geographically dispersed over a wide range of countries, including the US and Canada, Latin America, Europe, the Asian-Pacific region, and various emerging markets such as Russia and other assorted African and Latin American countries.)

The situation this global company came to me with included eight key "problem areas." These "problem areas" didn't just need to be resolved. The entire business needed to be looked at holistically in order to find transformational opportunities:

1. The margins on offerings were dwindling over the years.

2. Revenues were flat.

3. There was no innovation. Service offerings in the pipeline were little to none, and well thought-through new product introduction was nonexistent.

4. There were some major quality issues with products, yet there was no "feedback loop" to the product development teams on the problems being encountered in the field.

5. The organization structure of the services division was not optimal for executing its strategies, and many strategies were being developed in a vacuum.

6. Roles and accountability at all levels were not clear, which resulted in poor execution.

7. There was ineffective decision-making. Most decisions relating to customers were being made far away from customers; i.e., decisions were done centrally here in the US rather than empowering the "theaters" (field) to make appropriate decisions based on local needs.

8. Operating costs were high.

Despite the significant number of issues presented to me, I was nonetheless able to use the ten-step approach provided in this book to diagnose the problems. I led the organization through the process, step by step. As a result, we were able to achieve the company's desired state, beating all established goals for the project.

The results were felt by the customers, partners, the rest of the industry, and even employees outside of this particular division. In fact, most metrics went up across the board. Usually, when a company goes through a transformation of this magnitude many of the metrics take an alarming, if temporary, dip due to what I call "transformational distractions" before they begin to go back up again. In this particular case, the project execution was orchestrated so well that most readings were steady throughout the transformation process and, in fact, some even improved.

The approach helped the company lead the way! The transformation helped this Fortune 100 company raise the bar for itself and the industry. In fact, so successful was the transformation that it received the coveted JD Powers Award for Excellence!

My metric of transformational success is a simple one that starts with this question: Has the organization undergone a superficial transformation, one that will be short-lived? Or has it undergone a deep-rooted transformation, one that is likely to "stick?"

Organizations that have gone through a deep-rooted, DNA-level transformation actively continue to seek out opportunities for improvement at all levels on an ongoing basis (using the ten steps) and do not view transformation as a one-time event.

In this particular case, the company was able to change the very DNA of their organization, specifically they minimized complacency and a "false sense of urgency" to allow a "true sense of urgency" to kick in.

I am happy to report that since the completion of this major initiative over two-and-a-half years ago, *each* of the groups in the organization has sought out and *continues* to seek out change opportunities, and continues to respond to these opportunities by morphing their respective organizations on an ongoing basis. When a front runner is able to enhance the very DNA or culture of an organization using the ten-step process, it is a true transformational success.

Lap 1

Draft Your Transformation Charter

On the road to business transformation, the journey is as important as reaching the destination. Make the experience an enjoyable one for the employees.

As shared with you earlier, business transformation is not an event; it should, instead, become part of the organization's working DNA. To facilitate company-wide change, we must first consider "transformation" a key initiative—or official project—rather than just a familiar buzzword that gets passed around the employee break room with little to no action plan built around it.

In other words, transformation should not merely be a "to-do" item in the back of everyone's minds but a must-do item that requires its own specific charter as the official starting point of your organizational transformation. Only when the project has an official name does it become real; only when it becomes real will action be imperative.

Front runners don't approach the future on a crisis-by-crisis basis but, instead, see crisis as opportunity. What's more, they are constantly embracing changes to turn them into opportunities. In fact, these companies fully embrace a philosophy known as "operational excellence" (OE). They may even call their transformational effort "OE," which implies that they are going to strive for continuous and habitual change across all departments.

Many people say to me, "We would like to achieve operational excellence in our organization, Mahesh, so what do we have to do?" Well, the answers vary. Frankly, this is like saying, "I want to be the best, what should I do?"

The word "best" means different things to different people; as a result, the road to being the best can take you in many different directions.

There are many considerations that go into defining the operational excellence for any specific company. Here are just a few aspects to keep in mind:

- ❑ What is the current "pain" the company is going through? Is it in developing new products quickly? Or providing excellent customer support to customers?

- ❑ How high a bar would you like to set in those specific areas?

- ❑ What is the company's change readiness? In other words, is the maturity of the organization conducive to change?

Front runners in every industry have learned to make change a part of their organization's DNA. These front-running companies empower employees at different levels throughout the organization to identify potential crises, and in doing so prevent them from happening; it is a systematic approach versus a one-time approach. When unexpected crises do come their way, front runners turn them into opportunities.

Who makes up this special team of people? As one might expect, these are functional subject matter experts, movers and shakers within the company. They are revolutionary thinkers and, whether by past exploits, company history, or simply force of will, they have earned a tremendous amount of respect and/or trust from their peers, executives, and the rest of the organization. The most important element from any member of this team is demonstrable commitment to one driving factor: change. Later in this chapter, we'll explore individual roles that make up a successful team.

Define the Charter

Let's be clear: at the end of this chapter you will have all the tools you need to create what I refer to as a "transformation charter." A transformation charter is one that crisply defines the purpose, scope, approach, schedule, budget, roles and accountability, engagement model (how the various teams will be engaged on this initiative), governance model (how decisions get made), etc., for the transformation initiative/project. More details on this in the "The 10

Elements of the Transformation Charter" (page 6). This document, in essence, becomes the blueprint for change at your company, your division, your team, or your collective. It is, in fact, the written foundation for all that is to come next. Consider it a blueprint, of sorts—a blueprint for change. All of the rest of the steps that follow are based on this "blueprint" (see Illustration 1.1). To have a gauge as to what's to come in subsequent laps, refer to Illustration 1.2.

First and foremost, the purpose of drafting your transformation charter is to examine the primary purpose behind this business transformation exercise in the first place. In other words, what is the ultimate objective you want to achieve as a result of this charter (change)? Why are you thinking of transforming yourself and/or the company?

To simply draft a charter, throw a team behind it, and *not* focus on the end result would be worse than mere folly; it would be counterproductive to business on every level. Only if we force ourselves to think objectively about the transformation exercise can we document our goals and objectives clearly. Only if we document our goals and objectives clearly can we articulate with clarity to all key stakeholders and win their support.

Scope is critical to transformation; we must have guardrails if we are to move forward efficiently, effectively—even quickly. Defining what's in scope and what is out of scope will also help us put boundaries around the transformation exercise.

Team identification is also critical to mission success. Drafting your charter will help identify the transformation team (based on a criteria discussed later in this chapter), define the key roles of each team member, and establish accountability for all involved.

The downfall of many a workplace team is miscommunication. Who does what? Why? When? How? This charter-building process will help you define a transformation process that will become well understood so that everyone can align with the same procedure for change.

The process of creating a charter is nearly as important as the charter itself. Part and parcel of this process will be to assess the commitment level of the executive sponsor and other key team members. How committed are they to change? This process will assure you of their commitment or,

Illustration 1.2: Path of Transformation

Lap	Description	Relative Time to Complete	Relative Degree of Complexity	Suggested Participants
Lap 1	Draft your transformation charter—scope, roles & accountability, executive sponsorship, high-level timelines, budget, etc.	Medium	Medium	Executive sponsor, business lead, portfolio manager, division/group/department heads, communications manager, finance, HR
Lap 2	Gather outside-in data—JTBD, ethnography study of job performer, voice of customer, voice of partner	Long	High	Business lead, ethnographers, portfolio manager, interviewers (non-customer facing)
Lap 3	Gather inside-out data—voice of stakeholders, voice of employees, current state data, etc.	Medium	Low/Med	Business lead, portfolio manager, division/group/department heads, HR
Lap 4	Analyze data—Analyze data gathered, prioritize and categorize, growth strategy, investment strategy	Long	High	Executive sponsor, senior leadership, business lead, portfolio manager, finance, HR, division/group/department heads/subject matter experts, business analysts
Lap 5	Craft your future state—Vision, mission, values and objectives; communicate case for change	Short	Medium	Top executives, senior leadership; communicated to all employees, strategy and planning
Lap 6	Design your organization structure—Boxology, roles & accountability	Short/Med	Medium	Executive sponsor; senior leadership, division/group/department heads, subject matter experts, HR, finance and other key players
Lap 7	Assess competency of leaders and employees	Medium	Medium	Executive sponsor, competency assessment experts, senior leadership, HR
Lap 8	Transform products & services—Innovation methodology	Long	High	Product management, product marketing, engineering/development, IT, Finance, Manufacturing
Lap 9	Transform functions—Transform each function, craft engagement model & governance	long	High	All division/group/department heads, subject matter experts, process analysts, strategy & planning
Lap 10	Define measures and roadmap—metrics/measurements, reward systems; craft unified roadmap	Medium	Med/High	Executive sponsor, senior leadership, division/group/department heads, business intelligence, business analysts, finance, subject matter experts

conversely, their lack of commitment, in which case a more appropriate executive sponsor will need to be found.

When we take the time to create a process around drafting our charter, we also help define the constraints or specific guidelines we must impose up front for progress. In short, these are the "non-negotiable" elements and any other specific recommendations the executive sponsor would like to highlight before committing to the process.

Finally, the charter process helps us define precisely *how* decisions are going to be made during the course of the initiative or program execution. We will not only ask such questions as, What? Who? When? Where? More importantly, this process will help us answer those questions in advance so that the entire team knows the appropriate response.

The Direct Approach: Lay the Groundwork for Change by Selecting Your Core Transformation Team Leadership

The first order of business to accomplish during this initial step is to choose the executive sponsor to head your core transformation team. This is the team that is responsible not only for drafting your transformation charter but for implementing it; so, naturally, choosing the right people for the right job will be mission-critical to the success of this venture.

Like any initiative, it is absolutely critical to make sure the executive sponsor is not only committed to this transformation but also qualified to lead it. Don't be content with someone's resumé or reputation. Judge his or her qualifications based on real-time results you can see, touch, and feel.

Specifically, here are some of the traits expected of the core transformation executive sponsor:

❑ It is critical that he/she has the power to influence; has the ability to touch people's hearts and minds.

❑ He/she must be open-minded to ideas from other people.

❑ He/she must have earned the respect of everyone in the organization.

❑ He/she must have the necessary time to actively define and execute the mission.

❑ He/she must have determination and perseverance to deliver the results.

❑ Most importantly, he/she must have the authority to make critical decisions; there will be many critical decisions that need to be made during the course of this transformation journey.

The business lead and portfolio manager are the other two mission-critical positions on your core transformation team. (See below for descriptions of these and other key team positions.) The portfolio manager, with the help of the executive sponsor and business lead, should put together the actual transformation charter we've been outlining so far in this step.

Keep in mind that the charter being developed here will be a draft (a working document of sorts) leading to a final version at the end of lap four.

The 10 Elements of the Transformation Charter

Once your core team is assembled it is important to begin drafting the actual transformation charter they will follow to enact transformation on behalf of the company. It can be easy to fall into the all-too-common trap of putting our energies into simply building the team—but then what? The "then what" question, in this case, is easy to answer because the team is critical to success. It is the team's job to make the company's transformation a complete success.

To that end, here are the ten specific elements that go into the transformation charter:

1. Transformation or initiative name
2. Purpose or objective of the transformation
3. Overall transformation strategy and approach
4. Scope: what's in and what's out
5. Roles and accountability
6. High-level timeline
7. Budget
8. Communication strategy

9. Initiative governance
10. Risk management

For clarity's sake, let's take a closer look at what each of these ten items actually mean:

1. Transformation or Initiative Name: Make it Interactive

A critical initiative like this should be given its own identity, not just for internal purposes but for wider broadcast to the company at large, in order to elicit long-term and popular support, i.e., the "hearts and minds" of the people. You should choose a name that is easy to remember and that signifies what you are trying to accomplish.

Companies, media agencies, and even the military often give their "campaigns" names to increase solidarity and ensure support. Operation Flashpoint, Project Angel Child, Mission Possible, Desert Storm, Assignment Access . . . these are all vital and engaging campaign names that arouse action, interest, and participation on the parts of their participants.

A great way to engage everyone in the organization and jumpstart the initiative is to make the name-choosing process in itself very interesting. Ask people in the organization to come up with a good name. Make it fun, interesting, challenging, and, especially, interactive. Have teams or departments vote on a name before bringing it to committee. Next, announce that the top five names considered will get some interesting prize. Depending on the budget, this could be anything from a pack of ten movie tickets to overnight or even weekend vacations. By doing this, you subtly engage the entire team and/or company into transformation mode. This is change management in action.

2. Purpose or Objective of the Transformation: Making the Case for Change

What do you hope to accomplish through this transformation? What is the "case for change" or "burning platform" you must contend with? These are not mere questions for your own personal pondering but, instead, vital questions that must be answered by the core transformation team before progressing any further.

Without a powerful "case for change," you, as a leader, will not be able to take the entire organization with you on the transformation journey. Now more than ever, this case for change needs to be compelling and powerful. Here are a few compelling and powerful examples:

> "Our customer satisfaction ratings are going down and as a result we are seeing the impact on our sales. Our repeat customer sales have gone down by 70% in the past twelve months."

> "There is no innovation in the company—no new products or services are being offered—and the current products and services are becoming obsolete due to a shift in customer needs."

3. Overall Transformation Strategy and Approach

Keep in mind that the members of the core transformation team have not been relieved of their day-to-day duties while they're putting considerable time, energy, and effort toward the organizational overhaul. Therefore it is very important for you to customize the transformation approach based on urgency, specific employee time availability, and other constraints. After all, the organization is made up of people running various functions/aspects of the business; they are (hopefully) being measured against their deliverables (day-to-day job).

To engage the members in the transformation effort their involvement should not be over and above what they are doing already. If they are already putting in 100% of their time, you cannot throw more at them. (There is nothing like 150%!) To allow for maximum participation in the change charter, something in their day-to-day deliverables needs to be shifted or de-prioritized.

4. Scope: What's In and What's Out

Your definition of scope is vital to the charter's success. It is important to have an agreement on what is within the scope of the transformation and what is not. Is the entire organization going to go through the transformation—or only certain elements?

We need to pinpoint the depth and breadth of scope with specificity. In other words, if a department is within the scope, they need to know that; the team needs to know that. The same holds true for a department, team, or group that is *out of scope*. In or out of scope is not the same as popular or unpopular, or winning or losing; it is simply a specific detail that needs to be known so that proper budgeting of time and resources can begin.

But how do we determine what is out of scope? After all, shouldn't everybody be in scope? Not necessarily. That is why defining the reason(s) for undergoing transformation is so critical to the mission's success.

Share the importance of scope with everyone on the team and play a game with them to add items in the "out of scope" group. For instance, divide the organization into three to four teams and have each team think through what should be out of scope.

Every item proposed should be discussed by the core team and executive sponsor prior to inclusion. While they may get some very good objective determinations on what should be out of scope during this step, they may also get some not-so-bright ideas that should be dismissed.

While it is quite important to consider what items may go into the "out of scope" category, it is equally important to restrict what goes into this list. The more "out of scope" areas you have, the more you will restrict the transformation, which could potentially lead to a sub-optimal transformation.

5. Roles and Accountability

Pick only your "best and brightest" to lead this critical team. After all, this will be the most important initiative the company will work on for the next several months. Once a decision has been made to move forward with the initiative, it is absolutely critical to define certain key roles and identify appropriate people to fill them. Here are the types of team members your charter will require and the various attributes you should be looking for in these key personnel:

Executive sponsor: As shared earlier, this is the person who, at the end of the day, is accountable for the transformation initiative. This individual needs to have the power and authority to be able to drive change. You must select someone who is highly respected at all levels of the organization. This person's commitment in making this initiative a success is very critical and cannot be emphasized enough. When it comes to OE, this critical team member will set the direction for the transformation efforts and will be the go-to person for any critical escalations.

Business lead: This person is relatively senior in the organization (perhaps a level below the executive sponsor). While the executive sponsor will spearhead the initiative, the business lead will naturally manage the day-to-day operations of the initiative itself. This person plays the role of a strategist and has enough knowledge about the industry to perform duties at the expert level.

Portfolio (or program) manager: The portfolio manager develops the transformation plan and manages it. Therefore, this person needs to be someone very experienced in managing a portfolio of projects.

Key stakeholders: These are members of the executive team, whose support will be important for transformation success.

Subject matter experts: These are experts in specific areas; they will be leveraged from time to time, as appropriate.

Communications manager: This person develops a well thought-out communications plan and executes it.

Facilitators: There will be several group activities at multiple levels of the organization, so a pool of good facilitators is needed to moderate such activity. Preferably, they should be from outside the organization so they can remain neutral and objective during such proceedings.

Change management strategist: Someone who identifies behaviors within the organization that inhibit the organization from reaching its objectives.

These are not necessarily HR people, but some companies have HR team members who have been trained in this area. Again, objectivity is critical to this position's success.

Change ambassadors: When you want true change to happen at every level and function of the organization, you need to build a team of department representatives. These "ambassadors" check the pulse in their respective areas of responsibility and channel the information back to the initiative team. They also manage change within their respective areas under the guidance of the change management strategist (see above).

Measurements ambassador: The role of measurement ambassadors, or "metrics ambassadors," as they are also known, is to effectively be subject matter experts, change agents, and risk identifiers throughout the transformational journey.

Financial representative (someone from the controller's office): This vital individual studies the financial impact of the transformation throughout the transformation journey.

Human resources (HR): This person plays a critical role when we reach steps six and seven of the ten-step process. To that end, certain team members will inevitably take on a lead role for a given step, and then step into the background for the rest of the journey. For example, HR will take on a lead role in making sure that lap seven (Leadership Competency) gets done the right way. Similarly, measurement ambassadors will lead the effort, working with other teams in lap ten (Metrics and Measurements). I encourage the program manager to assign appropriate roles in each of the steps along the journey.

6. High-level Timeline

The timeline for any project obviously depends on that project's scope, budget, the charter team's availability, etc. This high-level timeline can be reset or the scope can be adjusted, depending on the detailed project plan.

The reason this is called a "high level" timeline is because it incorporates guidance from the executive sponsor. For instance, is this a quick, three-month transformation, or are we doing a more thorough transformation that may take six months or more? Since the executive sponsor is the gateway for all the vital information required to make such a determination, this decision will ultimately be his or hers.

As can be expected, this high-level timeline also depends on the "burning platform" (or strong case for organizational change), size of the organization, complexity of products and services, etc. So, again, this is just meant to be a guideline for the initiative (program) planners.

7. Budget

It is important to make sure the executives recognize the need for dedicated resources for the project and consequently set aside an appropriate budget for successful execution of the initiative.

The size of the budget depends on the size of the transformation and availability of dedicated talent within the organization to lead and manage the day-to-day administration of the transformation.

It is highly recommended an outside consultant(s) leads steps two through four so as to make sure the data-gathering is not biased in any way. Carrying this perception across the organization is quite important. Such consultants must be accounted for accordingly in the budget.

8. Communication Strategy and Plan

Change does not happen in a vacuum. For true business transformation to succeed, you and your core transformation team will need to communicate effectively within the team, through various departments and, occasionally, with the company at large.

Having a well thought-through communications plan is crucial to the success of your transformation. At this point, you may not have answers to fill in the entire template, as it will be a work in progress. However, using the template below will force you to think about the preliminary questions: what needs to be communicated, to whom does the change apply, when will it be appropriate to begin implementing change, and how will critical messages be communicated?

This person will, indeed, collaborate very closely with the executive sponsor, business lead, and change management strategist. Illustration 1.3 can assist you to think through elements you would like to communicate. Make this a working document and update it appropriately as you go through the transformation journey.

At this point, communicating the "case for change" is important. Keep in mind that currently it will still be at a high-level message. Once all the gaps are identified (in lap four), you will be in a better position to highlight the case for change with specific details.

9. Initiative Governance

Change is a process. In any transformation, certain critical decisions need to be made throughout the journey. The size and scope of these decisions and their impact on the company requires us to ask some pretty challenging questions long before we begin the process itself:

- ❑ What are the various categories/levels of decisions that need to be made?
- ❑ Who will make these decisions?
- ❑ How (or what process) will be used to make these decisions?
- ❑ How will the decisions be communicated?
- ❑ How will you define your plan to run the transformation initiative?
- ❑ Will there be weekly (bi-weekly? monthly?) core team meetings?
- ❑ Who is the core team?
- ❑ How will these meetings be run?
- ❑ Who facilitates them?
- ❑ What is the escalation process? This is a process that defines how to escalate matters toward resolution if and when there are issues.

Illustration 1.3: Communications Strategy and Plan

Lap	Communication objective	Audience	Who will create content?	Who will communicate?	Date to create content by?	Date to send communication by?	Communication vehicle	Success metric
Lap 1								
Lap 2								
Lap 3								
Lap 4								
Lap 5								
Lap 6								
Lap 7								
Lap 8								
Lap 9								
Lap 10								

In most cases, the executive sponsor is not part of the weekly meeting. In that case, how will the executive sponsor be kept in the loop? Also, how will the key stakeholders be updated on the progress?

In most successful transformations, the program manager takes on the role of facilitating these weekly meetings as well as delivering regular status reports/updates to the stakeholders. The business lead and the program manager together can update the executive sponsor on developments and escalations as the transformation progresses.

The program manager typically is the one managing the agenda for these weekly meetings and reporting on progress. For effective operation of the meeting, the team should be optimal in size—not too large, not too small. When determining size, see what makes sense for your organization. When picking the team, make sure to:

- ❑ Include strategists and revolutionary thinkers.
- ❑ Include key members from the leadership team that are resistant to the transformation idea (this is a classic change management strategy).
- ❑ Consider having someone from another organization (perhaps even from your stakeholder group) who does not have a vested interest in the outcome or process; this helps bring an unbiased view to the proceedings.
- ❑ Include members from middle levels of the management team; this will help in two distinct ways:
  1. It will give lower levels of the organization comfort that they have their interests represented and that the decisions are not just being made in an ivory tower.
  2. It will help with the adoption as well, as this person will help serve as a "change ambassador."

10. Risk Management

Finally, never lose sight of the fact that creating transformation is like performing leg surgery on a marathon runner while the patient is still sprinting toward the finish line! There are a lot of risks in doing transformation when in operation, so it is vitally important to highlight risk management as part of the charter.

We established early on that people aren't being taken away from their day jobs to be on the core transformation team but, instead, are being asked to perform additional duties. One potential risk is that of employees burning the candle at both ends. This very serious risk could result in the employee's work suffering in both areas. Other negative side effects include high burnout rate, lack of retention, etc.

Another potential risk in announcing a transformation is that employees may find this to be foreshadowing of "a sinking ship." They may try to jump ship before going down all together, resulting in high employee turnover due to uncertainty. This is why it is also exceedingly important to highlight the risk of *not* doing the transformation. Oftentimes this is more important than the inherent risks of doing it in the first place.

Next, identify others in the leadership team of the organization that, given their unique and varied life, work, and professional experiences, may contribute some beneficial changes. Engaging them with a draft will help them get a bird's eye view of not just the process but the impetus for change itself.

You may be surprised by how they may respond to not just the charter but the reason for its being. Their input in refining the charter is critical at this juncture. Besides, by doing so you are making them part of the transformation process. There is a better chance of adoption/buy-in if you engage the team members in a dialog and get their input during this early stage of the process.

5 Tips for Drafting Your Transformation Charter

Knowing what goes into your transformation charter is just the beginning. Actually drafting such an important piece of internal legislation can be challenging for first-time team members. The following five tips were designed to help you draft a transformation charter:

1   **Be committed:** Don't proceed with the transformation initiative without complete conviction that you have the commitment of the executive sponsor and the members of the core team. Timing—and commitment from the top down—is everything. If you have the time but not the commitment, going forward with the transformation could do your organization more harm than good.

2   **Consider a bonus program** for those directly involved with the initiative. Remember, these people are doing extra duty, not parallel duty. Even if their day-to-day deliverables are scaled down they are still present, and to get maximum results it is important to respond to employee realities. Consider recognizing and rewarding the transformation team based on milestones and results. Examine what motivates the people on the team.

3   **Customization equals optimization:** This step is applicable for all types of businesses, including small/medium businesses and large global enterprises. The key aspect that may be different is the scale or scope and the overall transformation strategy. Regardless of the type of business, you can customize each of the ten steps. (Of course, you need to read the entire book to understand them all.)

4   **Be honest, upfront, and reasonable.** When you are trying to make a case for change, you are trying to move your audience from a state of complacency to a state of true sense of urgency. Going overboard and putting pressure on people will cause an irrational or false sense of urgency, which could be detrimental.

5   **Benchmarks are beneficial:** Your team will need to see progress to stay motivated through an ongoing transformation, which, in my experience, can last from three to six to nine to twelve months (or more). While you don't need to constantly pep your team up, setting realistic goals and assessing progress through regularly published benchmarks will give executive team members a sense of accomplishment and pride. Consider throwing small celebratory parties every three to four milestones (depending on the budget and duration of the transformation, of course).

The 4 Kinds of People in Any Company

We all know them, that certain "type" who seems to pop up in every company, on every team, in every organization, on every board. While stereotyping or labeling employees isn't always beneficial, knowing what category a potential team member might fall into does have its benefits. For instance, there is no room for whiners, complainers, or slackers on a transformational team, so these would obviously be people to avoid. From my experience there are four kinds of people in any company:

1. **Those who are complacent**: These are people who are content with the status quo and absolutely do not see opportunities in crisis. In other words, they are not front runners and likely never will be. Complacency may seem like it's a benefit when things are going well, but as we all know things won't always go well. In that sense, complacency is like "interior rot," allowing

employees, teams, and entire departments to grow stale and tired.

2. **Those who have an irrational or "false" sense of urgency**: This is perhaps the biggest population in a corporation. These people think they have a solution to the problem without even understanding the problem all that well in the first place. They spend endless hours in meetings running around like chickens with their heads cut off. While this type of flurry of activity may seem productive, make no mistake: these are activities without a clear purpose. Such activities are driven by pressure from management that creates anxiety and anger. This is more distracting than useful. People mistake running around for a real sense of urgency (see below).

3. **Those who have a true sense of urgency**: These individuals look for opportunities in crisis. They come to work every day ready to cooperate energetically and they take pride in launching innovative initiatives. They do not believe in moving at 40 mph if 65 mph is required to win.

4. **Those who are completely unaware** of the situation the company is facing and hence maintain the status quo out of fear or ignorance. Though this is a smaller crowd than the other three categories, you would be surprised to know that such people still exist.

Change Management and Communication

I realize this step may seem superfluous to some change leaders who prefer action to contemplation. However, if I may add, it is one of the most critical parts of lap one. You don't intend to take your entire team to the new destination blindfolded, do you? So I urge you to take the time to not only complete the charter but, more importantly, to communicate appropriately along the way. After all, the more time you spend up front doing a thorough job on this, the better prepared the team will be to execute it and achieve the action you desire. I encourage you to begin cataloging your communications in a spreadsheet format similar to Illustration 1.3.

Information is vital to success, but not everybody in the company needs the same information at the same time. Once you have the charter ready, take the time to communicate elements of the charter only to key stakeholders at this point. (Communication to the entire organization will be done after lap four.)

Part of the plan should be for the senior-most person in the organization to participate in the communication to demonstrate the importance of the transformation. Remember, just because you recognize a true sense of urgency or case for change doesn't mean everybody else will. Having a top dog, head honcho, or VIP in the organizational chain announcing the transformation will increase the credibility and help with adoption.

Consider having the executive sponsor communicate the "case for change" at the highest level. Remember that it is critical we touch the hearts and minds of the key stakeholders (not just the minds, as is often done through data analysis). Make the communication as visual as you possibly can, perhaps through charts, graphs, Power Point presentations, and even accompanying printed reports. This will help make a strong and impactful case for change. We will do more of this in Lap four, when highlighting specific areas of transformation to the entire organization.

Case Study: Sponsor's Commitment Pays Off

Recently a leading network equipment company came to me with a true sense of urgency surrounding their unique case for change. I quickly realized that, given the parameters of their distinctive dilemma, they were ripe for the ten-step program we are utilizing in this book.

The case as stated concerned one of the larger divisions of this global company, which was facing a variety of very solvable issues, including:

❑ Dwindling profit margins

❑ Lack of a common unified vision

❑ An organizational structure that was not aligned to the vision or strategy

❑ Little to no innovation (i.e., no new services in the pipeline)

If you look at these items closely, you can see how a few were actually time-critical, and this is where the ten-step process is so vital to embrace fully and completely. Despite the time pressure to increase profit margins and get some new services in the pipeline, this particular company recognized its strong case for change and made the internal commitment to a transformation charter.

They took the time to build a charter and put together a team around the charter. Now, as is the case with many companies, some of the stakeholders were very pushy in moving forward to eradicate these problems quickly, but the executive sponsor managed the expectations and took the time to develop a sound charter to not only a.) solve today's problems but also to b.) avoid tomorrow's problems as well (i.e., he instinctively realized that change is not an event).

Perhaps the best part about this story is the level of commitment the core transformation team was able to get from key leadership positions. Case in point: to solicit ownership of the transformation and give it more credibility, the senior-most executive of the organization (a senior VP) was so passionate about the true sense of urgency involved in this transformation that while returning from a business trip to visit a major customer, he dialed in from the airport to "build" upon the case for change; he cited examples of his discussions with the major customer, and his enactment of his discussion with the customer helped the teams visualize the issues. He was able to make a compelling case for the transformation and the urgency involved in making it quickly.

The intent was to move the stakeholders away from complacency and yet not push them into a false sense of urgency—it is a fine balance, which is what the executive sponsor and the senior VP were able to do through this meeting. The leader was able to get everyone's attention by openly sharing what he heard from the field. He also did a fine job in positioning the case for change as an "opportunity" rather than a doomsday prophesy. An informal poll at the end of the meeting showed that 100% of the attendees were able to appreciate the issues shared by the leader and show eagerness in working with the leadership team not only to resolve these issues but also prevent them from happening in the first place.

What I love about this story is the commitment of the organization from top to bottom. Without some of the pressure from stakeholders, I'm not sure this company would have had the success it eventually did. Everyone was committed to "change" and, in particular, took the time to draft a sincere and effortful charter that truly reflected the unique opportunities for this company. As a result, all four of the critical challenges this company faced were turned around on time—and on budget—to put the company on the right track and, more importantly, to keep it there.

Lap 1 Key Takeaways

- Review and understand the ten specific elements that go into the transformation charter.

  ❑ It is necessary to take the time to create a charter (to enact change) now in order to drive change tomorrow.

  ❑ Change takes hard work upstream (now) to payoff big downstream (later).

  ❑ The case for change must be powerful enough to initiate the often painful process of real, lasting change.

  ❑ Time or money isn't enough to warrant change; a commitment to change must be made.

  ❑ Senior leadership buy-in and engagement is crucial.

  ❑ Key leadership positions must be chosen very carefully.

  ❑ Roles and accountability must be defined.

  ❑ What is in/out of scope must be defined to be truly effective.

  ❑ Highlight and communicate the high-level "case for change" to the core team and key stakeholders at this point. (You will need to communicate to the entire organization with clarity during lap four.)

  ❑ Benchmarks are critical to ensure success.

  ❑ Realistic goals are more important than lofty ones.

  ❑ The time to be aware of risk is now (versus later).

  ❑ Elevate the transformation effort to "initiative" status with dedicated resources and budget.

Lap 2

Gather Outside-In Data

*The greatest source of learning comes from observing your customers.
If you solve their toughest problems through your
products and services, they will solve yours!*

Customers have a job to be done. Do you know what that is? Clayton Christensen and coauthors wrote about the "Job to be Done" (JTBD) concept in the *Sloan Management Review* (Spring 2007), stating, "Most companies segment their markets by customer demographics or product characteristics and differentiate their offerings by adding features and functions. But the consumer has a different view of the marketplace. He simply has a job to be done and is seeking to hire the best product or service to do it."

A few years ago a good friend of mine attended a seminar hosted by Dr. Clayton M. Christensen, who is also the author of "The Innovator's Dilemma" and the person who coined the phrase "disruptive innovation." The latter phrase "describes a process by which a product or service takes root initially in simple applications at the bottom of a market and then relentlessly moves 'up market,' eventually displacing established competitors."

I was told that during the first part of his seminar he shared some great examples of disruptive innovation, and in the second part of his talk he encouraged companies to focus less on customer and product segmentation and instead ask the question, "What jobs are your customers hiring your products to do?"

He told a story of a fast-food restaurant that wanted to sell more milkshakes, so they did what many firms would do: they interviewed their customers to discover exactly what features they wanted in a milkshake. Then they took the results of that research and used it to build the perfect milkshake that their customers described.

The sales neither went up nor down! In spite of their building this great milkshake that they were sure was going to hit their customers' sweet spot, sales remained flat. So they hired a team of consultants to watch how people purchased milkshakes throughout the day, including how they came (drove or walked), how they were dressed, who they came in with, the time of day, etc. And they found something very surprising.

It turns out that the majority of milkshakes were sold early in the morning to customers who stopped by the restaurant alone and purchased only a single milkshake, on their way to work. Finding this interesting, they began to interview these customers, and they found that what the customers had in common was that each one had a particularly long commute to work in the morning.

It turns out that the job they were "hiring" the milkshake to do was to accompany them on their long drive to work. But why milkshakes? Well, as Dr. Clayton M. Christensen shared, if you wrote a help-wanted ad for the milkshake's "job," it might look like this:

Wanted: Reliable Food For Long Drive.

Must be sweet, cold, and filling. Must fit in cup holder, require only one hand to consume, and last for most of the trip. Must not make a mess in car or on clothes. Must be sugar-free and relatively low in calories. Coffee, bagels, candy bars, sodas, and breakfast sandwiches need not apply.

As you can appreciate, many of the milkshake customers had tried other products for the job, but none of those products had the unique combination of qualities that made the milkshake the perfect fit for their tacit job requirements. And it wasn't really even about the quality of the milkshake; it was about the general characteristics of the product that made it right for the job that the customers were hiring it to do.

So in an attempt to improve the sales, the restaurant moved the milkshake machine to the front of the store and made it self-service so that these customers did not have to wait in the breakfast lines. They could come in, get their milkshake, swipe their card, and go—all this in less than two minutes. They also increased the diameter of the straw so as to allow for pieces of fruit to flow through.

In the end, it wasn't about what features the customers thought would make a great milkshake. It was about discovering the unspoken job description in the customer's mind that made the milkshake the perfect candidate for that job.

Job Performers and Influencers

As shared in Illustration 2.1, you will need to gather both job performers' behaviors as well as their influencers' opinions. "Job performers" are those people who perform the specific task to accomplish JTBD. "Influencers" on the other hand are people who influence "job performance" in making decisions at appropriate steps leading to accomplishing a JTBD.

Illustration 2.1: How to Gather Outside-In Data

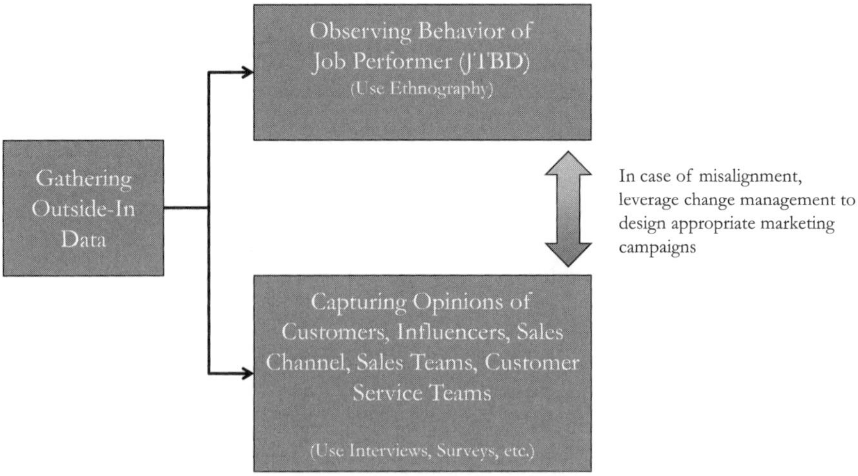

Gathering Outside-In Data

Observing Behavior of Job Performer (JTBD)
(Use Ethnography)

Capturing Opinions of Customers, Influencers, Sales Channel, Sales Teams, Customer Service Teams

(Use Interviews, Surveys, etc.)

In case of misalignment, leverage change management to design appropriate marketing campaigns

Let me illustrate through example: Let's say the JTBD is setting up high-end audio/visual equipment for home. In this case the job performer is a "prosumer" (*Pro*-fessional *Con*-sumer) and influencers are audio/visual equipments reviewers, audio/visual experts at specialty stores, audio/video enthusiasts, etc.

If you are an audio/visual equipment manufacturer looking to make success out of your product line, you will need to understand the true needs of the job performer (in this case a "prosumer") as well as the criteria used by the influencers to influence the job performer's purchase. This will also help you understand how far off the influencers' opinions are from the true needs of the job performers. You can then manage change by influencing the influencers in the right direction through appropriate marketing campaigns.

Apple understood very early the importance of influencers and the power of influencing. They built Apple stores where the "Apple Geniuses" took the time to influence and convert people one customer at a time.

Knowledge is Key

Front runners in the business world thrive on talent, motivation, skill, persistence, and a variety of other vital assets that propel their success. Each front-running company is unique in its own definition of, and journey toward, success. However, ALL front runners use the same basic fuel— knowledge—as energy to propel them to the top.

Data-gathering is a critical part of total business transformation. The key to remember here is that transformation cannot be done in a vacuum. First and foremost, the charter established in lap one exists to enact change on behalf of the company. Data-gathering is critical to that change.

There are two types of data-gathering:

1. **Outside-in Data:** is collected from outside the organization to effect change from within.

2. **Inside-out Data:** is collected from inside the organization to effect outgoing change.

Data collection takes considerable time and effort. If not done right, the problem you attempt to solve for the customer may be the sub-optimal

Illustration 2.2: Steps to Gather Outside-In Data

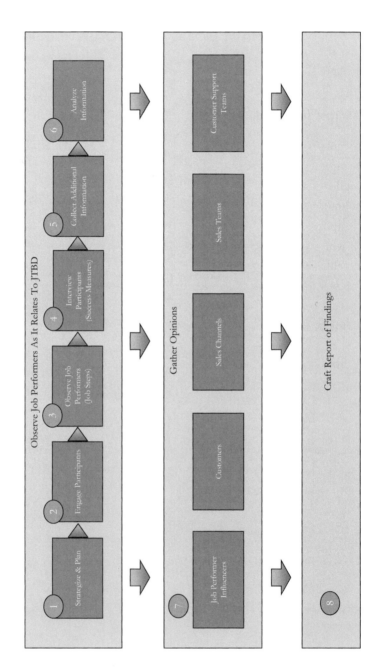

Observe Job Performers As It Relates To JTBD

1 Strategize & Plan
2 Engage Participants
3 Observe Job Performers (Job Steps)
4 Interview Participants (Success Measures)
5 Collect Additional Information
6 Analyze Information

Gather Opinions

7 Job Performer Influencers
Customers
Sales Channels
Sales Teams
Customer Support Teams

8 Craft Report of Findings

one or perhaps wrong one altogether. Remember, our job at this time is to identify the job our customers are trying to get done, to employ outside-in data gathering techniques. This will then determine the best way to help them get the job done. Approach this lap with caution and take the time to gather the (outside-in) data.

Observing Behavior

Ethnography is an art and science that is used in observing a job performer (including customer/potential customer) in completing his or her JTBD. Data collection is often done through participant observation, interviews, questionnaires, etc. For best results, however, you will need to hire a trained ethnographer who can provide the discipline associated with collecting qualitative data in the field and then accurately analyze the findings. Experts in this field are highly sought-after and can help you in gathering critical data that you would have otherwise missed.

This approach involves eight key steps, as shown in Illustration 2.2. Let's take a look at each of the steps to see what it entails:

1. Strategize and Plan

First you need to make some critical decisions:

What market segment would you like to focus on?

It is recommended that you consider focusing on all market segments that your organization plays in. In other words, all market segments your products and services are currently engaged in. This kind of effort, however, costs money and takes considerable time. If you have time or budget constraints, take the time to decide where you want to focus your efforts. Do not worry about new markets or new offerings as they will be dealt with in lap eight.

Who are the participants you would like to focus your study on?

Before answering this question, you will need to define the criteria to identify appropriate "job performers" to do this study on. It should be noted that there could be multiple job performers to get a JTBD completed. In this case you would study each of the job performers. It is important to understand each of the job performer's contributions to the overall JTBD.

Take care to make sure they are a good representation of the market segment you are going after. Pick those that use your competitors products or services to get their job done, as well as those that use yours. I highly encourage you to focus on identifying the right representation of job performers rather than just focusing on customers that bring maximum revenue and profit. Doing the study over a wide target audience within your market segment will help you understand where you stand relative to the competition.

How will you observe the participants (job performers)?
This can be covert (watching participants do a job without them knowing) or it can be overt (watching participants in front of them). An ethnographer can assist you with the approach.

When do you plan to observe the participants?
Depending on the product or service you are selling, you need to make a decision on when you want to observe the customers. Here are some suggestions:

> *Researching the product/service (pre-selection)*: This method looks at the participants' behavior prior to selecting the product/service. The data gathered will help you get information on how customers research products/services that will fulfill their need (or "job"). What website(s) do they go to? What search engine(s) do they use? What "key words" do they put into the search engine to do the search? When is this search done (in a proactive or reactive timeframe)?

> *Selecting the product/service*: This method looks at the participants' behavior in selecting the product/service. Who makes the selection? An individual or team? What role does the individual play? Who is the decision maker? What criteria were used for selection? What companies were

in the shortlist? How long did it take for them to make a decision?

Purchasing the product/service: What is the approval process? What questions came up (if any) during the approval/purchase process? How long is the buying cycle? What budget category does it come out of?

Unwrapping and installing the product: If this is a product, who unwraps or installs it? What was their unwrapping/installation experience like? How long did they take? What problems did they encounter?

Using the product/service: Who is the actual user of the product? When is the product used? What job is this end-user trying to get done? What key steps are involved? How long does it take to get the job done?

Servicing the product: If there is a service component involved, how does that get done? How do they know when to get it done? How do they schedule one? How do they pay for it? What budget does it come out of? Likewise, how do they get additional or replacement parts?

Disposing the product: If it is a disposable product, how do participants dispose of it? How do they know when to dispose of it? Where do they dispose of it? Who ultimately disposes of it (a community or state organization or a specialized or private trash or recycling organization)?

Where will you observe the participant?

In their homes, place of work, or a public place? It is important to note that in ethnography, you are observing people in their native environment, not in a lab or a "controlled environment" like focus groups.

How long will the study take place?

Remember you are trying to understand customer needs here, not gather statistical data. The quality of participants is more important than quantity.

Again, the above are just a few sample questions an ethnographer may employ when working with you to develop an overall strategy and plan.

2. Engage Participants

Once you have identified the participants that you want to study, then you will need to reach out to them and obtain their permission. Consider rewarding them for their time and valuable input. Make sure you explain to them the purpose of the study and what type of information you will be gathering, and most important, how the information will be used. Even if you are observing people covertly in a store or a mall or at the front desk, you will still need to approach the management or owner for permission.

3. Observe Participants

When you are doing an ethnography study you are trying to observe and take notes on how/what job the customer is trying to get done. Your job is to first of all understand what job the customers are trying to get done, and then understand the role of your product or service in the JTBD. You will also note what their expectations are. Are they using your product/service as it was intended? How does the customer appear to feel about the job they are getting done and, specifically, your product? What are the other products/services the customer uses to complete the job?

Here are some of the details an ethnographer takes notes on:

- ❑ Date and time
- ❑ Location
- ❑ What events or actions immediately (observably) led up to the job in question? What did the person do after the job was done?

❑ Sensory impressions: sounds, sights, textures, colors, smells, tastes, etc.

❑ Specific description of the "Job to be done" (very Important)

❑ Steps taken to achieve the job (also very important)

❑ Duration it takes to get the job done, and then the duration it takes to use the product/service

❑ Potential problems encountered

❑ Questions about people or behavior for further investigation

4. Interview Participants

Depending on the product or service, you may want to consider interviewing the customers soon after your observation. The key question to ask job performers is what their measure of success is at each step as well as for the overall JTBD? If for example the JTBD is getting tickets for a concert, then there would be a series of steps leading to completion of the job. In this case the steps could be browsing for all the concerts in your area, identifying the one you like, taking a look at ticket availability and then choosing a best seat before providing your credit card and purchasing the ticket. The overall success measure for the job is to get the best seating for the concert of your choice at the lowest price. Each of the steps leading to the completion of the JTBD may have its own success measures. It could be time, price, convenience, right seating location, etc. Ask follow up questions on success measures. If there are multiple people involved in completing the job, observe all of them and interview them as well.

These interviews can definitely provide additional insight. Take care to be sensitive to the participant's beliefs, opinions, and concerns. Do not make the participant uncomfortable at any point in time.

In some countries/states there are laws pertaining to recording or videotaping. Consult your general council, as appropriate. Later in the chapter there are specific interviewing techniques discussed that may be of additional value to you.

5. Collect Additional Information

Collect any additional information you might find that the participant is willing to share. For example: Software version number, process map diagrams, etc. This can also include competitor information, homegrown diagrams, manuals, and cheat sheets. These can help you paint a more complete picture.

6. Analyze Information

With all the information you have gathered on the customer, namely through a.) observing participants, b.) interviewing participants, and c.) any additional information you can find, now it is time to compile all this data and analyze it. Watch for patterns or trends that can help you hypothesize.

7. Capture Opinions

So far you have observed each of the job performers performing their respective tasks collectively leading to JTBD. In this step you will be gathering opinions of the following:

(a) Influencers

(b) Customers

(c) Sales Channels

(d) Sales Teams and

(e) Customer Support Teams

You can leverage interviews, focus groups, and surveys to capture their opinion. You can also use this opportunity to find out more about the customers' business. This can help you be ahead of the curve in seeing if the job steps or even the JTBD might change in the near future. In other words, this data can help you forecast trends, etc.

Later in this lap we will outline exactly how these opinions can be gathered through various approaches, including 1.) face-to-face interviews, 2.) telephone interviews, 3.) focus groups, and 4.) surveys. We will also discuss all the tools and techniques necessary to help capture this external data in an effective fashion, including what types of questions to ask and how to tabulate all the information for easy analysis downstream.

8. Craft Report of Findings

Steps one through seven may have to be repeated for each of the job performers that have a role to complete the JTBD in your target market. Once done, I would highly encourage you to validate your finding with a larger customer base. This can help you improve your accuracy.

The report of finding you will be crafting at this point will be overall for each of the key products and across the entire customer base as shared above. This documents your conclusion as well as recommendation(s). This information will be used throughout the transformation process— in almost every lap from this point on.

The Gift of Customer Intimacy

It's one thing to build change around a company's needs. Indeed, it's only natural that those needs come first. Neither success nor failure occurs in a vacuum. To truly effect change that lasts and increase opportunities, you need to set your priorities and goals consistent with the customers' needs.

The big question becomes, which of those customer needs align with your goals and can be profitably met? After all, companies don't exist merely to fulfill customers' needs, but do so in a way that aligns with the larger company vision. Lap two helps us capture the information we will need (now) to ultimately find the answers to these important questions (for use later in lap four).

The outside-in approach may seem antithetical to how corporations are run. But as we all know, it's vital to step out of our comfort zone and see how these high-level theories, hypotheses, and product launches are doing in the real world; thus, the outside-in approach becomes a valuable exercise for testing the realistic opportunities we've created for ourselves internally.

Gathering Opinions: Information is Power

Job Performer Influencers

As explained earlier in this lap, depending on the product/service, experts' opinions may be sought by job performers, especially for critical decisions. Understanding who these influencers are and what criteria they use for recommending can be a powerful catalyst in making your product a success.

While observing participants (job performers), be sure to observe which influencers they reach out to at each of the steps leading to the JTBD. Then interview these influencers as part of step 7 (above).

Customers

Let's face it. If you ask customers what features or solutions they want, they can lead you in a wrong direction, as seen from the milk shake example. However, the information they can provide is literally priceless when it comes to completing a transformation charter for your company. Why are their opinions important, you ask? Well, apart from making the customer feel loved by your reaching out to them, it will most certainly help you understand more about their business and how your products and services are helping or hurting them. It will also help you understand how far off their opinions about product features may be from their true needs. This can then help you market the products appropriately.

Broadly speaking, you can get valuable data directly from the customer through three sources:

1. Customer Satisfaction Surveys
2. Voice of Customer (VOC)
3. Social Media

Most companies conduct customer satisfaction surveys on a regular basis, either after the sale or on a periodic basis. The data you get here for the most part is "reactive" by nature—meaning the customers are giving feedback on existing products or services on a post-sale basis. Customer satisfaction surveys are something that the organization should be doing in the normal course of business (to spot check existing products and new product launch results), and are usually designed to address how well you are doing the things you are typically expected to do.

To fully acknowledge the level of transformation the organization is undergoing, it is critical to have VOCs that validate the customer insights you gather. Also, the voice of customer (VOC) information will help you proactively identify specifically that which is not working so well—perhaps long shipping cycles or poor customer service, etc. The idea is not to respond to customer complaints after the fact, but instead to be proactive and constantly innovative, so as to cater to the changing requirements of the customers with time. VOCs can be conducted through a formal, structured approach or through an unstructured, informal (ad hoc) approach.

In all the talk of high-tech data-gathering and social networking that's being batted about these days, it can be easy to jump on the bandwagon of what we now refer to as "social media," i.e., Facebook, YouTube, Tumblr, Twitter, LinkedIn, et al.

While the benefits of social networking are still being explored, personally I see social media as a great way to gather information. However, it is not ready for large-scale business consumption just yet. These sites, while popular, are not specifically designed from the ground up with businesses in mind, as they were originally intended for consumers.

Social media can and should be leveraged to engage everyone in your "business ecosystem." This, however, can be achieved only *after* businesses are able to better control/manage the information flow. A good example of where companies can leverage social media is in the area of product design and development, and we will be highlighting this in lap eight. Social media is a way to proactively interact with customers and gather their opinion.

Regardless of how you get it, or even where you find it, information is power. All the information you gather means nothing, however, if you do not analyze the information and take appropriate actions based on it.

Sales Channels (Partners, Distributors and Retailers)

Many companies rely heavily on customer information via outside channels to determine the VOC. For instance, major publishing houses regularly rely on their distributors—and major bookstore chains—to tell them what is selling a.) above expectation, b.) below expectation, or c.) just about as expected. This helps them mark trends, tailor their publication pipeline, and decide which books to publish next quarter.

Why not copy this successful business model for your own industry? Distributors, in particular, can help you determine VOC by region, and they can continually add to your body of knowledge concerning current customer demands on a region-by-region basis. Now, depending on the type of product or service you sell, you may or may not have a channel to help you sell the product. If you do use outside channels, they can often provide very valuable data and even provide insights on trends.

How can a distributor or retailer help you spot a trend? Think of, let's say, Croc shoes. While this comfortable, affordable fashion footwear seems to have come out of nowhere, feisty and fact-finding companies quickly caught whiff of this growing trend and were able to respond with Croc-like items, such as the generic-style rubber clogs found in the "Mart" stores and even Croc-like accessories. And these accessories attune to every imaginable need, such as little buttons—shaped to appeal to everyone, from Mickey Mouse fans to Star War fans—that pop into the ventilation holes on top of the shoes.

How did those first responders to the Croc wave of success find out about it? Did they have a magic ball? A psychic? Hardly. They were able to tap into their goldmine of information resource experts, like distributors and even retail shop owners, who are consistently feeding them information on what's hot and what's not.

Now, in the "what's not" department, Crocs are feeling a kind of backlash as many feel they are overexposed and bad for the feet. What will be next? In footwear or elsewhere? People know. And those people are quite often your distributors and retailers who have their fingers on the buying population's pulse.

Naturally, what goes for footwear trends (or even bestsellers) also holds true for gardening equipment, pet food, music and fashion trends, toys, games, etc. The key is to find allies in your channels and continually seek information from them. Ask them questions like:

- ❑ Given the changes in your country/region and industry, how do you see the customer needs changing?
- ❑ What are the current customer challenges?
- ❑ Based on early orders, what are emerging trends?

A Word About Your Customers: B2B Versus B2C

This lap is critical to companies of all sizes and types (B2B and B2C), as it is critical to know your customers to the fullest extent possible.

Oftentimes people struggle with the questions of "Who is our channel?" and "Who is our true customer?" For example, if your company manufactures mp3 players, selling through Best Buy and other retailers, who is your customer? In this case, the end-customer is the consumer and Best Buy is the channel.

Remember, in this case you are marketing your products to the consumer, not to Best Buy. In some instances, companies like Costco and Walmart resell products in their brand name and do considerable product customization and the necessary marketing to sell the products. In this case, these companies wind up being the customers.

The rule of thumb is: if a company that buys products directly from you adds considerable value (in this case, perhaps, product customization, marketing, etc.), then these companies end up being a customer. In either case, identifying the "end customer" is crucial to pure data collection.

As we delve deeper into this lap, I don't want you to get hung up on B2B versus B2C; we all have customers, and these customers provide us information. That information is the power we seek, not an endless debate over who, exactly, our customer is. So whether your "customer" is a VP at a Fortune 100 company or a little old lady buying her gardening supplies at a dollar store in Scranton, these principles—and this lap—will work equally well for you.

Also, in a B2B situation make sure you are gathering data from the right person. Give enough thought to who this might be—the actual user of the product/service or the decision maker (the person who signs the checks)?

Sales Team

While information and reliability can often be in question through your distribution and retail channels, you have a secret VOC weapon right under your nose—and on the payroll. After all, the sales team (YOUR sales team) meets customers on a regular basis. They understand the competitive landscape very well and, what's more, understand what the customers' unmet needs are. They can share with candor what customers feel about your products/services and can share what is preventing them from making a sale.

We all know what the sales folks, in general, always want: lower price with more functionality. Likewise, we know these broad strokes don't really provide answers to the higher-level questions we ask. In order to avoid hearing the "lower prices, more functionality" sales speak chorus, make it a priority to identify sales folks who are strategic in their thinking.

Mastering the 5-Why Technique

When engaging the sales folks in a dialogue, I often use the 5-Why Technique. By repeatedly asking the question "Why" (five times is a good rule of thumb), it is possible to peel away the layers of symptoms to identify the root cause of a problem.

Why five why's? Very often the first reason for a problem will lead you to another question and then to another. Although this technique is called "5 Whys," you may find that you will need to ask the question fewer times than five—or more than five times—before you find the issue related to a problem.

This technique works quite well to get to the root cause because with each question you're "drilling down" to the information you really seek. So, instead of focusing the questions internally, make them customer-centric. Here is a good example of the 5-Why Technique in practice:

Sales: The customers are not buying our products.

You: Why?

Sales: Because they are buying it from our competitors.

You: Why?

Sales: Because our competition has lower prices.

You: Why?

Sales: Because the competition is able to make the products cheaper by reducing the cost of goods (COGs).

You: Why?

Sales: Because they have eliminated a couple of features that we have in our product.

You: Why?

Sales: Because apparently they are not important to our customers.

As you can see, you can get a wealth of information from almost anyone who touches the customer using this simple 5-Why Technique.

Customer Service or Support Teams

In addition to your sales staff, you have another paid division in your company from which to draw valuable VOC resources. Customer service teams have a wealth of VOC information at their fingertips as well. They have case notes on product-specific support issues or even customer-specific data.

Customers share with them their frustrations about certain products, and sometimes even provide a "wish list" of products, services, features, or benefits they "wish" you would/could provide. If you analyze the data closely enough, you can gain valuable insights to recurring problems (quality issues perhaps) and identify interesting trends.

How to do that? Customer service departments are one of the most vastly underutilized divisions in companies across the globe. As I've stated previously, most companies use their customer service departments to "spot check" an issue that may be presenting itself or to time stamp a new product launch. This is back-runner thinking.

Front runners should engage customer service teams very early in the product development cycle to get their guidance on what feature designs might cause potential problems and how they can be avoided.

Front runners must thoroughly analyze and eventually organize their customer service departments to not only spot check and troubleshoot customer complaints, but also to analyze and sift through incoming data in order to:

- ❏ Spot trends

- ❏ Avoid problems

- ❏ Develop new products

- ❏ Reward customers for vital information

- ❏ Improve brand loyalty

Simply by adding an extra line to a questionnaire or by directing phone operators to ask one more relevant question—such as, "How did you learn of this product?" or "What do your friends think?" or "Would you recommend this product to a friend?" or even "What new features would you like us to offer?"—you can mine additional information at no extra cost, either to you or the consumer.

If you're a fan of Netflix, you're already familiar with this "one more question" technique. Oftentimes when I return my latest DVD, I will get an email asking, "When did you send in [insert title of DVD here]?" I am then prompted to click on a box next to a corresponding date; it takes me all of three seconds and, since I'm generally a satisfied Netflix customer, I willingly provide this information. Perhaps subconsciously, I assume that simply sharing this data will help them get DVDs to me faster in the future.

Reports

Many other reports can provide useful outside-in information. Often, the company already has such reports on hand. For example:

Quality Council Reports: If your company has these kinds of councils, then there can be some valuable data that you capture from these reports.

Industry/Market Reports: Most companies have stopped subscribing to industry and market reports these days, as the information is considered static and irrelevant. I am not a big fan of these either. However, if you are in an industry where this trend is different, by all means refer to them. While the data cannot be completely relied upon, it can certainly be looked at as another data point for our analysis in lap four. There is a good likelihood your marketing department subscribes to these reports. Before buying any new reports reach out to a few people within your company to see who might have them. If you do not have them, do not go overboard spending considerable amounts of money, as there is a good likelihood you can find most of the information on the Internet.

Product/Service Reviews: Sometimes this information can provide information on market trends, such as "the latest high-tech gadgets," "what generation Y is buying," "attracting the Boomer market," etc. Such analysis is compiled into reports, books, and/or articles available to the public for purchase (or borrow from libraries) from companies such as CNET, PCMag. com, Consumer Reports, etc. The goal is not just to read the reports and take them at face value but, instead, to analyze the data and apply it to your own unique company viewpoint.

Remember, the name of the game here is outside-in analysis, so do not hesitate to rely upon tried and true methods of gathering customer trend data through such avenues, especially from respected market sources.

The Internet

Nowadays, information on customer trends, buzz, and wants (what clientele really want) is often a mere two or three clicks away. The worldwide web can provide some interesting data on market trends, competition, pricing, etc.

If the products you make are targeted toward consumers or the component your organization manufactures goes into consumer products, there is a wealth of information in the customer feedback sections at websites like Amazon.com, CNET.com, PCMag.com, etc.

Customers on such sites are brutally honest, and if you are in the market with similar products, features, or services you can often learn what not to do at another company's expense.

Following the VOC Chain of Command

I'm not suggesting that you add insult to injury by both starting a complete business (or departmental) transformation AND revamp your entire VOC information-gathering protocol! In fact, I'm urging you to use the resources at your command and be completely mindful of your information channels'— sales and customer service departments'—existence within a kind of VOC "Chain of Command" in order to utilize what's close to you first before branching out to the actual consumers themselves.

So before talking to the customer directly, try gathering as much information as possible from your very own (and often internal) sales teams, customer service/support teams, and any other teams that touch the customer directly. Once you have educated yourself with key facts, start moving up the chain of command. That's right, in this chain of command the customers are at the top.

Here is how that chain might look: First, talk to the internal teams, then the distribution channel, and, finally, talk to the customers themselves. This will help you better prepare for meeting with the customer by asking the most relevant questions.

Not following the chain of command when you're seeking VOC information is a lot like shopping without your grocery list. If you're not prepared, you're likely to wind up with that all-too-familiar "kid in a candy store" syndrome in which you reach for everything in the store without knowing why. A proper list of items you want and need will help you make the most of your shopping trip.

Following this same metaphor, meeting with customers directly is like "shopping" for vital VOC information. The better prepared you are, the more customized, specific, and effective the results are likely to be. This will help inform your transformation with real-time results you can count on, as opposed to secondhand knowledge that has no relevance to you, your company, or your transformation efforts.

For instance, if your organization does regular customer satisfaction surveys, review them in advance, prior to preparing the questions; this will allow you to focus your questions better and help you come up with that "shopping list" you'll need. It also helps for the interviewer to read up as much as possible about the customer prior to conducting the interview.

If it is a progressive exercise and requires more than one interviewer to talk to all of the customers from the selected list, put one person in charge of selecting and supervising fellow interviewers. Consider bringing in a consultant to do interviews of all key stakeholders. Besides giving everyone the perception of the resulting data being unbiased, it will help gather sensitive information that people would have otherwise hesitated to share.

If you are a smaller company without a customer service department or one large enough to handle both their daily duties and an additional VOC information quest, why reinvent the wheel? There are companies that specialize in setting up processes, and even conducting customer satisfaction surveys—such as Walker Survey, Allegiance, NBRI, etc.

When it comes to the interview scenario, don't try to make it a day-long event. Try to capture answers to all of your questions in just one sixty-minute meeting. Remember, customers are busy and you will need to perhaps get back to some of them again (in lap eight, particularly), so do not use up all of their time now. This time limit will also force you to be thoroughly prepared so you can achieve your objective within a given timeframe.

It's also important to appropriately appreciate customers for taking time out of their schedules to answer these questions. And it's not just the customers you should be thinking about. Consider rewarding/compensating the customers, distributors, and even your retailer "insiders" for their time and valuable input.

For instance, you might offer them free tickets to local movies, theaters, or a sporting event; gift cards to various restaurants; or even discounts on your products. Check with your corporate legal department to make sure you are not violating any policies of your company or your customers. In most cases small gifts are okay.

The point is not to "buy" information but, instead, to enter into a partnership with customers, channels, and retailers alike so that they want to actively share information because they now have a personal, as opposed to just professional, relationship with you.

Master Your Medium: 4 Ways to Gather Information

When it comes to gathering information, you have quite a few options to choose from. For the purpose we are trying to achieve, I have included here four very effective ways of doing just that.

Which approach you choose depends on many factors, including the type of customer, your location(s) relative to customers, what level person you are speaking with (CEO versus manager), complexity of product/service offering, etc.

When soliciting such vital information it is important to remember that it's best to do it right the first time—and create a protocol for doing it right every time—rather than simply going through the motions and throwing a handful of people (or money) at the issue. So carefully examine the four following information-gathering means to determine which is most appropriate to help make your company a front runner:

❑ Face-to-face interviews

❑ Telephone interviews

❑ Panel interviews

❑ Surveys

Parting Words About the Interview Process

When it comes to the interview questions themselves, don't hand the customers a printed list of your questions, thinking it will put them at ease. It won't. It will only distract them.

Instead, allow every interview to be as personalized as possible. This works best in face-to-face and phone interviews, of course; but even a panel interview can become personalized when you delve more deeply into a consumer's response.

To that end, do not hesitate to ask follow-up questions during an interview, if necessary. Except for surveys, all of the other types of interviews allow for personalization and follow up.

Finally, consider what I call the interview "bookend" process. Assume that every interview has one bookend, the "invitation," and a second bookend, the "thank you." Send out the meeting invite from the executive sponsor (preferable) or someone senior within the company. The same is true for the "thank you" note (or present). In fact, ideally, the same person who sent the invitation should send out the thank-you note.

When Hi-Tech Meets Personalization: Alternative Interviewing Methods

Today we are fortunate enough to live in a world where the above four options aren't our *only* four options for interviewing customers to collect our precious data. There are other high-tech approaches that you could consider as well, such as "tele-presence" or "video-conferencing."

For instance, for high-tech consumers in high-tech markets, they might actually warm to a tele-presence or video-conferencing option in regard to their busy schedule or simply their personal preference.

In fact, for some customers, you may be able to enhance all of your data-collection needs online. You may send them an electronic invitation (an e-vite), for instance; set up an online tele-presence or video-conference using existing computer capabilities; and even thank them via an online gift certificate to their favorite movie theater, restaurant, online service—even Netflix!

The goal is not to enhance your comfort level so much as the consumer's comfort level; so, if you're in a low-tech business, if you have a low-tech customer base, or if you simply hit across a low-tech audience, don't push the online options as much. Again, know your audience; do what's best for them, not necessarily for you. While it may be more convenient and cost-effective for you to do things one way, you won't get reliable results if your consumers aren't in their comfort zone.

Eliciting Opinions and Additional Information: A Strategic Approach

In all of the above cases, make sure that the questions are well thought-through and relevant. Generic questions supply generic responses, while specific, thoughtful, and meaningful questions elicit the same in kind.

Also, before committing to a full interview onslaught, first find out if your company has reached out to customers/partners in the recent past. The last thing you want to do is repeatedly reach out to customers/partners with similar questions. This clerical oversight will reflect poorly upon the company by creating the perception that the left hand doesn't know what the right hand is doing.

Never forget the human factor in this type of technical interaction by overstepping your bounds and asking for too much "free" information. For instance, I mentioned earlier in this lap how impressed I was that Netflix bothered to ask me when my DVD was shipped or, on another occasion, about the video quality of the instant documentary I'd just watched online. Once or twice a month it's fine for them to nudge me for such information, but if they were doing it every other day—simply because one department didn't realize they'd just sent me a nearly identical email—I wouldn't be so "happy" about it.

There are two key aspects to keep in mind when reaching out to people (especially customers) and asking them for feedback:

1. Higher expectations: By nature, when you are asking people for input they automatically have a higher expectation of your organization; there is no going back from here. It is more damaging to the organization if true transformation does not happen (after customer feedback) than returning back to the status quo. You are setting an expectation by going through this initiative in the first place.

2. Realistic expectations: On the flip side, it is important for the customers to know that not every input they give will be adopted and executed. The input will go through internal analysis and get prioritized. Setting the expectation is a fine balancing act and needs to be handled with care.

To avoid setting unfair expectations or disappointing your personnel and employees, strategize how you are going to communicate the purpose of the interview. By "strategize" I mean to get very specific. Ask yourself:

- ❑ Who are we going to ask questions to at the customer site—a senior executive or a line manager?
- ❑ How many questions per customer?
- ❑ How many follow-ups?

VOC: A Step-by-Step Approach

Whichever approach you use, low-tech or high-tech, one-on-one or panel interview, you should make sure that you use the same approach consistently across the entire data-gathering exercise.

Mixing and matching various approaches will not get you consistent results. You will not be able to compare feedback like apples to apples. To make the information as valuable as possible, do not gather data using multiple approaches. Instead, use face-to-face interviews for some and use surveys for others.

Data gathered from a face-to-face interview, for instance, simply isn't the same as data collected using a survey. One is not necessarily better than the other. As we have seen, depending on the size of your company, experience of interviewers and even complexity of your product will guide your decision. A survey might be more appropriate for you over a face-to-face interview, or vice versa. The problem is blending various responses from various types of interview formats.

What is needed is a strategic approach that is used across the board, regardless of who the customer is, who the interviewer is, and even what type of interview you're conducting.

Specifically, when conducting a VOC here are the steps you need to consider:

1. Define the Objective

Before going on a mission and reaching out to customers by asking a bunch of questions, you should have a clear objective. After all, if we don't know the purpose for these questions, let alone what we're going to do with the answers, why should there be customer buy-in?

So ask yourself: Is the purpose of this exercise to truly engage customers in a dialogue so as to identify product/service gaps? Is it also to send the message to your customers that you are serious about the relationship, and you "finally" want to take some action?

It helps to highlight your "primary" and "secondary" purpose or objectives here. Be honest with yourself. After all, it's okay if your goal with these questions is more for the purposes of realigning your company versus making your customers feel warm and fuzzy (for now).

For instance, when it comes to transition, your primary purpose may be to "identify gaps" while your secondary purpose may be to "engage customers." Position the interviews appropriately, especially when you send out the invitations and begin the actual interview. Highlight the objectives appropriately with them. It's okay to be open and honest with them—it helps you build trust.

There is no such thing as getting "too specific" when detailing the interview process. It is always preferred at this point to ask decision-makers the questions. In lap eight you will get an opportunity to ask appropriate questions to the actual users of the product at the customer site. If your customers are end consumers, then gather as much data as possible in this step directly from the sales channels (for example retailers, etc.); then such consumers will be interviewed in lap eight with very specific product/service-related questions.

2. Decide Upon Your Information-Gathering Approach

If multiple people are interviewing, then it becomes critical to let all of the interviewers know the protocol concerning where and in what format to save the notes. You don't want Susan taping her interviews and storing them on disc, Robby taking copious notes on the laptop and backing them up only on his computer, and Sally taking shorthand that no one else can read!

You may want to go so far as to have a template or interview worksheet mocked up beforehand. Depending on the interviewer, it can be taken in longhand and recorded on the computer later or simply used as an open document on the computer and stored electronically afterward. Transcribe notes (Word or Excel format) from the interview and then save them on the server.

Whichever format you use, make sure these are backed up, perhaps once individually on a flash drive and again on the network server. Losing this data after the interviews can be disastrous. In large companies the interview data can be backed up on a commonly accessible site, while in smaller companies you may designate one computer for all the files and then back them up via disc or memory stick.

Next, decide on how—exactly—you are going to catalog/document the information captured. For instance, is the data collected going to be saved on interviewers' laptops or on the network? And, if it is on the network, make sure only the core team has access to it. Where on the network will the information be stored, and who will have access to it? Finally, be sure to decide on the document format—Works, Word, Excel, PDF, etc.

3. Prepare Questions

Once you decide on the approach for VOC, it is then time to draft the questions for the interview. This process must go in order because it is important to know the format before writing the questions. After all, questions on a survey will naturally be less open-ended than those in a face-to-face or phone interview. So decide on the format first, then write the questions. Remember that you are also trying to validate your observations from the ethnography study—so do not forget to take into consideration the findings from the ethnography study.

Sample Questions for VOCs or Surveys

These are just a few sample questions you may want to consider asking your customer. Please note that these are for B2B companies. Appropriate questions can be put together for B2C companies as well. Again, as mentioned earlier in this chapter, these are generic questions. You need to add specific questions to the list:

1. What are your customer's top business priorities and investment areas?

2. What changes in trends is your customer seeing in your industry? What impact does that have on the customer or customer's company?

3. What are the customer's top five strengths and weaknesses?

4. What are the top five threats and opportunities the customer sees for their company? How can we (your company) help?

5. What are your customer's key business issues (if applicable)?

6. What is the customer's problems/need?

7. How will your product solve the customer's problem/need?

8. What are the customer's specific needs that must be satisfied to address the customer's problems?

9. What are the priorities of these needs? What's most important to the customer in making a buying decision?

10. In thinking about your organization's competitors, which one company comes to the customer's mind?

11. As per your customer, what are the strengths and weaknesses of our product(s) versus the competition?

12. Who else from the customer's company should you invite for such a meeting? (Or . . . Whom can you work with in your customer's company to get specific feedback about your own products/ services?)

13. How does your customer receive pre-sales assistance for the product/ services you sell? How do you rate it?

14. How does your customer receive post-sales support for your products/services? How do they rate it?

15. How does your customer rate overall satisfaction with your products, services, support, and field sales?

16. Considering what you charge for your products, services, and support, how does the customer describe the price: a.) very low, b.) low, c.) moderate, d.) high, e.) very high, or f.) don't know/not enough experience.

17. How does the customer rate the overall value received from your product/service given what they pay? a.) excellent value for money, b.) very good value, c.) good value, d.) marginal value, e.) poor value, f.) don't know/not enough experience.

18. How would it impact your customer if your company did not exist and they had to choose a product from a competitor?

19. What is the likelihood that your customer would recommend your products, services, and support to a friend or business associate?

20. What is the likelihood that your customer will continue using your products, services, and support?

21. How do your customers describe doing business with you? Have the customer indicate their level of agreement (ten being the highest agreement and one being the least) with the following statements:

   a. Easy to do business with

   b. Customer-focused

   c. Innovator

   d. Cost-competitive

Add additional questions based on findings from the ethnography study.

Change Management, Communications & Other Tips

Here are some additional change management and communication pointers:

Leverage the wrong perception to reposition: As mentioned earlier in the chapter, we gathered data about the customer from two ways: a.) observing behavior and b.) gathering opinions and validating findings from the observations. If you find that your customers' opinions are different from the observations you have made, and especially if this "difference" was a trend you found across the customer base, then leverage change management to re-position and re-message your product/service appropriately.

Conduct dry runs: This is an important step that is often overlooked. Companies often create tools and templates for ethnography, as well as prepare appropriate interview questions, but do not take the time to conduct dry runs. A stage play wouldn't open on its first night without having a dress rehearsal, would it? That's because on stage, as in business, there are always contingencies we fail to plan for. Dry runs, or mock interviews, help eliminate such surprises.

Face it, you want to gather as much "precious" information as you can in the sixty or so minutes that you will spend with your customer. An experienced ethnographer and interviewer in the team can lead a "dry-run" session and train other ethnographers as well as interviewers so that none of that time is wasted and all of it is used to mine as much information as possible.

Instead of a boring Q&A session with a customer, dry runs can also help make it interesting and allow you to weave a "story" in which the customer is positioned at the center of the universe. Put yourself in the customer's shoes and remember that, for them, this is an opportunity to "get it off their chest" and let a corporate representative hear their point of view (for once). Pay attention to the flow of the interview and take cues for how to steer it back on point, if necessary, or even down a side street *if* that's leading somewhere valuable.

Time the "mock" interview and add a few additional minutes when scheduling the meeting just to be sure, as some customers may take you through a long and windy journey when answering questions. Make sure to moderate the sessions well so that you stay within the time—and on schedule.

Schedule observation sessions and interviews: When it comes to scheduling observation sessions and interviews, you must be specific and identify the person in the customer organization who knows your product and/or is the decision maker. Choose based on which of the customers have indicated they are willing to provide candid feedback. Be sure to include "friendly" ones as well as "not-so-friendly" ones in order to represent all target markets and segments you cover, as well as geographies.

Consider setting up meetings with the friendlier customers first. This simple tactic will help you iron out the kinks in the data-collection process, be they the questions themselves or simply to adjust the priority of the questions based on time constraints.

When you are scheduling, make sure to communicate the purpose of the observation or interview. Have this sent out from an appropriate senior executive from within your company with whom they currently have a business relationship. For example, the VP of Sales, a VP from Marketing, etc. See if it makes sense to let them know they will be rewarded for their time at the time of invitation.

Believe it or not, the end of the interview is as significant as its beginning. For instance, share the "next steps"—i.e., how do we "close the loop" with this customer once he or she has provided us with valuable data?

Do not commit to sharing the findings (from all other customers) with the customer being interviewed.

What you *should* commit to is taking their input and giving it serious consideration; and continue to keep them in the loop when appropriate. If they have volunteered to assist in giving specific feedback on products and services, then let them know you (or your company) will reach out to them at the appropriate time (lap eight).

With the customers, especially, do not set the expectation too high up front. Instead, show it through actions and results. Remind them in the communication that raw data will not be shared with anyone other than the "core team"—the information shared with internal stakeholders will be in an aggregated form.

Sometimes there will be a temptation or specific request to include your organization's sales people or support teams in the interview. I highly discourage that, regardless of how high of a position the request comes from. One reason is that customers generally may not be open enough if these people are around. I believe the customer should be able to highlight any issue, including sales or support issues, without fear of reprisal.

Logistically speaking, it is important to have somebody from your company confirm the interview meeting with the customer, preferably a couple of days prior to the interview.

To begin the process on the right foot, draft a communication along with the meeting invitation, including the following:

- ❑ The purpose of the meeting
- ❑ Date of the interview
- ❑ Who is being interviewed
- ❑ How the information will be used
- ❑ Confidentiality
- ❑ Who is the interviewer
- ❑ Who the interviewees can contact in the meantime if they have questions

Define roles: Identify the team members who will do the actual interviewing. Of course, this step does not apply if the data collection will be done through surveys. (In lap three we will discuss various free services to help you conduct surveys in search of the voice of employee, or VOE.) Some level of experience and skill is required to conduct an interview, especially if the interviewees are senior executives.

Typically, these should be neutral, objective people who do not have a direct interest in the organization's business. If hiring outside personnel is not in your budget at this time, use those employees who already have experience interviewing people, such as people from HR, for example—they may not, however, have the interviewing skill set, so bringing in an outside consultant for laps two and three will pay off if done right.

Give the interviewer as much support as possible. It is sometimes difficult for interviewers to conduct interviews as well as take notes.

Decide on how many interviewers will be utilized during this process. Naturally, the more interviewers you have the faster this step will go, but there are dangers inherent in using too many interviewers for this purpose. For instance, you may not get a consistently high level of information from the customers, meaning the quality of information collected may vary. It may be more beneficial to have fewer interviewers that you trust to do the job right than more interviewers who may provide a contrast in interview quality.

Inform stakeholders within the company that interviews are being done (sales, product marketing, etc.): It may seem like a no-brainer, but oftentimes we forget to let people who regularly interface with the customer know that we are conducting a VOC. When this happens, the contact person can look like he or she is being "left out of the loop" should the customer mention the interview and the contact person has no idea what they're talking about. Naturally, this can erode consumer confidence and increase employee tension, which is the last thing you want.

Conduct ethnography interviews: Keep in mind that most customers do not like to be either video- or audio-recorded during an observation session or interview. While it may be more convenient for you to tape the session and transcribe it later (i.e., no need for an additional notetaker), if it makes the customer uncomfortable the candor may be sacrificed. If you must tape the interview, remember to get their permission in advance and let them know that is going to be used only for transcribing notes.

Begin the interview by introducing yourself and the notetaker. If there are people other than the interviewee in the room, then get to know them before you begin the interview.

Reconfirm that the customer is available for the allocated time, and make him or her comfortable with water and/or refreshments, comfortable seating, adequate lighting, etc. Next, highlight the purpose of the interview and what the company intends to do with the information gathered. Assure the customer that his or her confidentiality is of the utmost importance to you and the company. This is also the appropriate time to inform the customer of how the information will be shared with others in the company.

Next, conduct the interview using the pre-arranged questions. Don't forget or be afraid to follow up with answers that go "off script" if they may provide a wealth of additional data. Also, don't be afraid to steer the interview back on track if you've got a talker!

Once the observation session or interview is complete, share the next steps and how you are going to keep them in the loop. Don't forget to thank them for their time. After the interviews are done, send out a "thank you" card or note along with a small token of appreciation (if appropriate).

Case Study: Poorly Choreographed Transformation Causes Chaos

This story was shared by a good friend in the consulting business. Recently a medium-sized manufacturer of industrial farm equipment out of the Midwest was faced with a drastic problem: their product quality was deteriorating. At least, that was the open market perception, and the CEO wanted to take care of the situation. He wasn't alone; the Board wanted to take care of this problem as quickly as possible as well.

To stem the tide of deteriorating quality at his company, the CEO naturally initiated a transformation initiative. One of his first steps was to ask various account sales managers and product managers to interview customers to get to the root of the problem. What was happening here? How could they rectify the situation? What was the problem, according to real-time customers queried by real-time employees?

While the intent was there, a process was unfortunately not. Indeed, there was absolutely no method to the madness. The transformation went forward without a charter being defined (i.e., they skipped lap one altogether) and hence, this snake had one too many heads. Without a charter, without a strategy, and without even a clear compendium of questions to ask, everyone involved was suddenly reaching out to customers willy-nilly, with different people asking different questions at different times.

One customer was approached multiple times by multiple people within the company. That customer said the company operated in a more chaotic fashion than he had previously thought imaginable by a modern, working company.

Ouch. The minute I heard about this single customer being approached by multiple company representatives on multiple occasions, I blanched. What kind of message does that send about your company?

We're panicking!

Nobody knows what we're doing!
I don't know what I'm doing!
Frankly, all of the above.

This is what I had referred to as a "false sense of urgency" in lap one. While the CEO had the right intention, there was no strategy to support it. Not only was there no charter in place—no reigning body to keep things in order and direct the transformation strategically—but the VOC itself lacked a common purpose, process, planning, and specifically-defined roles for those involved.

This is exactly what I mean by an ill-conceived transformational effort doing more harm than good. Rather than creating a positive perception of "Hey, we recognize there's a problem and we're committed through action and solidarity to fix it," the customer ended up having a worse image of the organization than prior to the attempted transformation.

As one might imagine, the damage control took considerable extra effort and time. It impacted the relationship with customers, morale of the employees, and most importantly it had an effect on the revenue as well. Not surprisingly, the company's transformation was delayed amidst all this, and with so many false starts and wrong turns, it's impossible to say how long it will be before their product deterioration turns around—if ever.

The lesson here? Any time you are working with customers, take extra care to make sure the interaction is well choreographed and thoroughly thought through. It needs to be coordinated and internally refined before being "road tested" with anyone outside the company. Anything else is counterproductive.

If only the company had gone through laps one and two before attempting to hit the streets, they could have soaked up as much information as possible and they wouldn't have faced such a potentially crippling issue by doing more harm to their cause than good.

Lap 2 Key Takeaways

- ❑ This entire lap is focused on gathering outside-in data. Data is collected from outside the organization to effect change from within.

- ❑ Observe customers' behavior through techniques such as ethnography.

- ❑ Gather opinions of influencers, customers, sales channel, sales teams, and customer support teams, through interviews, surveys, and social media.

- ❑ Decide upon an information-gathering approach.

- ❑ Gather as much information as possible about the customers prior to preparing questions—use customer satisfaction surveys and VOC data, and talk to internal sales and support teams.

- ❑ Educate yourself, talking to the channel prior to talking directly to the customers.

- ❑ Prepare questions and conduct dry-runs.

- ❑ Schedule observation sessions and interviews.

- ❑ Decide on how you will capture and archive all of the information from the interviews.

- ❑ Inform stakeholders within the company of the planned interview process.

- ❑ Conduct interviews.

- ❑ Send an appropriate follow-up note or gift to interviewees (like a thank-you note).

- ❑ Transcribe interviews.

- ❑ Pull together "Report of findings" based on the "observations" and "opinions" gathered. In other words, catalog the data your customers, vendors, partners, and other close external relationships offered.

Lap 3

Gather Inside-Out Data

If your business is like a vehicle, internal knowledge is like fuel for the journey. The more knowledge you put into the tank, the better and further along you will be to the desired destination.

Armed with the critical data received from the outside-in data discovered in lap two, the purpose of this lap is to capture data from the inside. By now we have cataloged what data our customers, vendors, partners, and other close external relationships have to offer.

Now it's time to solicit information from those with a more intimate knowledge of your company's internal workings. Here we must reach out to the employees and stakeholders themselves to solicit their input on what's working and, most importantly, what's not. This critical phase also helps us evaluate the organization's readiness for transformation.

It is all well and good to arm ourselves with outside-in data, but we can't stop there (though many companies do). If our inside-out data reveals critical cracks in our vision, strategy, organizational structure, roles and accountability, leadership competency, processes, success metrics, reward systems, etc., then the transformation process will help resolve them.

This lap will outline exactly how this information can be gathered through various approaches (many of them similar to those found in the previous section). This chapter will also contain the tools, techniques, and questions necessary to help capture the internal data in an effective fashion that will be easily transferable for the reader's core team. Generally speaking, inside-out data will come from two basic sources:

> **Voice of Stakeholders (VOS):** The approach for capturing the voice of stakeholders depends on many factors, including the location of the stakeholders, the level of detail being solicited, the seniority of the stakeholder, and how busy they are, etc. In some cases it can be done via in-person and phone interviews, in other cases a survey may suffice.

> **Voice of Employees (VOE):** Depending on the number of employees, data collecting can be done either in person, for smaller companies, or through a web survey, for larger companies, which will also help preserve anonymity and therefore foster more honest responses (without fear of reprisal).

Data gathered from both sources will be viewed from all angles and analyzed at a later point. How? Broadly speaking, input from either the employee or the stakeholder will fall into one of the following categories:

- ❑ Vision and strategy
- ❑ Organizational structure
- ❑ Roles and accountability
- ❑ Leadership competency
- ❑ Initiatives, portfolios, and projects
- ❑ Products/services
- ❑ Processes—engagement model and governance
- ❑ Success metrics
- ❑ Financial
- ❑ Function specific—marketing, sales, customer support

This is not a rigid structure, but more of a guideline. There may be some that span across multiple categories such as "quality." The business analysts in your core team can help guide you on how best to categorize the data being gathered during lap four. Every organization's needs and findings are different. See what makes sense for your organization.

Also, keep in mind that some of the interviews may result in follow up meetings with each of the stakeholder groups, especially if the information we are looking for exists in employees' heads but is not documented in the form of example processes, governance, execution roadmaps, etc. Such information is critical for business analysts in lap four in order to identify issues. Where requested information does not exist at all, it is important to highlight it as a gap and make sure it is cataloged in lap four.

Hearing the Voice of the Stakeholder

Obviously, the customers—be they B2B or B2C—will not have visibility into the inner workings of your company. And getting only one view of your company would be like only looking one way before crossing the street. You might be fine on the right-hand side, but if you don't look left first you could be blindsided by a speeding bus!

The best way to begin capturing this inside-out view is to interview those who manage the inner workings of your company, those who see the company's feats and foibles every day of the week. Even so, you must do so with a careful and judicious eye. In most companies, such input is rife with politics, highly self-serving and biased. You will need to assess and validate the information you develop in this phase of the process before taking any appropriate action (see lap four).

A stakeholder analysis is a technique you can use to identify and assess the importance of key people, or groups of key people, within the organization who may significantly influence the success of your transformational activity or project. You can use this technique alone or with your team members.

First Things First: Who is a Stakeholder?

Who are the stakeholders you'll be involving in lap three? We can begin by analyzing the word itself: "stake-holder." These are leaders—or teams of individuals—who have something at "stake" in the process. So we're looking at folks or teams who will be directly affected by the transformation itself.

If the people or teams you identified in lap two as being "in scope" of the project include sales, marketing, and R&D, then these are your primary stakeholders. Doing what we call a "stakeholder analysis" allows us to work within these main groups to first identify and next sort these stakeholders based upon how they will affect the transformation process, how they can specifically help, and who can help the most. Clearly, defining who the stakeholders are and prioritizing them based on both access to—and influence upon—the project is a first priority in lap three.

The reason it's so important to define stakeholders early on in the process is that their data is critical to the mission itself. Identifying stakeholders and collecting data from them fully engages them in the project. The data gathered needs to be both collected accurately and later analyzed thoroughly.

Next Up: Refining the Choice of Stakeholders

Now that you know what a stakeholder is and who they are in your company, it is important here to refine the list of stakeholders you'll be speaking with, both for the sake of convenience and accuracy. What I suggest is defining a specific and limited core team of stakeholders from whom to draw these interviews. For the purposes of this exercise you want to be thorough and exhaustive, but not *exhausted!* By that I mean not everybody who qualifies as a stakeholder should be interviewed; instead, work hard upstream to identify a representative core team of stakeholders to solicit information.

When creating this team it is important to have ample representation of all stakeholder groups that will be directly impacted by the transformation.

Depending on the organization, keep the interviewee list to about twenty stakeholders comprised of an equal sampling of senior executives and line managers. Too long a list will increase the time to complete the interviews.

Also, from my experience, I have seen that after interviewing about twenty people, the chances of you capturing new information drastically reduces. In fact, by this point almost 95% plus of the data is captured. (If you have identified the right stakeholders, that is.)

How to Choose a Stakeholder

It is a misconception to think that the stakeholders interviewed in lap three *always* need to be senior executives. What I have found from experience is that, for large companies, having two to three people from each of the groups you interface with is most beneficial. (For small- to medium-size companies, one to two people should suffice.) One of these stakeholders should be a senior leader.

Oftentimes the issues or problems highlighted by executives are different than those shared by people further down the chain (those working in day-to-day operations). Senior executives can provide strategic input while the line managers can provide more tactical information. Having representation from multiple levels will help you a.) understand issues at each of the levels, b.) understand any misalignment at various levels, and c.) be able to separate facts from emotions.

It is also important to consider how the core team you built back in lap one participates. These are true stakeholders, so make sure to capture input from the core team as well. As always, maintaining their anonymity is critical to ensure an accurate and open exchange of ideas.

There is always a balancing act between efficiency and effectiveness. A lot of employee time and energy is being spent on this interview process, but it is vital to get accurate information. How many people will you interview to get that information and how long will it take?

Having a long list of stakeholders to interview takes time, so be pragmatic. Depending on the size of the transformation, especially for large companies, limit the number of stakeholders to no more than twenty to twenty-five; at a more medium-size company limit the number of stakeholders to no more than twelve to fifteen.

In order to fine-tune your list of stakeholders (and gradually whittle down the list of potential interviewees), start with the groups or organizations that your organization engages with. First list all of them, then begin identifying people in each of the groups who might make appropriate interview candidates.

In finalizing the list, make sure that you have people who (from your perception) are supporters as well as detractors. As they say, keep your "friends" close but your "enemies" closer. In this case, the idea is to go in with an open mind to honestly try to understand the issues.

Eyes on the Finish Line: What You Want to Accomplish in Lap 3

Lap three is a critical step in the transformation process. If we were to liken it to a road race, this would be the lap where you begin to build up steam, and once you have heard from the stakeholders and gathered accurate and usable inside-out data, look out; your company or organization will be nearing the head of the pack, as few of your competitors will devote the time and energy to take this step.

That said, there are a few aspects to accomplish in this lap. We need to identify various issues/problems, as seen by the stakeholders—those issues that are currently preventing the company from reaching its goals. We also need to capture potential "landmines"—i.e., transformational risks—as seen by all of the stakeholders, as well as their thoughts and ideas on how some of the problems can be resolved. Last, we must understand the stakeholders' motivation for supporting or not supporting the transformation effort.

The intent here is to also catalog the following:

- ❑ Organizational structure—current roles and accountability (with job descriptions, if possible)
- ❑ Key processes
- ❑ Key vision, strategy, roadmaps, objectives of each of the groups in the organization
- ❑ Success metrics of each of the groups in the organization and how they are aligned to the overall organization's success metrics
- ❑ Personnel review/appraisal information of all key managers (including executives)
- ❑ Financial details of each of the groups
- ❑ All interesting high-level ideas the stakeholders share regarding the "future state" of the company

The Inside-Out Approach: A Step-by-Step Process

What's fortunate going into lap three is that we have likely mastered the art of interviewing customers back in lap two. In fact, many of the things we learned in lap two apply here as well.

Again, there are a few different ways to conduct these interviews. First we will review the steps required to interview your company's stakeholders, then later in this chapter we will review the steps required to interview your company's employees. In this case, I would not recommend using the survey method, as it is far too impersonal for this group of high-level individuals. The most appropriate ways to interview and gather input is in a.) face-to-face interviews, b.) telephone interviews, or c.) panel (or group) interviews.

1. Define the Objective

Before you identify a single stakeholder or arrange a single interview or ask a single question, first determine why you are engaging in this exercise in the first place. You will likely have already determined the objective of this exercise in lap two, but perhaps doing it again will refine the objective for you here, in lap three.

2. Determine Your Approach to Gathering Data

We talked earlier about the three types of data-gathering you'll use with stakeholders in your company, namely, face-to-face interviews, telephone interviews, and panel interviews. Now it is time to determine which approach is best based upon the individual stakeholder or team of stakeholders being interviewed. For instance, perhaps it will be more appropriate to interview the five to seven executives on your core stakeholder team on a face-to-face basis, or maybe one or two will prefer to be interviewed by telephone.

3. Prepare Your Questions

Once you decide on the information-gathering approach, it is then time to draft the questions for the interview. This process will be very similar to that used in lap two. However, you will be asking questions about your own company versus someone else's company.

It is sometimes tempting to share the information you are gathering with the key stakeholders, but it is important that you refrain from doing this, as the information can be taken out of context and interpreted the wrong way.

A complete picture of this will be shared in a more well-thought-through, methodical fashion in lap four.

Remember, we are talking inside out, here, as opposed to outside in. Using our original list of questions from lap two, consider altering them to be more appropriate for our internal core team of stakeholders. For instance, here are just a few ways those earlier questions could be specifically altered for this group (by all means feel free to amend and personalize the following list for your own needs):

1. How would you rate the level of pre-sales support for the products/services we sell?

2. How would you rate the level of post-sales support for the products/services we have sold?

3. What is your estimation of our customers' overall satisfaction with our products, services, support, and field sales?

4. In what areas can we improve?

5. Considering what we charge for our products, services, and support, how would you describe the prices? a.) very low, b.) low, c.) moderate, d.) high, e.) very high, or f.) don't know/not enough experience

6. How would you rate the overall value customers receive from us given what they pay? a.) excellent value for money, b.) very good value, c.) good value, d.) marginal value, e.) poor value, f.) don't know/not enough experience

By now you can likely see how a question-by-question comparison with customer responses versus internal responses could be beneficial in illuminating any disparities between the two. Imagine, for instance, your team of stakeholders having great confidence in your post-sales service while customers relate quite the opposite trend. How illuminating might this be for a transformational team to consider when moving away from lap three?

As we move forward through the interview process, here are some additional questions to consider, specifically as they apply to your company. I have arranged them in categories to help you focus on the objective for each series of queries:

Lay the Foundation:

1. Which groups within the company do you interface with?

2. What is your overall experience interfacing with them? For each of them, on a scale of one to ten (ten being the best) how would you rate them?

3. What are our top three challenges, as you see them?

4. Two years from now, there is an article written about the organization in *Business Week*. What do you think the article will say?

5. In comparison to the vision you just articulated (above), where do you think we are currently (ten being the best)?

6. In the roadmap to achieving the above vision, what do you think are the top three objectives we need to achieve in the next twelve months?

7. What are our top five strengths of the entire company?

8. What are our top five weaknesses of the entire company?

9. What opportunities do you see ahead of us?

10. What threats do we face?

Structure:

1. What are the common points of friction or bottlenecks between our two groups or departments? Or, what type of collaboration needs to happen that is not currently happening?

2. From an organizational structure—looking at roles and accountability within the company—what changes should we consider and why?

Process:

1. What are the key processes in our organization that are not optimal?

2. How are decisions (governance) across boundaries being made? How are escalations being handled?

Success Metrics:

1. What, in your opinion, should be our success indicators?

2. What metrics do you watch to see if there are potential problems?

3. What additional or different measures would you suggest?

People:

1. How would you rate the quality of people in the organization on a scale of one to ten (ten being the best)?

2. Does the leadership team have the right competency? If not, what in your opinion do they lack?

3. What needs to be improved?

General:

1. Is there anything else you want to share that has not yet been discussed?

2. Given everything we have discussed, what are the top three priority issues that should be addressed?

4. Conduct "Dry-runs"

Scheduling mock interviews is extremely important for your core team of interviewers. Particularly when executives and C-level employees are going to be asked to devote precious time and energy, either in person or via a phone interview, it is critical to have the kinks worked out of the process and the system running smoothly.

5. Schedule Interviews

With several interviews to perform, scheduling should begin early and be prepared to accommodate for various missteps, cancellations, and last-minute schedule changes. Keep in mind that this is an internal exercise so you can be more flexible in where, when, and for how long you meet each of your interviewees.

6. Decide How to Collect and Archive Data (Including Backup)

Data collection and archiving is extremely critical to this stage of the process, so having a system in place will assure both the accuracy of your information and its safety upon retrieval later.

Perhaps you want to use the same system devised in lap two. If that is the case, this step of the process will go smoothly. Then, too, since these are internal interviews, you may require a much simpler system for collecting and archiving data. Try to develop a system that will stand you in good stead as we progress through the rest of these laps as well, since data will be key to every step along the journey.

7. Define Roles

Who will do what? When? Where? Defining roles is a critical part of lap three. Particularly because you're dealing with stakeholders, consider your various team roles carefully. It may still be prudent to hire outside interviewers to conduct this process, as doing so internally might cloud the issue and taint the results. Keep in mind that while hiring outside consultants can be costly, the payoff in getting accurate, timely, and, most of all, honest feedback is worth its weight in gold. An independent consultant can be unbiased in interviewing subjects objectively.

As a reminder, maintaining confidentiality before, during, and after the interview process is extremely important at this stage. Finally, assign business analysts to capture all information gathered during the interview process. Interviewing consultants is one thing, but additional analysts are needed to understand and process this data. This is an art form unto itself.

Whatever you do, do not position this as an audit. Have the CEO or a senior executive in the organization send out an email to perhaps just the line managers (as these are the people who understand the inner workings of the company), requesting their assistance in documenting the "current state" of their department. Then set up one-on-one meetings with these line managers. Remember, do not confront or provide guidance at this point; merely ask questions, listen, and take notes. Anything else will be counterproductive (no analysis at this point; that will be done in lap four).

8. Conduct Interviews

Aside from eliminating the survey option for the data-gathering process, the way you conduct interviews in lap three should discreetly mirror the same process from lap two. However, noting that these are inside employees versus external customers shouldn't be the only variable to take into account.

If the stakeholders are assured that only the consultant will have access to the feedback and that everyone else will see the information in its aggregated form (such as "25% of the stakeholders felt that XYZ is an issue . . ." and so on), they will be much more likely to speak openly and freely throughout the interview. And this is, of course, the ideal scenario for any interviewer. Furthermore, regardless of how efficiently you store this data electronically, it will be important to provide written transcriptions of each audio interview to share and collect data amongst those who are authorized to view it.

Hearing the Voice of the Employee

Executives and management are a vital part of understanding the voice of the stakeholders (VOS). But there is another voice to be heard in lap three: the voice of the employee (VOE). After all, it is just as important to keep your hand on the pulse of those working the front lines in your company to monitor perceptions and employee morale throughout the transformation journey. In this case, the survey approach would be most ideal and effective in capturing this data.

Depending on the complexity and size of the transformation, you may want to do the employee survey three times:

> **Baseline survey:** done prior to making the general announcement to the entire organization about the transformation.
>
> **Midpoint survey:** done after lap seven in the ten-step process.
>
> **Post transformation survey:** done three to four months after the completion of the ten-step process.

Uniformity of these three surveys is critical to their effectiveness. As you begin to design your employee surveys, make sure the questions are the same in all the above surveys. Otherwise, it will be impossible to compare the results once all three surveys have been completed.

Managing the Peaks and Valleys of Transformation

Business transformation is challenging for everybody, and while the end result frequently exceeds expectations, oftentimes the peaks and valleys along the way can put everyone under strain. Every situation is different, of course, but many of the metrics will take a dip during the transformation before coming back up, even stronger than before, after the transformation is complete.

The reason why it dips in some cases is because people exhibit anxiety when confronted with uncertainty. And transformation, especially in the initial phases, causes uncertainly. After all, most people will not have the bird's eye view of the transformation approach that you and the rest of the charter team will have. Getting the VOE will help keep your finger on the pulse of the rank and file while also helping them understand not only your commitment to change but the various benefits of change itself.

Hence, to minimize the dip, it is critical to manage effective communications. You've got to make employees aware not only of the ten-step process itself but also where you are in the process. (Knowing which lap you're in gives employees both ownership of that lap and lets them see a light at the end of the tunnel.) It is also highly critical to highlight the significance of each of the steps.

As shared in lap two, there are many great (and free) survey tools available on the Internet; leverage them, as appropriate. For instance, over at www.surveymonkey.com they have a single purpose: "To enable anyone to create professional online surveys quickly and easily." Why not take them up on the offer?

Here are some survey best practices that you may want to keep in mind as you determine the VOE at your company. Specifically, the following are the steps you want to consider when doing an employee survey:

1. Define Survey Objective

It is important to know what you want to learn from the survey before you begin crafting it, so that your questions and goals align. No one has time to waste, and this information is critical to your cause for change. Take the time upstream to define the survey objective so that everyone benefits.

Being specific about the needs of your survey will not only help you design questions appropriately, but will also help people taking the survey understand how the information will be used on the processing end.

Be specific and compose a legitimate and formal objective before crafting a single survey question. For example:

> The purpose of the survey is to better understand our employees' perception of how our company is being run. Based on the information gathered, we can identify the right aspects to transform and define our change-management strategy.

This lets people know, at the outset, why they are taking the survey and why honesty and openness is so important to its success. To help solicit honest and open feedback, also define how you intend to use the information gathered from the survey.

2. Identify Your Audience

Once you have a well-defined purpose, you can define the target audience for your survey. Just as you thought long and hard about who to interview for the VOS, take some time now to consider your audience for your VOE surveys.

In this case, would the audience all be employees of the organization—at all levels? Would it be all employees, except the executives? Would it include janitorial, secretarial, and support? What about long-term contractors (non-employees)? These are some of the decisions that need to be made before question one on the survey is ever considered.

Why? Because knowing who the survey is for helps you write it more effectively. For instance, if you're not including executives in your target audience, you can tailor your questions for middle management and below. If you are including executives, you must include another audience in your question generation.

3. Communicate to Your Audience

What will your audience know about the survey before they take it? It is vital that you and the rest of the transformation charter set the proper context for the audience so that they know why they're being asked what they're being asked and, more importantly, why their responses matter.

A simple mission statement at the beginning of the survey isn't enough to accurately convey this message to all parties. Instead, communicate prior to the actual survey. Educate the audience through repeated communications and, when appropriate, leverage staff meetings to communicate further—all prior to distributing surveys.

In an effort to accurately convey the importance of the surveys, have all managers mention the following points in their respective staff meetings:

Introduction: Explain the reason why the survey is being done. How is the information going to be used? Why is it important for the company?

WIIFM: In other words, What's in it for me? Highlight the relevance for each employee. What's in it for *them*?

Confidentiality: Be sure to stress that the results of the surveys will be used only in-house, and that no names will be linked to provided information.

Instructions: Provide instructions for taking the survey, with the URL link clearly provided (if taking an online survey).

Who to contact: Identify the person(s) within the organization that can be contacted in case the interviewees have technical and/ or business-related questions. Remember, the support staff should be instructed not to provide answers but, instead, to provide help in interpreting the answers or provide help in interpreting the answering or technical assistance.

When and how results will be shared: It is highly encouraged to share the data even if it means at a high level. If you do not close the loop, they may not (willingly) take part in surveys in the future.

4. Design Your Survey Questionnaire

Designing survey questionnaires is an art form unto itself, but with the right audience in mind and the proper goals at heart, you too can create a survey that will make it easy for respondents to respond—and transformation to occur.

The "flow" of the survey is very important; it shouldn't jump around willy-nilly but, instead, follow a logical order that keeps like-minded questions "clustered" to encourage appropriate and open feedback. Here are some types of survey questions you might consider:

Qualitative versus quantitative: Which kinds of questions will you ask: "qualitative" (subjective; i.e., up to the survey participant's interpretation) or "quantitative" (objective; e.g., rating one to five, multiple choice, etc.)? Think through which questions are qualitative and which are quantitative.

Multiple choice: If you are designing quantitative questions, think through the multiple choices you are providing in the answer portion of the survey. Will you give the option to provide custom—or "other"—responses? And, if so, will your survey provide for an extra blank space or screen to explain "other" reasoning?

Rating and ranking: Rating and ranking questions allow you to create a question matrix where the respondent is asked to evaluate multiple items against the same scale—e.g., poor, fair, average, good, excellent; one to ten scales (ten being best) or five-point scales; low–medium–high, etc.

Open-ended: Open-ended questions are very helpful for collecting richer, more detailed information, and may yield valuable input on issues not specifically queried.

Surveys are meant to flow so that they can be taken relatively quickly. Confusion, long-windedness, and lack of clarity are not appreciated by survey takers and tend to skew the results, as they dissuade openness and honesty. Use simple language, and specifically avoid acronyms that may elude some of the employee's understanding and/or pay grade.

Clarity is key when conducting VOE surveys. Avoid double questions that add to confusion or don't provide an option for explaining one's answer. For instance, "Do you like silver exterior with black interior?" These are actually two questions, not one, and one can't answer accurately if they a.) like a silver exterior but not a black interior or b.) like a black interior but not a silver exterior. If you want to know whether they like a silver exterior, ask them; if you *also* want to know if they like a black interior, ask them— just do so separately.

Also, avoid suggestions in your questions. In fact, avoid leading the respondent to give any type of answer at all. For instance, "Didn't you think we did a great job at our leadership summit?" That is a suggestive question. How should they respond? The logical, unwritten answer for any "loyal" employee would be "yes," but how does that foster openness and honesty on the rest of the survey?

Remember that the ultimate goal for designing this survey is NOT to design the ultimate survey to end all studies but, instead, to bring about transformation in your particular company; design it accordingly, and quite personally. With that on the table, be sure to ask questions keeping in mind the future state of the company, and not just the current state of affairs.

In constructing your survey, have no more than ten to twelve questions. That is why the questions themselves are so important. With so few of them to answer, the questions must be top rate. The trick to getting accurate, open, and enthusiastic responses is to make sure that it does not take more than five to seven minutes to respond.

Here are some sample survey questions that might give you a starting place when crafting your own survey:

- ❑ What organization are you part off (make this multiple choice for consistency)?

- ❑ What is your title (make this multiple choice for consistency as well)?

- ❑ Do you understand the organization's:
    a. Mission
    b. Vision
    c. Strategic objectives

- ❑ Do you understand your organization's roles and responsibilities at xx level (define these levels or use what is appropriate in your organization)?

- ❑ Are you getting the information and communication needed to do your job effectively?

- ❑ Does the current organization structure help you align more closely with XXX organizations?

❑ Does the organization structure support successful execution of the XXX (parent organization or CEO's vision and strategy)?

❑ Do you believe your organization is effectively achieving its objectives?

❑ Are you confident in the ability of the management team to implement your strategy?

❑ Would you say that this is a great place to work? Do you want to continue growing your career in this organization?

5. Conduct a Pre-test Survey

Much as we did a "dry run" with the executives interviewed in this lap and customers (either B2C or B2B) in lap two, consider conducting a pre-test survey before going "live" with the official survey. Before sending out the survey, test out the survey with just a few respondents.

This will give you an idea if there is a bad link or page on the survey, if something is misprinted or misleading, or if various questions are giving employees trouble. Better to confuse one or two employees now, in a controlled environment, before doing a rewrite for more than one hundred or two hundred employees later because you didn't do a test run.

Finally, to ensure participation across the board, make sure there is a compelling case for everyone to complete and submit the survey, such as making it a team effort in every department or part of their day-to-day duties on the job.

6. Set Up a Survey Hotline

Depending on the survey method, see if an internal hotline is required to provide assistance for people taking surveys. Some survey approaches, like the "telephone survey," may not need this.

7. Execute the Survey

Regardless of how you are running the survey, be it online, the phone, or in the mail, send out the survey per your plan. Encourage managers to request their respective teams to actively participate; the message needs to be trickled down that, "This survey is important for the good of the company." Employees will actively participate IF they sense that their input matters. Giving clear and regular guidance will encourage their active participation.

Remember to monitor the response rate closely. It is important to see which departments are responding, how often each department is responding, and how many employees are responding. This allows you (or managers) to prod or "nudge" those with low response rates to encourage everyone to complete the surveys. If response rates are low in one department or another, or even across the board, send out reminder communications from senior executives, as appropriate.

To increase response rates and reinforce the message, send the survey out with a message from the senior-most executive, perhaps the CEO, if possible. This lends credibility to the project and makes it a priority for people to finish promptly.

8. Analyze the Results

The actual analysis of the survey happens in lap four, but I am taking the liberty of sharing some aspects of "survey analysis" in this chapter, as part of best practice.

Results should be analyzed differently per the type of question asked. For multiple choice questions, for instance, you analyze frequency. An example might be, "36% of the respondents felt that the vision and strategy did not exist; 26% felt that collaboration was not happening amongst their peers; etc."

For ratings/rankings use the respondents' average. For example, "The management received an overall rating of 3.2/5 for keeping the employees in the loop on short-term plans." The same is true for open-ended or "numeric" questions, an example of which might be, "Employees spend an average of thirty-five minutes for their commute (each way)."

Quantitative questions should be analyzed per their frequency. Example: "25% of the respondents felt that their customer support was an issue."

Since we are measuring quantitative results, be sure to accurately address the sample size taken and make sure it is large enough to be considered a fair and reasonable sampling.

9. Report Results

Once the analysis is done, it is time to present the material formally to both the senior management/executives as well as the rest of the organization. If you are reporting mid survey or on the second survey, show in your chart the numbers in the base-line survey for comparison. Similarly, in the final survey show both baseline and mid-survey results.

When it comes time to formally present the results, it is important to prepare multiple versions of the report: detailed ones for the internal core transformation team and management and an abbreviated version, perhaps, for the rest of the organization.

Change Management and Communication

From my experience, I have seen that by reaching out to the stakeholders, they feel that their voice is heard. This is critical because their engagement this early in the transformation process is a strategic move to gain adoption.

Consider updating and leveraging illustration 1.3. Stakeholder management is critical to transformation success. Give it enough attention and it will pave your future path.

Case Study: Stakeholder Engagement Key To Success

Change is never easy. Just ask "Gerry," the brand new CEO at a very profitable medical devices company. After the CEO of twenty years retired, Gerry was brought in to steer the company into the future.

Granted, there was a lot to like about this company. It was profitable, for one, and the employees there liked it that way. They also liked the feelings of inclusion and ownership when it came to making not just departmental but organizational decisions. The company had an "open" feel and, as a result, employees worked uniquely well together.

Gerry started his new job with a bang. He did not take the time to understand the inner workings of the organization, nor identify the organization's strengths, weaknesses, opportunities, and threats (SWOT). Turns out Gerry's management style was one of being a "know-it-all" task master.

Without consulting with the rest of the leadership team, Gerry quickly made drastic changes to the organizational structure, putting new processes and a heavy governance model in place. Suddenly, the way decisions were being made at the company was entirely new and uncharted. The problem was that Gerry was not a subject matter expert and he did not bother consulting with many of the key people who were specialists in this field. As a result, the decisions made were not always information-based.

Gerry's decisions caused anxiety among employees, and particularly frustrated some. Remember, this was a highly profitable organization that enjoyed a very open culture, where people were empowered to make appropriate decisions; this environment, in turn, helped improve the customer's experience. They even enjoyed collaborating amongst themselves. However, there were clearly areas where the company could have improved—distribution and shipping, for example.

Shortly after Gerry took over as head of the company, employee attrition was on the rise. Many of the experts, who were actually quite well known in the industry, began to leave the company. In a little over five months, a staggering 70% of the leadership team had left the company altogether. Many of the line managers left as well. The morale of the company was at an all-time low.

Company profits fell over 50% within a year; many major customers left for the competition. Eighteen months after he was hired, Gerry was fired and the company was able to bring back one of the former executives as a CEO.

This company learned the hard way to engage the stakeholders in a steady dialogue, particularly when change is involved, and keep them engaged in that dialogue. Understand their concerns; ask them for their insights.

Remember, business transformation can never be one man's journey; you need to take others along with you. Unfortunately, Gerry failed at doing that. What's worse, the entire company paid the price.

Lap 3 Key Takeaways

❑ This step is about getting input from stakeholders (VOS) and employees (VOE).

❑ Define stakeholders (Who are they? How many are there?). Make sure the list is not too long nor short.

❑ Catalog input specifically around organization structure, key processes, vision, strategy, success metrics, etc.

❑ Steps for conducting interviews:

◆ Define objectives

◆ Decide upon an overall approach for gathering information

◆ Prepare questions

◆ Schedule interviews

◆ Decide how to collect and archive data

◆ Define roles

◆ Conduct dry-run

◆ Conduct interviews

❑ Gather employee (VOE) feedback through surveys—conduct them in the beginning, midpoint, and then a few months after completion of the first transformation cycle.

Lap 4

Analyze Data

In analysis, you expose. In implementation, you resolve.

Gathering data is one step in the transformation process, but it is useless without a close and perceptive analysis of said data. Therefore, the data gathered from our 1.) outside-in and 2.) inside-out analyses are eventually compiled together for closer scrutiny.

This is not just any data, nor is this just any analysis. In fact, compiling and organizing large amounts of data such as this for analysis is nothing short of an art form. Therefore, it is critical that we engage our best data analyst to help pull this information together in a way that will be both meaningful and impactful for our core charter team.

Keep in mind that front runners don't treat such data as an afterthought, nor do they scrimp when it comes to investing in quality data collectors and/ or analyzers. Remember, data is knowledge, and knowledge is the fuel for our success.

Before the actual analysis begins, it is important to craft the organization's vision, mission, and value statements as well as strategy and objectives. Without these critical elements we will not be able to catalog the gaps that exist in the organization. We need to know the destination of our transformational journey in order to catalog what will prevent us from achieving that destination. Illustration 4.1 shows how and why laps four and five need to evolve in a parallel timeframe.

Illustration 4.1: Need for Working on Lap 4 and 5 in Parallel

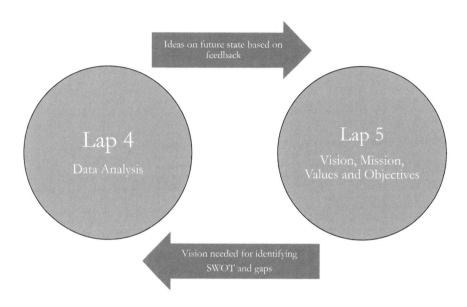

A typical organization going through transformation will have a considerable number of gaps. There are many factors that determine how many of these gaps we want to resolve. The two key limiting factors are resources and time.

We could prioritize and take a phased approach instead of attempting to "boil the ocean." The prioritizing exercise can be complex and perhaps even politically charged. Prioritizing based on predetermined criteria such as impact, time to resolution, budget or head count needed, etc., can be an effective approach to get the final prioritized gaps list that everyone on the team can align with. Illustration 4.2 shows the overall approach for this lap.

Once the list of potential gaps in our organization is identified, a detailed root cause analysis can be done to identify options to address each gap. Solutions are then developed to "plug" these gaps.

An experienced program manager will be able to scope out projects and tasks to assist in the execution of these proposed solutions. A roadmap with interdependencies highlighted can be a good way for everyone to understand

Illustration 4.2: Process for Analyzing "As Is" Data

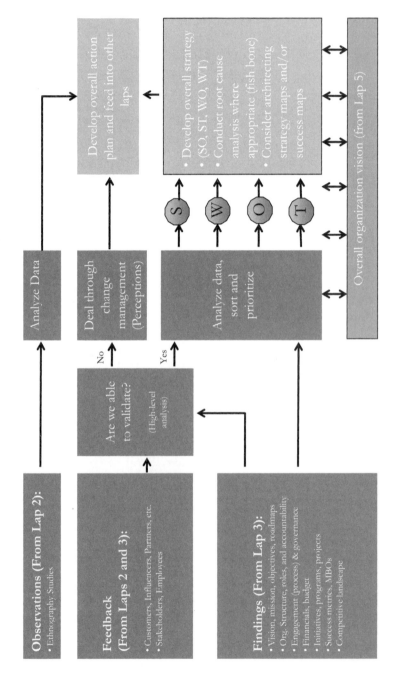

the overall picture. This should be done in conjunction with laps five through ten.

Purpose: Cataloging, Analyzing, Categorizing and Prioritizing Data

The purpose of this step is four-fold: to catalog, analyze, categorize, and prioritize the data captured above, from laps two and three. This process also includes (see Illustration 4.2):

❑ Cataloging and analyzing VOC, VOP, and VOS data as well as your VOE survey. Incorporating the findings into the overall picture.

❑ Capturing the key elements of the current state, including current vision, mission, values, organizational structure, processes and success metrics, etc. Maintain a table similar to Illustration 4.3 (so everyone in the team has visibility).

❑ Cataloging any interesting ideas shared by customers, partners, stakeholders, and employees on the "future state," and then feeding them into lap five for architecting the vision, mission, values, etc.

Illustration 4.3: Information Gathered & Potential Sources

Type of Information	Potential Sources (Organization & individual)	Last Updated	Document Location + Additional Comments
Market Data			
Product Data			
Consumer Data			
Marketing & Sales Data			
Financial Information			
Engagement & Governance			
Quality Data			
Research & Development			
Customer Support Data			

❑ Identifying a SWOT Analysis for each of the categories.

❑ Analyzing high-level root causes for each of the gaps and further prioritizing, as appropriate.

❑ Developing a high-level strategy (draft).

❑ Communicating the "burning platform" with the entire organization and mobilizing toward a more unified front. Unifying and engaging the entire organization to understand the "burning platform" and moving them into a "true sense of urgency state"—by winning the "hearts and minds" of employees.

❑ Sharing roadmap and next steps with employees.

Strategy . . . in 10 Words or Less

All change starts with strategy. What is strategy? Over the past several years alone (to say nothing of the previous decade), literally hundreds of books have been written on strategy—some as thick as 500 pages or more. These can be very intimidating. My definition of strategy is quite simple: **strategy is a path that gets you to your vision**.

We will talk more about the vision in the next chapter. For now, let's look at it this way: vision is where you would like to be in the future, say two to three years from now. What markets would you like to be in? Who are your target customers and what "job" for these customer will you try to get done? What will your competitive differentiator be?

Defining the strategy next sets you on the right trajectory to achieve your vision. Realistically, though, the timeline to achieve your vision is in the two- to three-year range, and so the strategy should be developed for twelve to twenty-four months. This should put you in the right trajectory. If we had to simplify, the vision answers the "what" and the "by when" questions, while the strategy answers the "how" questions. Tactics, on the other hand, will help you develop a six to twelve-month plan, keeping the strategy in mind. This is often referred to as "fiscal year plan" in many companies. (Lap ten will elaborate more on this.)

At the end of the day, your strategy should be able to answer at least the following questions:

- ❑ What markets should you focus (both new and existing) for you to achieve the vision?

- ❑ What "job" are you trying to help get done for the customer? Or in other words, what "pain" are you attempting to solve for your customer? (What is the value proposition?)

- ❑ How are you planning to solve the pain? (Through what products and services?)

- ❑ How will the "pain-killer" be delivered?

- ❑ How will you differentiate your products in the market? This is referred to as "competitive differentiation." How can you sustain the "competitive differentiation?"

- ❑ What are your objectives, goals, and targets? How do you measure your success?

- ❑ How should the organization be best structured so as to develop and deliver value in the most cost-effective way?

- ❑ What core values will get you to the vision?

- ❑ What are the risks and how will you mitigate them?

- ❑ What competencies are expected of the leaders in order to achieve the vision?

- ❑ How should you best engage with your customers, partners, stakeholders, and employees? This is known as the "engagement model."

- ❑ How will decisions be made across various disciplines? This is known as the "governance model."

Approach to Analyzing "As Is" Data

Let's begin the process by taking a look at the overall approach for analyzing the data. As you can see from Illustration 4.2, it's vital to develop both feedback (from laps two and three) and turn those into findings (from lap three) before attempting the type of high-level data analysis we're crafting in lap four.

Making sense out of the data collected and being able to connect the dots is key for transformational success. By now you have huge amounts of data collected. It is literally an art to convert this data into powerful knowledge. If I had to make a comparison, converting this data into powerful knowledge is similar to archeologists sifting through tons of information at an archeological dig—bone fragments, broken pots, and other artifacts—and then taking just those that are relevant to connect the dots from there.

So, for instance, not every clue will help uncover who was buried there. Some bits of bone, for instance, come from harmless animals while others come from kings and queens of a reigning civilization. Some broken pots were simply water jugs, while others are more priceless artifacts, revealing articulate paintings of the culture life during this time period.

Spending too much time on irrelevant data—data that does not further the cause—is almost as hazardous as not collecting the data in the first place. This is why data analysis is so critical to transformational success.

Data validation is a critical step. After all, just as at a crime scene, not every piece of data we gather is perhaps accurate and/or valid (more on this in subsequent paragraphs). If we aren't able to validate the data, we must deal with the inconsistencies through change management. We do this with a specific SWOT analysis to determine the organization's strengths, weaknesses, opportunities, and threats (more on these later in laps).

Before we begin working on identifying your organization's strengths, weaknesses, threats, and opportunities as identified by customers, partners, stakeholders, and employees (from laps two and three), let's take some time to identify the vision, mission, values, and objectives for the organization.

After all, for you to do a SWOT, you need a reference point. What are the strengths that will help get you to the vision? What are the weaknesses that will prevent you from achieving your vision? And so on. This interdependency between laps four and five forces you to work on them almost in tandem.

Let me again elaborate upon this point by referencing Illustration 4.1. As you can see from the figure, this is not an either/or proposition, but a concurrent, two-part analysis in which each lap feeds off the other. For instance, the data analysis discovered in lap four provides ideas on the future state based on feedback for lap five. Likewise, lap five provides the vision needed for identifying the SWOT analysis and resulting gaps that may arise.

Specific information you got from observing customers, feedback from partners, stakeholders, and the rest of employees, etc., with relations to the "To Be State" (aka "Future State"), which will be cataloged in lap four can be used as input for defining vision in lap five. There are interdependencies within laps four and five, the two often evolving in a parallel and symbiotic timeframe, that ultimately lead you to your vision.

Now that the vision is defined, you will take the output of laps two and three and sort them into strengths, weaknesses, opportunities, or threats. This will take a little bit of thinking. The definitions are as below:

> **Strengths**: current attributes of the organization that are helpful to achieving the new vision (identified in lap five).
>
> **Weaknesses**: current attributes of the organization that are harmful and will prevent you from achieving the new vision.
>
> **Opportunities**: external conditions that can/should be leveraged and are helpful to achieving the new vision.
>
> **Threats**: external conditions that could pose as road blocks in achieving your new vision.

The idea is for the company to remedy and convert weaknesses to strengths; leverage strengths to exploit opportunities while eradicating threats (see Illustration 4.4).

The Small Group Setting Approach

How will you determine your organization's specific strengths, weaknesses, opportunities, and threats before moving forward with your organizational transformation? One approach I have seen work well for this analysis is to do this in a small group setting. Let me elaborate:

Pick three to four people from the core team, preferably senior analysts, to take on the arduous task of parsing the massive amounts of data collected into a form that allows for further detailed analysis. Remember,

Illustration 4.4: SWOT Analysis

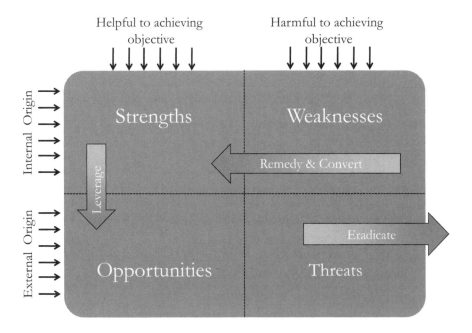

the information needs to be kept confidential (so to ensure trust and confidentiality you need to use people from the core team).

Consider leveraging the template shown in Illustration 4.5. Have an individual from this small team of three to four people enter the data onto the template while the others read out the feedback from customers, partners, stakeholders, and employees one by one. As each person is reading out the feedback to each of the questions, have everyone collectively discuss and analyze the information. Given the vision (this is important!), parse each unique item of feedback from each individual interviewed or surveyed as a specific strength, weakness, opportunity, or threat.

Consolidate common feedback/observation themes so as to avoid repetitions, and give one unique theme per row in the spreadsheet. Make sure to pay attention to nuances and separate them, as necessary. For example, it might be tempting to lump "long customer-support hold times" and "wrong problem identification and resolution" into a single theme, but this will weaken the significance of both. The first one is probably due to too few customer-support representatives available, whereas the second perhaps

Illustration 4.5: Consolidating, Categorizing and Prioritizing Data

Consolidate based on unique themes (reflected in each cell)

These columns will have multiple sub-columns to represent each of the entities—customers, partners, sales, marketing, R&D, customer support, etc. Gives you an indication for who is feeling pain the most

Mark "X" if feedback or findings is a "Strength," "Weakness," "Opportunity," or "Threat"

How critical is this to business?

What work effort category does it come under? Vision, Org. design, process, metrics, etc.?

#	Feedback or Finding	Number of people in each entity that share this view	Percentage of people in each segment who share this view	SWOT Category				Impact to business (Low, Medium, High)	Work Effort Category
				S	W	O	T		

touches on competency. So in this case, combining two critical issues only helps you solve one; specifically, the one that fits closest to the theme. The other winds up being an "orphan," which of course negates the reason for doing such an intense analysis in the first place.

While consolidating, make sure to highlight where the feedback is coming from—i.e., customers, stakeholder group, employees, etc. If multiples of these groups have mentioned an issue, then highlight them as such.

Capture the number of people within each of the categories who have given the feedback, then calculate the feedback percentage—i.e., the percentage of people in each entity or group who have given the feedback. For the percentages to be statistically relevant, make sure you have interviewed an appropriate sample size. For example, if there is feedback given on "poor customer service," you will naturally highlight where this feedback is coming from the most often. If it is coming from the customers, then which segment? Identifying the entity that is highlighting this issue also helps you to understand the "disconnects." For example, let's say that 62% of customers said that "poor customer service" was an issue but only 15% of the customer support team interviewed and only 20% of senior management interviewed said that customer service was an issue. Can you see how it helps us see where the disconnect lies between multiple data segments (in this case outside customers and internal management/leadership)? This is the type of information we're looking for. Repeat the same table and discussion/resolution for each of the "feedback" items or "findings." Make sure that you are preserving anonymity (at the personal level). It's okay to mention the group source, but not an individual's name.

Data validation is a key step in this process; make sure you are validating the data as you go along. For example, if a "reseller" says that he or she has a 50% return rate on products as a result of defects, then let's make sure we are validating the information—confirm in fact that the product indeed has a return rate of 50%.

Clearly, you can see how a small group discussion lends itself to a valuable exercise when analyzing this data. This step is critical in ensuring that the data you have collected in laps two and three is filtered through trusted and professional individuals and can be used credibly.

As one might imagine, this is neither a quick nor expedited process. In fact, depending on the amount of data you've gathered in the two previous laps, this may be a three- to five-day exercise. There are no shortcuts, so please take care and have patience!

Once this is done, arrange an extended team meeting consisting of people representing the following:

- ❑ The entire transformation core team
- ❑ All executives within the organization
- ❑ Key line managers within the organization

The purpose of this meeting with the extended team is threefold:

1. To educate key people on the findings you've gathered.

2. To leverage key subject matter experts and influencers in the organization to further analyze the data and help prioritize issues as well as identify root causes.

3. To engage key experts and influencers to improve adoption of the changes as they are part of the process. This approach is referred to in change management as a "high engagement model."

Once again, time is critical here and this is a process that should not be rushed. The meeting with the extended team may take up to three days off-site. Whether you conduct your strategy sessions at some far-away resort or in a rented conference room just down the street, be sure to get away from the office.

Why off-site? You'll want to avoid interruptions, certainly. I highly encourage this meeting be done outside your office so there are no distractions. Also, getting out of the office helps change the environment to stimulate creative thinking by removing the planners from their day-to-day, operational setting.

The analysts (above) who compiled the list should review the list (row by row), helping everyone in the extended team to understand the feedback (they are the moderators).

It is important to moderate the session so the data review does not become emotional and/or defensive. After all, if you have asked people for input you should be ready to at least hear it. As we have seen, you will have already committed to a large chunk of time and energy on this process and the only way to realize your investment is to view the findings with an open mind. Without objectivity, true change is rarely achieved.

Having the change management strategist (or "change agent") in the meeting will help. For instance, this individual can take notes on people's perceptions and behavior, which will help develop appropriate strategies for transformation adoption.

Make sure the entire team has printed copies of your vision/mission draft from lap five that you have worked on in parallel with lap four. This will serve as a critical reference as you review each of the (theme consolidated) feedback and findings.

As you are reviewing the data, ask the team to keep an eye out for information that is minimally relevant to the business transformation effort. These will be filtered out through a prioritization process highlighted below.

The Categorized List

What did you find as a result of your meetings? What pressing issues face your company in the immediate future and what challenges await further down the line? By now you should have a list of issues such as "customer support," "distribution," or "sales streams" that require your attention; this is called simply, "The List" (see Illustration 4.5).

Don't let the length of the list bother you at this point. A longer list does not necessarily mean that the transformation is going to be more challenging, while a shorter list won't necessarily make things less challenging.

To move forward, however, we need to now highlight what the impact of each of the feedback/findings is on the list by considering its "impact to the business." Take the team through the exercise of categorizing each item on the list as having a "low" "medium," or "high" impact to business.

As you prioritize items on the list, consider filtering out low-impact feedback and findings. By prioritizing your efforts to surround medium- to high-impact items on the list you will likely alter and even remedy those low-impact items.

A Strategy Pairing Exercise

First, consider splitting the team into four groups, each group representing all the various functions of the organization. I encourage you to identify the teams in advance so you do not waste time during the meeting.

The purpose of having cross-functional teams representing each of the groups is to allow you to take several aspects into consideration while building your strategy. As you will shortly see, each team has a vital mission to achieve and the results of that mission could greatly affect the transformation.

Make sure the groups have a good balance of people who have left/right brain dominance—creativity, strategic thinking, tactical planning, pragmatic thinking, etc. These skills will allow your teams to not just read or see the data but to actively interpret it.

It is also important to have the organization's top talent represented here. Include executives as well as line managers. Make sure that all groups within the organization are included as well.

In order to encourage participation, collaboration, and creative thinking, you may want to consider setting aside awards for active participation and be sure to set up quite a few of these awards so everyone feels that they have a chance to win.

To increase the level of employee ownership, let the participants vote for each other. Make it interesting by breaking up sessions with mini or even major "awards ceremonies" to provide breaks. It's important to short circuit the feeling of monotony that might accumulate after several days of these meetings.

By now each row in the list (see Illustration 4.5) has been categorized into strengths, weaknesses, opportunities, or threats. Sort and cut the list into these four categories. Each of the four teams (see below) takes a list. Give each team an interesting name (see below) to provide identity and verbal/visual cues throughout the meeting. For instance:

1. The Almighty (for Strengths)
2. The Underdog (for Weaknesses)
3. The Optimist (for Opportunities)
4. The Patriot (for Threats)

These teams work together in pairs to work on SO, WT, ST, and WO strategies (see below for further explanation). Let's start with SO and WT strategies. Each team's job is to make sure their interests are well understood, analyzed, and considered in the development of each of the four strategies, namely SO, WT, ST, and WO.

The SO Strategy

Now, the "strengths" and the "opportunities" teams will get together to define the SO strategy. In other words, they will examine and leverage strengths identified to take advantage of the opportunities (that have not been mined so far).

Since you are leveraging your strengths into opportunities with this step, these are usually short- to mid-term strategies, meaning you can reap your rewards relatively quickly.

Some examples of SO strategy include:

1. Expand globally
2. Increase sales staff
3. Enter new markets
4. Develop new products
5. Diversify, etc.

The WT strategy

The "weaknesses" and the "threats" groups will work together on the WT strategy. So, in this case, the team wants to ask the collective, "How do we avoid threats and the impact of weakness?"

In other words, how can we convert a weakness into a strength as well as avoid future threats? This is a defensive strategy that often takes time to overcome. If, for example, your organization has a "weak customer support" system and your strongest competitor recently received a "best customer service" award in your industry, then in your WT strategy you should look at ways to strengthen your customer service. In a situation like this, a "fish bone" technique, also known as an "Ishikawa Diagram," named after the inventor of the process, is provided for your convenience. (See Illustration 4.6 for a visual representation of a typical problem: low customer satisfaction.) These can be used to get to the root cause of your weakness.

In this case, low customer satisfaction is labeled a weakness. Three separate categories have been determined as leading to this weakness:

> **Low-quality product**: a result of poor materials, bad design, and incompetent employees.
>
> **High pricing**: comes from ineffective marketing and cost of materials.
>
> **Poor support**: results from wrong answers, long hold times, and fee structure.

WT strategy examples include:

1. Divest
2. Reward employees
3. Retrench
4. Restructure
5. Downsize, etc.

Illustration 4.6: Causes of Low Customer Satisfaction (Weakness)

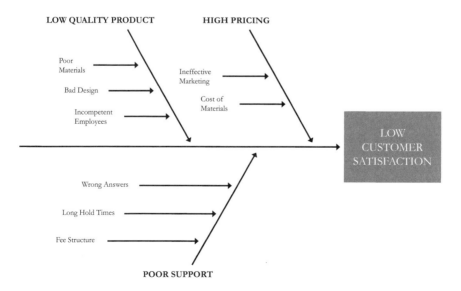

The WO Strategy

The "weakness" and the "opportunities" groups will take on the task of building a WO strategy. In essence, they will take on the responsibility to address weaknesses in order to exploit opportunities.

These are considered "gaps" and, hence, need to be "filled" in order to convert weaknesses into strengths. Let's say you are in the business of developing Bluetooth headsets and your data suggests that your customers do not like your product because of its battery life (which they consider "short" when compared with other, similar products). There is a new technology being developed by a Bluetooth chip vendor that doubles battery life. This would be exploiting the opportunity to take care of the weakness. You can leverage the "fish bone" technique, as appropriate.

This level of detail is necessary to understand not just the weakness (W) but how to turn that weakness into an opportunity (O).

- ❑ Name the problem (or in this case weakness) that you are trying to solve. In this case, we used "low customer satisfaction."

- ❑ Next, decide the categories of causes for the weakness. For a starting place, I always suggest that companies consider the six Ms: Manpower (personnel), Machines, Materials, Methods, Measurements, and Mother Nature (environment). See which of these make sense in your case.

- ❑ Next, brainstorm with the team for a more detailed root cause. For instance, determining that "poor support" is contributing to low customer satisfaction is helpful, but far from a solution. Determining the root cause—wrong answers being delivered by agents, long hold times, hang-ups, and fee structure—helps you turn weakness into opportunity.

- ❑ Complete the exercise shown in Illustration 4.6 to pinpoint each issue and target a resolution. For instance, under "poor support" you may list "wrong answers," "long hold times," and "fee structure."

- ❑ Consult with subject matter experts, as appropriate, to resolve each issue.

❑ Review the diagram for completeness as you solve each issue.

❑ Color code, as appropriate, to highlight criticality. For example, not every issue is created equally. Under "poor support," solving the problem of "wrong answers" might be as simple as printing up and distributing the latest product catalog for each service employee and testing their knowledge. This could take a weekend or, at most, a week. However, for an issue contributing to "low quality product," like "poor materials," it might take significantly longer to find "better materials," hence it might need to be highlighted for criticality.

WO strategy examples are:

1. Joint venture
2. Acquire competitor
3. Expand nationally
4. Backward integration
5. Forward integration, etc.

The ST Strategy

Strengths
Threats

The two might seem at odds with one another but, as we all know, in business it is our job to use what works best to avoid problems down the line. To that end, the "strengths" and "threats" groups will work together in leveraging strengths to avoid or eradicate threat.

ST strategy examples include:

1. Diversify
2. Acquire competitor
3. Liquidate
4. Expand locally
5. Re-engineer, etc.

Combining Strategies for Maximum Effectiveness

Once each group has thoroughly brainstormed every strategy pair, namely SO, WT, ST, and WO, next have someone from each of the four groups present their respective views to the entire team. It is critical for the leader of the entire organization to join this session.

For each paired strategy, make sure the group thoroughly discusses the data; specifically, consider thinking through some of the following questions:

- ❑ What are our guiding principles in developing this strategy? (Clearly, this needs to be done up front.)
- ❑ What are the benefits of each of the points being discussed?
- ❑ What are the respective risks? Pros and cons?
- ❑ What are the root causes of gaps or issues showing up in WO and WT strategies?
- ❑ What is the (approximate) financial impact of each of the items being considered?
- ❑ What is the impact on the organizational design as well as any new competency expected of the leaders/employees?
- ❑ How will the specific points being discussed impact our engagements (processes) and governance (decision-making)?
- ❑ How will the specific points being discussed change our existing product/service strategy?
- ❑ How can we measure success?
- ❑ How long might it take to achieve success?

The key strategic leaders will then take the time to craft the overall strategy for change, which could be a combination of one or more of the above strategies. Again, this process is very critical and often takes time.

When their critical analysis is complete, the same leaders will come back and share the overall strategy with the entire team. After all, the team has put in a considerable amount of effort on this initiative, and so it is critical that you provide closure—you need to close the loop with them. It is beneficial for the organization to give them the satisfaction of their effort, resulting in something tangible.

As part of the strategy and planning exercise, I highly encourage you to engage the above team back into doing a start-stop-continue-change exercise. The point here is to highlight the following as a result of the new strategy:

- ❑ **Start:** What specific effort do we need to begin?

- ❑ **Stop:** What current efforts should we stop working on?

- ❑ **Continue:** What current efforts should continue?

- ❑ **Change:** What is working to some extent and what would benefit from minor change?

Obviously, the crisper you are with this exercise the better. This will help everyone get a better picture of the "to be" state This needs to be communicated to everyone at the all-hands meeting (discussed below).

Finally, as we enter into this critical phase of pre-transformation, it is important to understand that the strategy/strategies that we are working on will continue to be a draft; aspects may be tweaked as we go through further laps.

Where to Invest

A common question I am often asked while consulting with companies that want to be front runners is, "Where is the best place to invest the money in the company? Should we put our money into developing new products, or should it go into improving existing products?"

I look at these kinds of questions very differently. I often ask the client, "Where are the best (most qualified) *opportunities*?"

That's where the money should go.

I don't care how big or small the company, there is only ever so much money to invest. Even an Apple or Microsoft has to determine every year, "Where is the money going to go?" While it may seem like these ultimate front runners have billions to throw around, we all know that if money is squandered, the front runners will fall behind faster that you can imagine.

Not all opportunities get you the same kind of return, and many of them have different timelines for success. You need to analyze the opportunities to see what works best for your organization. Illustration 4.7 represents what I call the Product/Services Opportunity Matrix. As you can see from the chart, opportunity comes in the form of new products/services and/or markets. This chart, and this section, will help you determine which is more prudent for you to invest in at this time: products/services or markets.

What combination of strategies you employ depends on the vision for your company. If the prevailing idea is to position your organization for a sale in the next six months—in other words, to maximize your return on investments with potentially minimum costs—the SO strategy may work best for you.

Another aspect to be considered is how equipped the company is in developing new products/services versus developing new markets. Where does your ability to develop new products/services and your ability to enter new markets fall in the SWOT analysis? Is this your strength or a weakness? Don't forget the time it takes to develop new products versus the time it takes to develop new markets. Your objectives should dictate the choice. Having said that, it may not be necessary to compromise and make that choice. One could do both.

Remember the ethnography study for your current products you did in lap two? Leverage the information in the report of finding to see if you want to consider getting into developing new products, or prefer getting into new markets with existing products or both. I strongly urge you to conduct appropriate new ethnography studies before investing into new products or new markets. This will considerably reduce your risk.

Also, if you have taken a long-term view, are you willing to exploit opportunities despite weakness in specific areas? This is a rather longer-term strategy—the SO strategy can often fund the WO strategy.

The ST and WT strategies are relatively short-to-mid-term and mid-to-long term strategies (see Illustration 4.8). Of course, there are always exceptions to the rule, but they should serve as a good guideline.

As we see in the Product/Services Matrix (Illustration 4.7), the further away you go from the "current" box the riskier it gets, requiring both time and resources. If you do it right though, you could reap huge rewards.

Illustration 4.7: Product/Services Opportunity Matrix

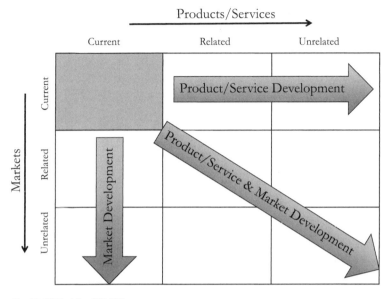

Illustration 4.8: Time-centric Strategies

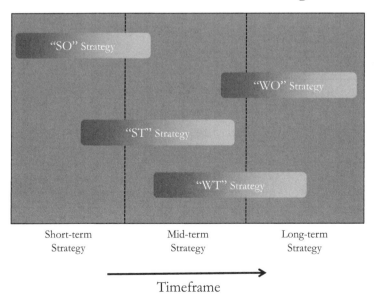

Marketing the Microsoft Way

Take the example of Microsoft. Marketing is definitely one of its strengths. As we all know, Microsoft has dominated in the software space but was growing somewhat eclipsed in the portable media market by heavy hitters like Apple, whose iPod singlehandedly revolutionized the marketplace (to say nothing of the overwhelming initial success of their new iPad).

When Microsoft considered getting into the new markets, like music and video players, it made a strategic decision to move diagonally rather than horizontally. Specifically, it took on the burden of market development (or marketing) while deciding to partner with Toshiba for the actual product development of the device that would later be known as the Zune, Microsoft's answer to Apple's iPod.

By sharing the burden of product design and development with an established company like Toshiba, Microsoft considerably reduced the risk of hardware design and manufacturing to its own bottom line. Obviously, this is not a permanent partnership. With more experience on the product side over time, Microsoft began designing specific aspects of the product internally while still partnering with a contract electronic manufacturer for the manufacturing side.

Cisco, another hi-tech giant, adopts the same philosophy, oftentimes getting into many related market adjacencies offering new product/ services or vice versa. Unless you are a behemoth with (almost) unlimited resources, and excellent brand image, you may be taking considerable risk. A conservative approach is to take a two-step approach (see Illustration 4.9).

As another example, Microsoft's "Sync" product for the automobile industry was a huge success. In this case Microsoft was entering into an unrelated industry with related products (software). Now, would Microsoft succeed in selling farm equipment (unrelated products) to farmers (unrelated industry)? I will let you be the judge!

Keep in mind, a more detailed analysis around products or services will be done later, in lap eight. For now, the intent is not to nail down the strategy, but more so to set the direction. As you work on the next few laps, you will get closer and closer to the 100% mark that will bring you the transformation you desire.

Illustration 4.9: Product/Services Opportunity Matrix

Also, it should be noted that if the vision and strategy are drastically

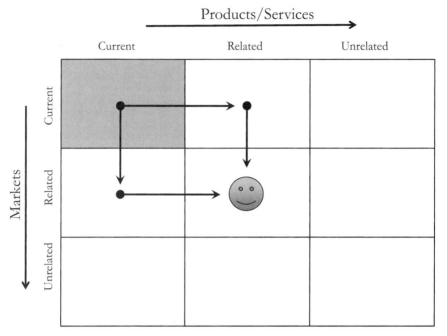

different than the current one, consider conducting a quick impact analysis; understanding the impact of a new strategy on customers, employees, and shareholders is important and should not be taken lightly. If there are any risks, manage them appropriately.

Assessing and Investing in Innovation Opportunities

In all the years that I have led innovation projects, I have never been able to understand why even experienced leaders use DCF (Discounted Cash Flow) or NPV (Net Present Value) as a way to assess innovation investment opportunities. Worse yet, they use these numbers to compare against projects that are chartered for incremental improvements.

For those of you who may not be familiar, Discounted Cash Flow (DCF) analysis uses future-free, cashflow projections and then discounts them (most often using the weighted average cost of capital) to arrive at a present value, which is used to evaluate the potential for investment. If the value arrived at through DCF analysis is higher than the current cost of the investment, the opportunity is said to be a good one.

Let's analyze this for a moment here. Discounting a future stream of cash flow into a present value assumes that a rational investor would be indifferent to having a dollar today as compare to receiving a dollar plus the interest (or return that could be earned by investing a dollar) a few years from now. This makes perfect sense to assess the investment by computing $(1 + r)^n$, where "r" is the discount rate or the annual return from investing that money and "n" is the time period.

The problem, however, is with the assumption of the baseline. We are assuming here that not investing in the innovation will have no negative financial effect on the company. Now we all know in real life this is not true, and that lack of innovation over time will result in the company losing margins, revenue, and even market share. You should assume that your competition will invest in innovation regardless of whether you invest or not.

There is an interesting article titled, "Innovation Killers," by Clayton M. Christensen, Stephen Kaufman, and Willy Shih that elaborates on this exact topic. They go on to highlight that it is tempting but wrong to assess the value of a proposed investment by measuring whether it will make us better off than we are now. It's wrong because if things are deteriorating on their own, we might be worse off than we are now after we make the proposed investment but better off than we would have been without it (see illustration 4.10).

Also, another area I have a problem with is forecasting models. It blows my mind as I sit through presentations from entrepreneurs and seasoned product managers to see them highlight elaborate charts and spreadsheets to explain their forecasts for the innovation products. Let us not kid ourselves here: identifying future cash flows generated, especially from disruptive innovation, can be extremely difficult to predict, making investment decisions that much harder. Unfortunately, most managers make up these numbers so as to look good and get funded. The big question however is, are we setting the innovation project up for failure with perhaps unrealistic

Illustration 4.10: DCF Trap

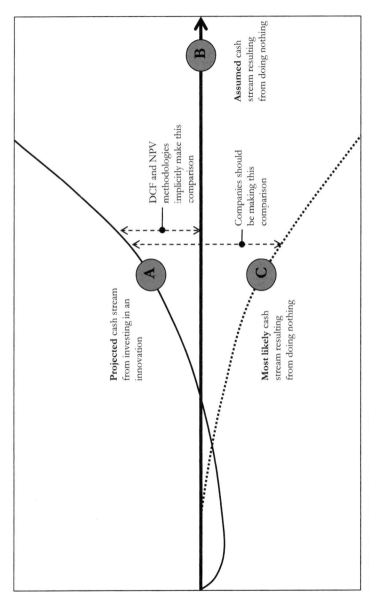

A — **Projected** cash stream from investing in an innovation

B — **Assumed** cash stream resulting from doing nothing

C — **Most likely** cash stream resulting from doing nothing

DCF and NPV methodologies implicitly make this comparison

Companies should be making this comparison

Adapted from Harvard Business Review January 2008
"Innovation Killers" by Clayton M. Christensen, Stephen P. Kaufman, and Willy C. Shih

expectations? I will let you answer that question based on your experience working on innovative projects.

While there is no perfect approach to remedy the anti-innovation bias, here are some aspects you can keep in mind while assessing and executing innovation projects.

❑ Your annual strategy-planning process should involve identification and execution of innovation projects (new business models, new processes, new products/services). Allocate a certain percentage of your revenue for these innovation projects.

❑ The leaders need to change the way they assess and approve innovation-centric investment opportunities. The leadership team needs to take the time to develop a culture that supports innovation. Consider rewarding those who innovate within the organization.

❑ Most companies have rigid product development life cycles or new product introduction life cycles that are typically suitable for incremental improvements. Once a year, they start with a large list of projects they want to work on. They go through various steps that filter out the less viable ideas for more "promising" projects, but based on skewed logic. The process takes them through several gates with preset approval criteria. The unfortunate part is that the criteria used for making the decision at each gate is biased against innovation. Managers who want to take their innovation projects through the gates make up unrealistic revenue and profit numbers, or even tweak key assumptions as appropriate just to get their projects through the gate and to get the funding. While these measures are easy to show in incremental improvement projects, they are harder to show in innovation projects, leading to an anti-innovation bias.

❑ Proposing to create growth through potentially disruptive technologies, products, processes or even business models can't always be supported by hard metrics, at least in the initial stages.

For this reason, I encourage you not to measure innovation projects with the same yardstick as mature projects chartered around incremental improvements.

❑ Avoid making assumptions that the strategy you came up with initially for the product, service, or business model innovation is the right one. Unfortunately in most companies, if after the launch the product/service fails to meet the "unrealistic" goals, the leaders are sometimes quick to cancel the project even if the ideas have potential. The problem is that except in the case of mature products/services that go through incremental improvements, the right strategy may not be known well in advance. Sometimes you just have to row the boat in order to steer it. You will have to refine your strategy a few times for it to click. The leaders should be patient and supportive, asking the innovation team all the right questions and removing any roadblocks that might prevent success. I will share some specific approaches in lap eight that can help you improve your odds of success with your innovation projects.

❑ Consider developing an inhouse methodology for identifying and developing innovation projects based on your need. This is different from methodologies used in making incremental improvement for mature projects. If you do not have the expertise inhouse to develop such a methodology, then leverage models that exist, like the "Discovery Driven Planning" or "D4" models. Look them up on the web to find more details about them.

❑ Set aside a dedicated cross-functional team to work on innovation. Make sure the team is hand-picked and has the right entrepreneurial skills. Give the team an identity, just as you would for a startup. Consider defining and communicating criteria and processes for moving the projects mainstream as they reach the pre-determined trigger point.

❑ We have highlighted in the earlier chapters that people buy products and services to get jobs done (customer need). The idea is to align company strategy to the satisfaction of customer needs. The better your product or service in fulfilling the need, the better the chance of the customer buying your product.

❑ In crafting your financial calculations, consider starting with business objectives; for example, target company growth at 20% in revenues and margins. Next, identify new markets that are large enough to get you to the target growth. Just to clarify, "market" is defined as a group of people with similar JTBD. This will then help you define opportunities in the selected markets where you can develop products that meet customers' needs (JTBD).

❑ If you do not have expertise or the technology to build appropriate products for the newly targeted markets then consider leveraging the WO strategy (explained earlier) to perhaps license the technology or even acquire a company to meet your objective.

Change Management and Communication

A Step-by-Step Guide to Communicating the Burning Platform

You have worked hard to follow this lap and use the findings from two previous laps to develop a deep and dense data pool. You have further used these findings to develop what I call your "burning platform."

What, exactly, is the burning platform?

Let's say you're staying in the penthouse suite of a strange hotel when an alarm wakes you in the middle of the night. Your eyes open to find the blinking of red and blue sirens reaching your window. You sit up and smell smoke wafting through the front door. You don't know where you are, you haven't examined the exit strategy on the back of the front door and it's too late now. You stagger blindly into the hallway and reach for the nearest door that, fortunately, leads to a stairway.

Unfortunately, the stairwell below you is on fire, leaving you only one choice: to climb out onto the roof. There you become trapped. Flames are already consuming the stairs you just walked up and are flickering around the edges of the building, leaving you no choice but to walk to the edge and contemplate your only other alternative: to jump.

This hardly seems reasonable. Twenty-four stories separate you from certain death, but as firefighters scramble below and fire engines race to put out the fire, you spot a patch of grass that might soften your blow. Behind you the heat is intense, the flames threatening to reach you at any second.

What do you do? Stay and face certain death at the hands of a raging fire or leap to a possible death, hoping a postage-stamp size swatch of lawn might soften the blow? Most people would jump because, for most of us, the mere chance of survival beats that of certain death.

The point here is that many companies, unless compelled by a literal "fire alarm," a dip in profits, an irate shareholder phone call, a red flag, or other emergency, won't change unless they absolutely have to. The burning platform is the literal danger forcing you to make one decision or another: stay where you are and be consumed by the fire or jump into the unknown and have a chance to find salvation.

When it comes to your company, the burning platform is what you've determined in your SWOT analysis to be the critical factor(s) around which the change initiative will take place. Now, with these findings under our belt, it's time to communicate your "burning platform"—or your case for change—with the employees.

As with most game-changing events, this is a crucial step. In fact, it's not enough just to communicate the platform, but further thought needs to be given to what, when, and even how to communicate.

Let's break this down further for clarity:

What to communicate:

- ❑ Celebrate your accomplishments thus far.

- ❑ Highlight where you want to be two to three years from now. What does success look like at the end of the journey?

- ❑ Share where you are, relative to the vision, based on the feedback and findings.

❑ Highlight no more than three to five key reasons for the transformation, based on the findings. What happens if you don't change? How will it impact the organization and the employees? Keep it simple and easy to understand and remember to avoid information overload.

❑ Create and share an easy-to-understand roadmap of things to come.

❑ Highlight the immediate next steps.

❑ Share how you will continue to keep the employees engaged and informed. Employee participation is crucial to success.

Who to communicate to:

All part-time and full-time employees, contractors, consultants, etc.

When to communicate:

❑ Make this a half-day event.

❑ From my experience, nine a.m. to noon is the best time, as everyone will be present. Consider doing it on a Friday in order to leverage a more relaxed atmosphere.

❑ You may have to plan this half-day event well in advance, especially if you want everyone to be present (as some, especially sales and marketing folks, may have travel plans).

❑ Provide lunch, breaks, and refreshments or snacks, as appropriate.

How to communicate:

❑ I have yet to hear of a successful transformation without active engagement of all the employees.

❑ You will not be able to get that unless you can get their "hearts and minds" interested in the transformation.

❑ Make the presentation as visual and interactive as possible—studies have shown that people tend to remember visual and interactive experiences more.

Tips for Effective Communication

You've seen who, what, when, and how to communicate, but what are the specific steps you need to follow to do just that? Here are some additional tips for effective communication:

1   **Minimize the usage of Power Point slides and high-tech** gadgets to deliver your information. Don't get wrapped up in sharing too many charts or Power Point slides with numbers and jargons.

2   **Take care in choosing the right speakers** for the occasion. Remember, it is not so much about bringing in speakers who are flawless in their language and technique, it is about who can speak to the hearts and minds of the employees.

3   **Trust can play a key role** in choosing the right people. You will need three to four key speakers to deliver this content. Consider including line managers as speakers; this will help avoid the perception that all of these changes are merely coming from the "ivory tower," or from the powers that be on high, rather than with consideration to the common man.

4   **It is critical that the CEO or division head be included** on the speaker list. This will ensure that employees can see how important the transformation effort is to even the most senior people.

5   **Consider showing a condensed and edited video** of what the customers, partners, analysts, etc., are saying about your current products and potential. This will require hiring an outside company to video customers/partners and compile a twenty-to-thirty-minute documentary from that footage. I have seen this to be a very effective way to help employees understand the customers, especially people in groups that never see or touch a customer or have visibility into the market; for example, folks in manufacturing, shipping, finance, accounting, HR, etc.

6   **Change Ambassadors:** Consider leveraging change ambassadors to craft the WIIFM message. Remember, these ambassadors are influential people that everyone trusts, and they know the inner workings of their respective departments.

7   **Highlight WIIFM** (What's in it for me?). In other words, why should employees support the transformation process? What's in it for them? This needs to come out clearly during your communication efforts.

8   **Weave a story** to communicate the tremendous growth potential the company has because of the transformation process. Let the employees know how they play into that potential, and just how valuable they are in the process. Employee ownership of the transitional phase is critical to its success.

9   **Consider recognizing employees** who have made great contributions so far and reiterate that their contributions are appreciated.

10   **Make some of the sessions interactive** so the information is not delivered all in one way (see agenda, below, for more details).

11   **Share the results** of the employee survey (high level).

12   **Devise an interactive and engaging way to communicate** the transformation progress. As the transformation is likely to continue for some time and the team participation elements of these exercises may "wear off" for the day-to-day employees not involved in the transition team, consider starting an internal blog to keep employees apprised of current goings-on as they apply to the transformation. One of the core team members can be assigned to update the blog, say, on a weekly basis, simply so that employees so inclined can stay updated on the process.

Your Sample Agenda

Wondering what one of these half-day, "all hands" meetings might look like? Wonder no more. Here is a sample agenda for such a meeting:

> **Frame the meeting** (done by the moderator): Let attendees know why they're here and lay down ground rules for the meeting.

> **One of a kind vision** (done by the CEO): Provide a rousing message that explains the reason for change and outlines what the company will look like after change.

> **Current state findings** (done by the transformation initiative sponsor): Discuss the current state of the company and allude positively to the future state.

> **Roadmap to the future** (done by one of the line managers): This lays out the actual strategy, or road map, of the transformation itself.

> **Employee engagement:** An opportunity to invite employee participation by engaging in brainstorming or Q&A activities.

> **Closing** (done by the CEO): Send folks off with a positive message "from on high" to compel them that this is a top-down transformation.

We have spent a great deal of time discussing communication strategies for sharing data with employees in every department. As we wrap up this lap, however, it is important that you get a sense of where each of the stakeholders is in the placement map.

The idea of the **stakeholder analysis** (Illustration 4.11) is to understand where each of the critical stakeholders stands with respect to the transformation relative to where they should be. Illustration 4.11 provides a great way to provide stakeholder analysis. For example, perhaps the VP of customer service is at the "awareness" level, but you need to get the person to the "committed" level. The gap (between the two states of being: awareness and committed) in this case is large, and an appropriate plan of action is required to influence this critical stakeholder. The tool in Illustration 4.11 can also help you think through the steps. The change management strategist,

Illustration 4.11: Stakeholder Analysis

Stakeholder	Criticality to transformation			Current placement	Future placement	Gap (Small, Medium, Large)	Issues
	Make or Break	Influencer	Directly Impacted	Irrelevant	O = Not on life cycle, A = Awareness, U = Understanding, D = Desire, B = Buy-in, C = Committed	O = Not on life cycle, A = Awareness, U = Understanding, D = Desire, B = Buy-in, C = Committed		

Name Stakeholders here. Arrange based on groups if appropriate

Map criticality to transformation

Where are they now on the transition cycle?

Where do they need to be on the transition cycle?

Placement gap between the current state and the desired state

Stakeholder issues to be aware of

Message—What??	Message—Who?			Message—How and when?		Status
Message key points	Who will create?	Who will approve?	Who will deliver?	Vehicle?	Delivery date?	

or change leader, in your core team can leverage this tool (Illustration 4.11) and take the necessary steps to begin the transformation process.

Here are two sample email letter templates that should go out to all the employees. The CEO or head of the division should send these letters:

Sample letter 1: Invite the employees to a company meeting. The letter should:

- ❏ Be two to three paragraphs long.
- ❏ Encourage employees to join the meeting, in which the CEO will be sharing some critical plans for the future, etc.

Here is what a "real world" invitation might look like:

> Dear Employee,
>
> Something BIG is in the works, and we'd love to get you involved. You may have heard rumors that change is in the air. Well, for once, the rumors are right!
>
> Change IS in the air and we need your help to maximize our efficiency and grow to even greater heights. As part of this exciting transformation initiative, we want each of you to actively participate and contribute.
>
> Over the next few days we will be holding strategic planning sessions designed around key areas in which senior management feel there should be some changes. We invite you to attend our first meeting, where the leadership team and I will be sharing some critical plans for the future.
>
> The meeting will be held this Friday between noon and 2p.m. Check with your department head for details, and we'll see you there.
>
> Sincerely,
>
> John Myer
> President and CEO

Sample letter 2: Thank-you message. This will be sent to everyone after the company meeting. Here are some suggestions for drafting this letter:

- Consider sending the letter via email.

- Thank the employees for joining the meeting.

- Highlight five to seven key takeaways that identify the reasons for why this transformation is critical.

- Request employees to participate actively in this transformation.

- Inform employees on how they can get the latest information:
  - From their managers
  - Link to the blog
  - Milestone-based town hall meetings

- Link to where they can find the information shared with them at the company meeting.

- Set aside awards to encourage employee participation.

- Highlight immediate next steps.

- Identify the next meeting date (if possible).

Now, here is what a sample of the above template might look like in a "real world" thank-you message:

Dear Employee,

Thanks so much for attending last Friday's meeting, which I think we'll all agree was a major success! Your participation was greatly appreciated by the leadership team and by me.

As a result of everyone's input, the core team has agreed that the following items will require transformation throughout the coming months:

- ❑ A customer service upgrade
- ❑ More accountability concerning inventory

- ❑ Faster delivery times
- ❑ Bigger incentives for recruiting senior personnel
- ❑ More flexible schedules for production employees

As an active participant in last week's meeting, we're sure you'll share our enthusiasm in making these departments even more efficient and productive than they already are. But we still need your help! In the coming weeks we will be inviting employees to participate as we further hone our plans for each of these items. Will you help?

Your manager or department head will keep you up to date on not just the latest changes but how you can actively participate with suggestions, additional meetings, and hands-on initiatives to further change. You can also check into our new company internal blog [insert specific URL here] at any time for weekly updates, and stay tuned for another company-wide "town hall" meeting to be scheduled soon.

Want to know exactly what was decided as a result of last week's meeting? The following link, [insert specific URL here], will tell you everything you want to know—and then some—including vital feedback that was provided thanks to you! As mentioned at the meeting, departmental awards are being finalized now not only for your previous participation but your continued participation as well.

In the coming weeks you may notice some changes in your department and/or related departments. These will be due to the following immediate action steps that resulted from last week's meeting:

- ❑ While customer service reps take a three-day class on Wednesday, Thursday, and Friday, temps will be filling their positions;

❑ Production on the central line may be interrupted next Tuesday and Wednesday while an outside team begins the process of refitting outdated metrics;

❑ The warehouse will be closed, starting Thursday at 3p.m., through Friday afternoon to begin a preliminary inventory.

Again, due to YOUR active participation, this company-wide transformation is well under way. Stay tuned to the internal blog and incoming emails to keep apprised of our next meeting, to be held one month hence. Until then, your continued support and patience is appreciated.

Yours,

John Myer
President and CEO

Do You See These As Gaps In Your Company?

Consider the environment: It is imperative that in this day and age you consider creating an eco-friendly strategy for your company. Taking the time to do a transformational effort without addressing the very real, very near impact of the environment just means you'll have to address it in the near future anyway, so why not take the time now? In short, make sure you build strategies that do not just embrace eco-friendliness but also have it as a central theme. Consider the "carbon footprint" of all new initiatives not only to make sure they comply with national, federal, or local laws (which are rapidly changing), but also to ensure that your company is socially responsible (see below).

Corporate social responsibility: Having a clearly defined philosophy or mission around your company corporate social responsibility (CSR) only makes sense in these trying times. Consumers, vendors, even business partners want to do business with companies who are modern, and who have specifically strong values and a coherent sense of CSR.

Case Study: Grass Roots Enthusiasm Delivers High-level Support

This is truly a case in restructuring an organization from the bottom up. A division of a major telecommunications company was struggling to build an identity. I was called in to consult and coach a frustrated VP named Jim Brown (fictitious name), the division chief.

Jim was facing a crossroads at his company. While he was in a senior position himself, he was battling the age-old specter of internal politics. Through several initial meetings, Jim was able to vocalize his frustrations with how his organization was performing. The senior management in the company did not perceive much value coming out of the customer advocacy division. They had given Jim four months to either turn it around or be ready to disband. Jim had several aspects to work on to truly turn around the company.

First of all, there were several "pet projects" of the company's senior elite members, initiated over the years that were sucking the resources. These eclectic projects collectively added little value and relevance to the division or the overall company. These "pet projects" were in fact not only distractions, but adversely affected the profits. The chaotic environment deeply impacted the morale of the employees.

Jim suspected the problem, but needed a way to communicate these issues with the senior leadership team and the rest of the employees without making anyone look bad.

After getting a feel for Jim's personality, I realized it would be ideal to craft and share the "new" vision with his employees, staff, and personnel in order to rally their support and focus in on what the root problems confronting the organization really were.

With Jim's help, we created a very well-choreographed presentation for the "all-hands" meeting(s) (those meetings attended by everyone in the division) to share the vision and the "burning platform" with the entire organization and engage the audience in a dialogue that was both healthy and productive.

Jim did an exceptional job of building the story, which is so critical to making the transition phase personal to employees. He started by explaining the importance of the vision, and then articulated his vision for the organization. Next he highlighted the gaps that currently existed, engaging the audience in a SWOT exercise, followed by a root cause analysis.

Enthusiasm and instincts are one thing; data and black-and-white analysis are quite another. Through determining the root cause analysis he was able to quantifiably pinpoint proof that what he suspected was dragging the company down were, in fact, the culprits.

He even invited some of the key stakeholders and customers to share their views live with the entire organization. This was not an organization that was open about doing such things but, through his enthusiasm and belief in the success of the eventual transformation, Jim ultimately prevailed.

By doing so, Jim was able to accomplish two things in one step:

1. Engage the employees in the most effective way—by capturing their hearts and minds.

2. Help solicit the input of the subject matter experts in determining the root cause.

Through this employee-centric data analysis, Jim was truly able to take the crisis (a potential shut-down of the division) to his advantage by killing initiatives and projects that were not delivering any value (thereby creating an opportunity). This had been a considerable challenge in the past because many of the initiatives shut down were his leadership teams' pet projects.

Further analysis helped Jim to truly prioritize the "burning" objectives and, as a result, he was able to successfully weed out dead wood in his organization and instigate a complete restructure while keeping the customer in mind. He was able to influence his leadership team to develop a well-articulated vision, mission, and objectives, and align the same with the stakeholder groups' objectives.

Jim was also able to mobilize employees at the grass roots level. As a result, those employees were proactive in the transformation process and participated in identifying the gaps and finding the root cause.

By developing and articulating a clear value proposition, each of the groups within the organization actually helped save the organization from layoffs that the entire organization was previously facing. Why? Because through his presentation style and the active engagement of the team meetings, the senior management clearly saw the value of the transformation and grew committed to seeing it succeed.

All in all, the high-engagement model helped in rapidly transforming the organization. Other senior leaders within the company who saw this were encouraged by Jim to try this out in their respective departments. While it was an investment of time, money, and certainly Jim's energy, he has shared with me on multiple occasions how rewarding it was to him to see those efforts pay off—not just in the corner offices, but throughout the entire company.

Lap 4 Key Takeaways

❑ Catalog and analyze data gathered from observing job performers as well as data from VOC, VOP, VOC, VOS and VOE data.

❑ Lap four and five progress in a parallel fashion.

❑ Catalog, analyze, categorize, and prioritize the feedback.

❑ Catalog any interesting ideas shared by customers, partners, stakeholders, and employees on the "future state" and feed them into lap five for architecting the vision, mission, values, etc.

❑ Identify SWOT (strengths, weaknesses, opportunities, and threats) for each of the "feedback items."

❑ Engage high-level root cause analysis for each of the gaps and further prioritize, as appropriate.

❑ Draft a high-level strategy (SO, WT, etc).

❑ Communicate the "burning platform," with the entire organization and mobilize employees.

❑ Engage employees. Unify and engage the entire organization to understand the "burning platform" and move employees into a true sense of urgency state—in doing so, win the hearts and minds of the employees. Share a detailed roadmap and the next steps of the process with employees. Regularly update employees and thank them for their participation.

Lap 5

Craft Your Future State

Business management is like a team sport—there is a leader (coach), there is a strategy (playbook), and there is a method for scoring; but at the end of the day, the success of the transformation initiative all boils down to executing the plays in unison.

If three years from now, *Business Week* decided to write an article about your organization, what would you want it to say?

Front runners don't pause to think when asked this question; they don't have to. In fact, they all have a very clearly defined **vision** about where they would like to take the company and, frankly, an even better **mission** for what they'd like *others* to say about their company.

What's more, they have a firm set of company **values** in place. In other words, they know their destination and how to get to it. They know how to take appropriate detours if faced with challenges. They know how to turn challenges into opportunities.

While collecting data and bridging gaps, it can be easy to get bogged down in the day-to-day duties of business transformation. When the trees are our only focus, however, we can quickly lose sight of the forest and, in fact, lose our way altogether.

What do your vision, mission, and value statements say? In their simplest terms they should each communicate the following:

❑ **Mission statement:** Says who are you and what you are doing **today**.

❑ **Vision statement:** Highlights what you would like to achieve in the future.

❑ **Value statement:** Defines how the work gets done in your company and how you will need to behave in order to achieve your vision.

The biggest problem, though, is that most of these statements are just a bunch of feel-good business buzz words and industry jargon. They have nothing unique or courageous to say. Try pulling a few of these statements from your own industry—you could almost swap your company's vision with another from your industry and you would never notice the difference. Over the years they have been "templatized," so to speak. I would say you are better off not having these statements at all than having one that is generic in nature and feels like you copied from the Internet.

What often gets neglected in all these statements is **your sustainable competitive differentiator**. Does your company have one? There is a good chance you do, especially if you have done reasonably well all these years. Either your company has it by design or, perhaps, it grew organically—it is that special aspect that attracts customers to buy from you rather than your competition. If your customers are unable to identify and highlight your competitive differentiator, you either have a weak one or do not have one at all. If this is the case, you may have to first craft it.

If done right, these three statements will help you build your **brand positioning**. Take, for example, Disney's mission statement: "Our mission is to provide a wide range of entertainment options to families and children of all ages."

Their competitive differentiator, however, is the overall experience. They brand themselves to be the "happiest place on earth," "the magic kingdom," and the place in which "dreams come true."

So, for example, to define your vision, it is critical, therefore, to answer the following questions:

❑ What are you trying to achieve?

❑ By when do you want to achieve it?

❑ Why are you trying to achieve it?

❑ What is your sustainable competitive differentiator?

❑ How will the end-state look when you achieve it?

This is a critical step that defines the ultimate destination, or vision, we want to achieve for ourselves, for our company, for our team, for our employees—for our customers. This will then allow us to pave the path to the destination (i.e., define an effective strategy) through the rest of the steps outlined in this book.

Now that we know where our company is headed, this is a good time to bring together a cross-functional leadership team that is strategic and out-of the box in thinking to identify opportunities.

Case Study: Successful Mission, Vision and Value Statements at Work

Vision is just one part of the future for a successful company. In addition to stating the vision, companies must further distill that global message and create a mission statement as well as a value statement.

While we will dig deeper into all three such statements in this lap—vision, mission, and value—the following anecdote may serve to illustrate them quickly and easily before we start digging in much deeper. In many of my working sessions I often use the following example to illustrate what vision, mission, and value statements mean for an organization:

Imagine that you are waiting to catch a flight and you run into a friend of yours at the airport. As it's been a long time since you've run into this person, you quickly exchange notes on a personal front. Afterward, you inevitably start talking about work. Your friend talks about his background and expertise, and suddenly you perk up. It just so happens that your company has been looking for someone just like your friend to fill a critical role.

Now comes the tricky part. Your friend has quickly and succinctly summarized his qualifications; now it's your turn. He asks you whom you work for and you mention your company by name. Then your friend asks, "Sounds good, but what do they do?"

You mention that your company is into building solar panels for companies and commercial properties all over the US—its customers are Fortune 1000 companies. You go on to highlight that your key differentiator is a solutions approach that allows for appropriate product selection, installation, management, and maintenance in addition to reducing the client's carbon footprint, thereby qualifying them for valuable carbon footprint credits. What's more, the technology your company uses and their customer service is second to none.

At this point you are very excited about the prospect of working with your old friend and busily laying the groundwork in convincing him to join your company. You continue to talk about how bright the future is for the company, highlighting the fact that the management is looking at doubling the revenue in the next three years with plans of hiring close to one thousand people.

"Our goal is to be number one in our market segment by doubling our revenues in the next three years," you conclude breathlessly.

"Wow," your friend comments, "the management must be good."

"Oh yes," you say, "they are very good at understanding and delivering on customer needs with excellent fiscal responsibility. In fact, the entire company is built around honesty and integrity. The culture supports creative and innovative thinking and rewards people who deliver results."

Stop, freeze frame, and now . . . rewind. Many companies struggle for hours, days, and even weeks at great cost of time, energy, and even money to pitch the company vision, mission, and values as you just did in the above example. And what's more, you utilized all three of the statements we'll learn to craft in this lap.

You initially pitched your mission, "company is into building solar panels for other companies and commercial properties all over the US—its customers are Fortune 1000 companies;" then your vision, "Our goal is to be number one in our market segment by doubling our revenues in the next three years;" followed by the company values, "they are very good at understanding and delivering on customer needs with excellent fiscal responsibility. In fact, the entire company is built around honesty and integrity. The culture supports creative and innovative thinking and rewards people who deliver results!"

Purpose of Lap 5

Yes, believe it or not, sharing your company's mission, vision, and value statements can be as simple as that. Unfortunately, most companies over-complicate this process. There is no need to, and in this lap we will discuss how to make this process as simple, quick, and easy as it can be.

The Strategic Approach to Writing and Implementing Mission, Vision and Value Statements

Illustration 5.1 not only shows the strategy used for distilling your company vision, but it also shows the sequence of events that both precede and follow it. At the very left we see how both your company's mission and vision (more on both shortly) affect or reflect the company's values, whichever the case may be.

Notice how the mission, vision, and value statements don't just sit in a box by themselves but flow outside the box into more meaningful and practical action streams to include "high level strategy," "objectives," and eventually "tactics." (More on all three later in this chapter.) Finally, notice (at the bottom) how the feedback, findings, and recommendations from lap four inform and color the steps we'll be taking in lap five.

It is absolutely critical that you either have a separate "sustainable competitive differentiator" statement or you can embed them into your vision, mission, and value statements. The competitive differentiator impacts your overall strategy and your objectives.

Crafting Your Company Mission Statement

In my interactions with executives over the past several years, I often ask executives what the most valuable "underused" asset in business is. Here are the top three answers I usually get:

1. Human Resources
2. Mission statement
3. Customer data/feedback

Illustration 5.1: Vision Strategy Execution Sequencing

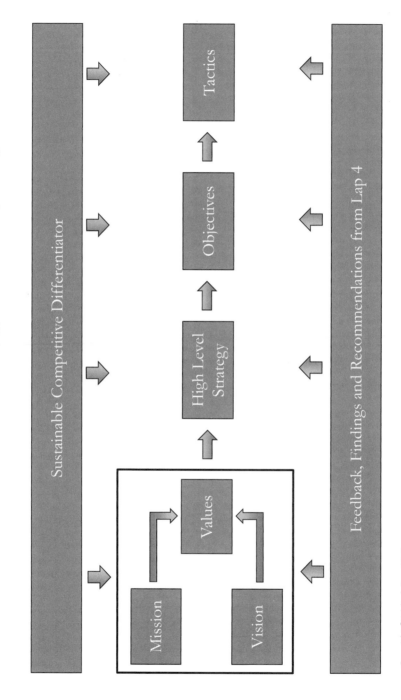

Often the mission statement is seen as just another "internal-facing" statement about the organization or company *for internal use only.* Many researchers feel (and I tend to agree with them) that a mission statement should be an introduction to all those who come in contact with the organization.

Why miss a golden opportunity to share yet another aspect of you or your organization with people? Rather than just another statement turned inward, toward yourself, the mission statement should be your face to the world; it is a way for you to let the world know—in just a sentence or two, if not less—who you are as an organization.

In this sense, "the world" includes employees, contractors, vendors, customers, business partners, and even the general public (even stock holders). The mission statement should inspire all of these groups to support and work with the organization to carry out its mission, creating a sense of partnership and even a feeling of ownership, where applicable.

Some companies take the "mission" aspect of drafting a mission statement a little too seriously, literally creating a company-wide task force to create a twenty-page document in which the mission statement itself gets lost amidst the various facts, figures, charts, graphs, and inevitable business buzz words. Instead, a mission statement should be a brief, clear picture about why your organization exists. It should give the organization a framework for devising the products and services it offers its customers in fulfilling its mission.

See Illustration 5.2 for some example mission statements that work. As you see in these examples, a mission statement is precise *and* concise. It highlights the reason for the organization's existence and what sets it apart from the competition. Once you read a successful mission statement, there should be no question as to what the company does, let alone how it does it.

While I'm all for giving mission statements their due, please know that writing the mission statement shouldn't be a week-long, let alone month-long, exercise. I don't believe it's an exercise worth bringing in an outside consultant for, either; it's something you can do, quite simply, in a day or even half day. Likewise, mission statements are never perfect. And more does not always equal more here; spending a week on something that you could have done in a day is not necessarily going to make it better.

Illustration 5.2: Example—Mission, Vision and Values

Company	Mission	Vision	Values
Medium hi-tech company	Supporting the growth of internet-based businesses by providing a suite of logistics software *that require minimal maintenance or training*, efficiently and effectively handling all processes from "click-to-ship."	Within 3 years our company will be among the top 5 custom internet-based logistics software companies (that target all companies selling products online) in the USA in terms of customer base and revenue. *The products offered will require zero training and zero maintenance.*	Our values are: fiscal responsibility, dedication to get the job done right, innovation, and accountability.
Large healthcare company	Our mission is to keep our members healthy in mind, body, and spirit. *Promoting wellness is the most effective and proactive way* to keep our members and communities healthy. Our health education programs are the embodiment of that belief. Our mission is to inspire people, inform their choices, and improve their health.	In 4 years we will double our membership to be the #2 provider of healthcare in America, focused on improving the health of our *members through proactive and preventive care* in the communities we serve.	Our values are: trust, integrity, honesty, and respect.

Note: The underlined statements highlight the competitive differentiator.

What can a mission statement do for your company? Illustration 5.3 reveals what a mission statement can communicate to each of the entities that an organization deals with.

Many companies fiddle with their mission statement every time there's a new competitor on the market, a new change in the wind, or a new report out from their favorite business magazine. But in my experience, a mission statement rarely changes, unless you are drastically changing what the company is all about.

The 4 Key Elements Every Mission Statement Must Have

Too many mission statements are oblique for the sake of obliqueness, or wordy for the sake of wordiness. Often this seems to be because few companies have ever stopped to learn the true essence of what a mission statement should—and could—be. After this lap your company will no longer have that excuse!

Here are the four key elements a mission statement should have:

1. What is the reason for the organization's existence? *(What is it that you do?)*

2. Who does the organization serve? *(Who is your primary customer/ client?)*

3. What is the organization's competitive differentiator? *(How competitive are you in the current marketplace?)*

4. What is the overall value of the organization? *(What is it that you do that no one else does?)*

To further illuminate each point, let's take the first example from Illustration 5.2 and analyze its mission statement according to the above four questions:

1. The reason for the organization's existence: *To support growth by providing a suite of software solutions.*

2. Who the organization serves: *Internet-based businesses.*

Illustration 5.3: Building Your Mission, Vision and Values

	Mission	Vision	Values
Customers	• What is the reason for its existence? • Who are the customers it serves? • What problem does the organization solve? • What is the current competitive differentiator?	• What can the customers expect in the future? What direction is the company taking? • What is the sustainable competitive differentiator?	• How will the company interact with customers? • What values/beliefs does the company operate on? Does this resonate with customers?
Partners	• What is the reason for its existence? • Who are the customers? • What products/services are being offered? • What makes the organization unique? • What channel will be used for serving the customer?	• What direction is the company taking and why? • What role will partners play?	• What are the behaviors expected of those representing the organization?
Employees	• Why does the organization exist? • What makes the organization unique? • What products and services are offered? • How can we maintain the competitive differentiation?	• What direction is the company taking and why? • What expectations are set? • What areas of specialization will be expected in the future?	• How will the products/services be created, offered, and supported? • What are the behaviors expected of those representing the organization? • What values need to be exhibited in order to maintain competitive differentiation?
Shareholders	• How big a problem are we solving for the customer? • What products/services are being offered? • What makes the organization unique?	• What is the future direction of the company? • How big is the future potential?	• What values/beliefs does the company operate on?
Public	• Why does the organization exist? • What do we want everyone to know about us (aka what is our "brand")?	• What direction is the company taking and why?	• What values/beliefs does the company operate on?

3. The organization's competitive differentiator: *Easy to use and maintain— no training required!*

4. The overall value of the organization: *To efficiently and effectively handle all processes from "click-to-ship."*

Lack of Clarity Leads to Lack of Mission

We see them all the time—mission statements that read more like movie taglines, which, while creative, give no hint as to what the company does, who it serves, or even why it exists. For instance, "Making each day count for you and your family." This is a real mission statement for a real company. Is it effective? Hardly. Why? Because it raises more questions than answers. For instance:

❑ *How* are you going to make each day count for me and my family?

❑ *Why* are you going to help us?

❑ *With* what product or service are you going to help us?

❑ *Who* are you?

Other creative yet similarly unclear mission statements for companies include:

❑ "Serving your needs for over 50 years!" *What* needs, exactly, have you been serving? Plumbing, copying, accounting? Be specific!

❑ "Because life is too short to wait!" Wait for what? A good plumber? Or a five-star vacation?

❑ "When everyone else lets you down, call us!" Call you for *what*, exactly?

Make sure your mission statement is not just a tagline. The tagline is similar to one-line "teasers" used on movie posters. For example, "In Space No One Can Hear You Scream." Such one-liners have nothing to do with the mission.

How is a tagline related to a mission statement? It may be an offshoot, but it will never deliver the whole package the readers need to see, and feel, to understand your company's true mission.

For instance, "Serving your needs for over 50 years!" might be a significant factor of a company's mission—trading on its rich heritage of service and customer loyalty, for example—but how would we know that without the rest of the mission statement?

To avoid creating a tagline in place of a true mission statement, and to develop a compelling mission statement that really works, here is a method you may want to consider:

- ❑ Invite the leadership team to participate in creating a mission statement for the business; divide them into three groups.

- ❑ Have each group answer the above questions in their own way—this allows for different individual, group, and eventually team interpretations of what the company does, who it serves, and what its key competitive differentiator is.

- ❑ Have the teams come back and share their answers with everyone (including other groups); this allows for them to get feedback from everyone before going to the next step.

- ❑ Next, have each of the teams independently work on weaving their answers into a concise mission statement.

- ❑ Have each of the groups present their mission statement to the team.

- ❑ Finally, the team picks the best statement and further fine-tunes it, as appropriate.

- ❑ If you are a group or division of a larger company, make sure that your department or division mission aligns to the overall company's mission.

- ❑ When developing a mission statement, the drafters should think of what the organization is trying to accomplish rather than the "nuts and bolts" of how it will get done. Note the following examples:

- ◆ NO: "Our mission is to put gardening tools in the hands of every local senior citizen."
- ◆ YES: "We hope to enrich the lives of our local seniors through the habit-forming gift of gardening."
- ◆ NO: "Our mission is to redistribute leftover food from local restaurants and deliver it to the homeless."
- ◆ YES: "We strive to enrich and fulfill the lives of local homeless families by providing food from local restaurants through a joint community effort."
- ◆ NO: "Our mission is to provide local schoolchildren with free dental supplies for a week."
- ◆ YES: "We want to reinforce the importance of good dental hygiene by empowering school-aged children."

Remember, a well-written mission statement is more than just another item on the new CEO's to-do list; it is actually an important communication tool. Specifically, it communicates: 1.) what the organization does and 2.) why. It also helps articulate what the organization can and cannot be involved in when it comes to specific work.

The Importance of Vision

Thomas Edison once famously said, "Vision without execution is hallucination." It's equally true, however, that "Execution without vision is chaos." These principles are two sides of the same coin—like yin and yang—and necessarily belong together, since having one without the other renders both unusable. Alternatively, combining a powerful vision with strong execution creates an unstoppable force for achieving your desired outcomes.

Which comes first: the mission statement or the vision statement? I think the answer depends on the maturity of the business. If you have a new start-up business, new program, or plan to re-engineer your current services, then the vision will guide the mission statement and the rest of the strategic plan.

If you have an established business where the mission is well known, then many times the mission guides the vision statement and the rest of the strategic plan. Either way, you need to know your fundamental purpose for your mission and vision statements and how these statements provide opportunities for growth and progress.

Creating a Vision Statement

Many academicians say that your vision statement should represent an organization's five-year benchmarks. I disagree. In fact, I think that's way too long. After all, so much can change with the company, the competitors, the business climate, etc., in four or five years. That makes it hard to know the environment beyond three years, so my recommendation is to stick with two to three years and validate and fine-tune your vision every year.

This is not some esoteric vision of the untethered goals you might like to accomplish, but instead a very set and specific bit of language tied to 1.) a time and 2.) some type of measurement.

Here are some examples of vision statements (see Illustration 5.2 for more examples):

Example 1: "Within three years, Smythe Auto Body will be the number one auto body repair company in the San Francisco Bay Area, with revenue exceeding $26M..." There are so many (great) qualifiers here! See for yourself:

- ❏ "Within three years..." (timeframe)
- ❏ "The number one auto body repair company..." (measurement)
- ❏ "Double its revenue..." (how much)
- ❏ "In the San Francisco Bay Area..." (where)
- ❏ "Increasing its profits by 150%..." (how much)
- ❏ "In California..." (geographic focus)
- ❏ "With revenue exceeding $26M..." (how much)

Example 2: "Within three years, Guarantee Bank will double its revenue while increasing its profits by 150% and become known in California as a premium Internet-based Bank..."

I encourage you to consider highlighting your sustainable competitive differentiator in your vision statement. See Illustration 5.2.

Rather than get so specific, many companies usually go in the opposite direction. In other words, we often get tempted to use vague/generic terms that may confuse the audience—we do not want the statements to be misinterpreted. Avoid using popular, if but toothless, buzz words like "leading edge" or "high customer satisfaction" or "high quality." These terms sound good but say little.

4 Key Questions Every Vision Statement Should Answer

A well-written vision statement should answer the following four key questions:

1. Where do you want to be two to three years from now?

2. What measurement defines the destination (time required/allotted, degree/percentage of change, increase in dollars)?

3. What is your long-term sustainable competitive differentiator?

4. Is the organization's message in realistic and credible terms?

See more validating questions in Illustration 5.4.

We've seen great examples of the first three so far, but let me visit question four for just a moment before moving on. "Is the organization's message in realistic and credible terms?" It is so important to dwell in reality while going through the exercises introduced here.

For instance, can your auto body empire *really* amass profits of $26M in two to three years? Can you *really* increase profits by 150%? We do not have a crystal ball, of course, but by using past performance, opportunity ahead of us, and the team's ability to execute, you should be able to gauge, within a few decimal points, just how much market share or profit you can gain in twenty-four to thirty-six months. This is why having teams split off into groups is so helpful; hearing from every corner helps season your vision statement with plenty of reality!

Just as in your mission statement, alignment is key. So if your group comprises a small division of a larger company, make sure your vision

Illustration 5.4: Validating Questions for the Mission, Vision and Values

	Validating Questions
Mission	1. Is it concise and easy to understand? Can it be communicated easily? 2. Does it explain why the organization exists? 3. When the mission statement is shared with people who do not know the organization, do they get the message? 4. Does it provide focus while still providing some level of flexibility? 5. Is the statement you are making true? 6. Is the competitive differentiator clear? 7. Has the leader of the organization signed off? 8. Has rest of the leadership team signed off on the statement? 9. Have you analyzed how the customers, partners, employees and shareholders may perceive from the mission statement?
Vision	1. Is the statement inspirational? 2. Is the vision realistic yet pushing the envelope a little? 3. Does it have the key measurement you would like to improve in a specified time? 4. Is your long term sustainable competitive differentiator clear? 5. Can you look at the statement and say with conviction that your organization is not there yet? 6. Have you taken into consideration the external threats and opportunities over the timeframe for which the vision is defined? 7. Have you analyzed how the customers, partners, employees and shareholders may perceive from the vision statement?
Values	1. Do the values identified align to the mission and vision? 2. The values if demonstrated will help us achieve our mission 3. Do these values resonate with customers and partners? 4. Is it realistic for the organization to demonstrate these values if not now at least in the near future? (Remember if current and expected values are far apart, it will take some time to reach there requiring change management strategies)

ties to the overall company's vision. Some of the phrases to be avoided in developing a mission and vision statements are mentioned in Illustration 5.5.

Values

Finally, let us turn our attention to the crafting of the third kind of statement that is so critical to your organization's success—and to lap five. Unlike a mission or a vision statement, a value statement should focus on articulating the **core values**, **traits**, and **qualities** the employees of your company should have; and by "employees" I mean executives, managers, and the rest of the employees.

For small companies, these are often a reflection of the values/beliefs held by the founders/owners. For medium and large companies, these values and beliefs are, perhaps, reflected through corporate culture.

4 Key Questions Every Value Statement Should Answer

A well-written value statement answers the following questions:

1. What is the company's competitive differentiator as perceived by customers and partners?

2. What aspects of the company's culture and values help achieve this competitive differentiation?

3. What behavior will support the long-term sustainable competitive differentiator?

4. How do employees, managers, and executives behave?

You can see by the nature of these questions that this statement really should address your company's core values. In short, a value statement defines how employees are expected to behave when representing the organization inside (to peers, colleagues, managers, etc.) and outside (to customers, partners, community, etc.). It addresses how the employees should support the mission and vision. These also define how decision-making is done, how customers are treated, and what the employees are rewarded for.

Illustration 5.5: Words and Phrases to Avoid in Mission, Vision and Value Statements

Best-managed	Solve problem
Blue-Chip Clients	Customer-centric
Technologically advanced	Huge increase
High margin	Grow aggressively
High revenue	Leading edge
Culturally aware	Major force
Cost basis	No-compromise
Cost-effective	The most
Cutting edge	True partnership
Complete package	Drastic increase
Capture market	Improved focus
Despite controversy	Established leader position
Grow rapidly	Best in class
Full-service	Never done before

If, for example, you say that you are a "family friendly" daycare, then flex time is something that you should definitely offer your employees. Company policy should align with the value statement—walk the talk.

Here are some examples of value statements (see Illustration 5.2 for more examples):

Example 1 (the medium public software company): "Our values are fiscal responsibility, dedication to get the job done right, innovation, and accountability."

Example 2 (the large global management consulting company): "We value integrity, customer service, taking pride in our work, presenting accurate information, and sharing creative ideas."

As always, if you are a group or division within a larger company, make sure your values align to the overall company's values. To see what a value statement can communicate to each of the entities that an organization deals with, see Illustration 5.3.

> **Tip**
>
> Share the mission, value, and vision statements with people who do not know your business and ask them what they make of it. If they are unable to nail down who you are or what your company does, then there is a problem—you will need to fine-tune the statements.

Now that you're more familiar with the examples of vision/mission/value statements I've shared throughout this chapter and, in particular, in Illustration 5.2 and 5.6, take a fresh look at your company's current vision, mission, and values to determine what is missing. Ask yourself:

- ❑ Could we be more specific?
- ❑ Could we have more quantifiers?
- ❑ Is this really a mission statement, or is it more a vision statement?
- ❑ After reading this/these, would someone from the outside know what kind of company we are?

Finally, I urge you not to spend too much time on this exercise. Yes, it's important, but not at the cost of the rest of these laps. You will never—I repeat, *never*—write the perfect mission, vision, or value statement. If you are close to being perfect that is okay!

Strategy and Strategic Objectives

The above statements might as well be hidden beneath glass and protected by a velvet rope if you don't create strategic objectives for implementing them company-wide. These objectives communicate your ultimate tangible purpose, or intention, for devising the strategic plan. Where does this plan come from?

You develop the strategic objectives from your:

- ❑ Vision
- ❑ Mission

Illustration 5.6: Example—Mission, Vision and Value

Vision	Mission	Strategy	Objectives
I see a world where . . .	In that world we intend to . . .	We will achieve this mission by . . .	The strategic objective is to . . .
Gaphu Solar's vision is to design, develop, and mass produce the *most technologically advanced solar panels capable of producing over 4500 Watts per square feet in three years time*, which will help the company capture 25% of the USA commercial market, while maintaining a 10% year over year profitability improvement	Gaphu Solar's mission is to research, develop, manufacture and deploy the *most technologically advanced solar solution in the industry* and a clean and reliable alternative energy source for companies and commercial property owners through research and development	• Raising money • Pouring considerable funds into R&D • Expanding physical presence (offices) • Increasing sales staff, • Increasing marketing • Exploring acquisitions as a way to rapidly expand sales/service • Developing new cost effective products • Scaling manufacturing to a bigger plant overseas	• Raise money by taking the company public in the next 12 months, bridge financing in the interim • Hire top talent in sales and marketing who have extensive experience in renewable energy • Identify target acquisitions • Identify locations to expand • Identify manufacturing partners for cost effective high quality manufacturing

Overall Strategy – "SO" & "WO"

Note: The underlined statements highlight competitive differentiator

Copyright © Mahesh Rao, 2010

    ❑ Outcome from observations, feedback, and findings (from lap four)

    ❑ Sustainable competitive differentiator

    ❑ SWOT (pairing strategy) recommendations

Here are the specific steps you need to take to develop your strategic objectives:

1. Recall the "pairing strategies" output from the exercise in Lap four (see page 97).

2. Work on crafting a "strategy-map" and/or a "success map" (we will touch on this later in this lap).

3. When developing your strategic objectives, ask yourself the following questions:

    ◆ Do they align with the overall strategy developed in lap four?

    ◆ Does the objective support the mission and vision? In other words, by fulfilling the objectives, will we meet our mission/strategy?

    ◆ Do the objectives help sustain or, better yet, increase the competitive differentiation?

    ◆ Can the objectives be well understood by all employees, without any room for misinterpretation?

    ◆ Are the objectives tangible enough so as to be able to craft specific tactics and goals?

4. If you recall, we went through an exercise of "Start-Stop-Continue-Change" and created a list from that exercise. It is now time to validate and fine-tune that list based on the strategic objectives just developed.

5. Continue building the "success map" (in subsequent laps).

Crafting Your Balanced Scorecard

Over the years there have been many approaches and techniques for measuring business and transformational success shared by many measurement gurus. One of the most famous techniques that many companies still use is the Business Scorecard, developed by Dr. Robert S. Kaplan and David P. Norton. They published their work in early '90s and published their first book in 1996. Indeed, they had come up with a way to tie all of the metrics together.

Kaplan and Norton introduced the notion of a "strategy map" that tied strategic objectives into four main categories (see Illustrations 5.7 and 5.8). The idea is that the learning starts with people—employees and partners. It encourages the identification of measures that answer the question, "How can we continue to improve and create value?" As these people are educated to accomplish the strategic objectives, they then help accomplish the pre-defined strategic objectives of the second category—internal business processes. At this stage it encourages the identification of measures that answer the question, "What processes must the company must excel at in order to satisfy the customer?"

This then helps align to the third category—customer perspective. Identify measures that answer the question, "How do customers see us?" This in turn aligns with the financial perspective that encourages key high-level financial measures. Strategists looking to put this together are encouraged to choose measures that help inform the answer to the question, "How do we look to our shareholders?"

Once this structure is in place, mission-critical projects, initiatives, and core processes can be identified and addressed. Subsequently, measurements—commonly called "key performance indicators" or KPIs—can be defined, assigned target levels, and monitored.

One could also argue that executives do not really have a strategy but rather a vision of where they want their organization to go. The linked strategic objectives, like the musical instruments in a Beethoven symphony, then become the strategy.

This is not about every instrument playing loudly, but rather playing together in harmony, regardless of the volume. The strategy map becomes the sheet music that instruments (teams and processes) follow. This way each "note" of music is interpreted as it was written.

Illustration 5.7: Strategy Map—Cause and Effect

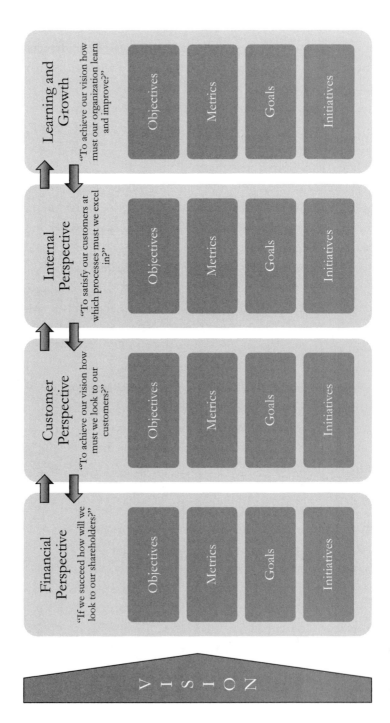

Financial Perspective
"If we succeed how will we look to our shareholders?"
Objectives
Metrics
Goals
Initiatives

Customer Perspective
"To achieve our vision how must we look to our customers?"
Objectives
Metrics
Goals
Initiatives

Internal Perspective
"To satisfy our customers at which processes must we excel in?"
Objectives
Metrics
Goals
Initiatives

Learning and Growth
"To achieve our vision how must our organization learn and improve?"
Objectives
Metrics
Goals
Initiatives

VISION

Illustration 5.8: Example of Strategy Map for a Fitness Equipment Company

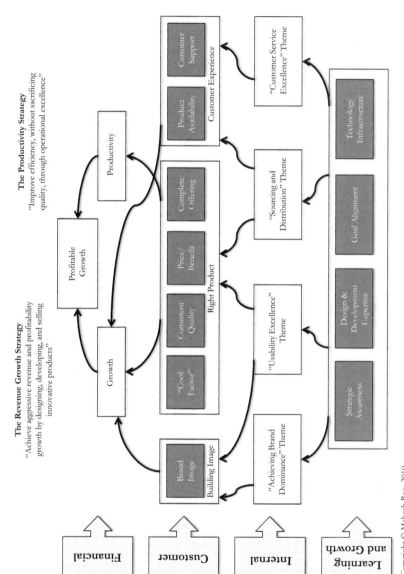

The Revenue Growth Strategy
"Achieve aggressive revenue and profitability growth by designing, developing, and selling innovative products"

The Productivity Strategy
"Improve efficiency, without sacrificing quality, through operational excellence"

Financial

Customer

Internal

Learning and Growth

Profitable Growth

Productivity

Growth

Right Product

"Cool Factor"

Consistent Quality

Price/Benefit

Complete Offering

Customer Experience

Product Availability

Customer Support

Building Image

Brand Image

"Achieving Brand Dominance" Theme

"Usability Excellence" Theme

"Sourcing and Distribution" Theme

"Customer Service Excellence" Theme

Strategic Awareness

Design & Development Expertise

Goal Alignment

Technology Infrastructure

It is said that over 50% of large global corporations still use a balanced scorecard methodology. Unfortunately, many of the organizations do not follow the best practice in developing and deploying such a scorecard framework.

The nine logical, key steps to develop and deploy a balanced scorecard methodology are:

1. Organization assessment
2. Vision and strategy development
3. Strategic objective(s) identification
4. Strategy map development
5. Performance measure(s) identification
6. Target(s) identification
7. Balanced scorecard education and training—cascading
8. Strategic initiative(s) implementation
9. Monitor and control implementation

Depending on the complexity of each step in the process, this can take anywhere from a few months to beyond a year. I have interviewed many Fortune 100 company executives in the past few years, asking them how their balanced scorecard projects were going and, most importantly, what was not working.

Here are just a few aspects that were highlighted during these enlightening conversations:

❑ Some of the companies who implemented a balanced scorecard felt that they had less focus on the "intangibles," regardless of how critical they are; perhaps this is due to the fact that the balanced scorecard methodology focuses on strategy as opposed to results.

❑ Many leaders expressed that their strategy was written in vague business/technical jargon; therefore, they struggled to highlight tangible results implied by the strategies. As a result, they measured what is easy to measure, regardless of where the methodology might take them as a company.

❑ Many companies revealed that their measurements focused on activities like "development of leadership competencies" or "improvement of service quality" or even "improvement of brand image" rather than clear outcomes.

The above activities can mean different things for different groups and people in each group (within an organization). It takes considerable effort to define these and identify appropriate measures; i.e., it takes more than just a couple of brainstorming sessions or copying from an Internet site/ book. It takes deep understanding of the result or benefit you are trying to achieve. There are other factors that go into the thinking as well, such as the availability of data, measurability of the metrics used, etc. The entire organization needs to understand the meaning of these measures and the linkages. In the case of a balanced scorecard, it is relatively hard to explain the linkages to the day-to-day tasks being completed, especially tasks done by individuals who are way down in the value-chain. Also, this learning will not be a one-time event but, instead, needs to be ongoing. This takes up considerable effort and ties up resources. In real-life situations, organizations simply do not have this luxury.

As you can see, creating a balanced scorecard is not a one-time event. The ongoing rigor required for a balanced scorecard to work is considerable— it is a long-term commitment required not only from the organization's leaders but from every employee. Unfortunately, many organizations fail to recognize this, and because of this lack of commitment over time the balanced scorecard becomes less effective and eventually fades away into the dark, going down in the history of the company as yet another "fad" that has come and gone.

I am not suggesting that you throw out the baby with the bath water. A balanced scorecard is not all bad. The strategy map is a very good way to draw out the linkages between the four categories it highlights. In my honest opinion, however, you may want to augment it with some other methodologies that will help distill the strategy down to day-to-day activities.

One such approach that I have found over the years is a technique I call the "success map." This technique will help you not only "connect the dots" better amongst the various groups within the organization but, more importantly, it makes our strategy more measurable all the way down to specific projects and activities.

Creating A Success Map

Most organizations begin with the executives defining the vision and strategy. Usually, this exercise ends with them defining key critical success factors or balanced scorecard perspectives; then, for each of these factors or perspectives, high-level goals are crafted along with the appropriate metric (see Illustration 5.9a).

Next, I recommend that executives communicate the overall organization strategy (see Figure 5.9a) to their direct reports. The idea is to allow the information to cascade down the hierarchy within the company with the understanding that each of the groups or lines of business (next level down) will take the strategy and translate the message further into division- or function-level (marketing, sales, engineering, etc.) strategies (see Illustration 5.9b), tactics, and activities. The functional managers are then asked to contribute to the achievement of the overarching strategy.

With respect to customer focus as it pertains to an IT Department, for example, this would mean improving the customer satisfaction and resolving the case faster, which is great. If ITs job also includes maintaining and managing the internal network, personal computers, as well as servers, then maintaining the availability of the general network and, in particular, Support Desk, CRM, and email servers, over 99.5% of the time will help in serving the organization's customers better.

However, with respect to improving profitability, the IT department may reduce its manpower as well as capital expenses despite an increased number of projects in the pipeline. Why? Because they are trying to contribute to the overall strategy of the organization. So as you can see with this method, some of the departments may be forced to contribute to the overall strategy regardless of relevance. While blindly following the overall organization's strategy, they may also overlook what may be critical to the department's success.

When facilitating strategy sessions at the group (or line of business) level, I often hear the leaders ask the question, "What should our department's expense goal be?" Instead, we should be asking ourselves, "In what ways does

Illustration 5.9: Organization Strategy

Illustration 5.9a: Overall Organization's High-level Strategy

Key Focus Areas	High-level Goals for Next Year	Key Metrics (KPIs)
Customer Focus	Increase customer satisfaction to 90%	Customer satisfaction index (5-scale rating)
	Reduce resolution time by 25%	Mean time to issue resolution (days)
Improve Profitability	Increase profits 20%	EBIT (earnings before interest & tax)
	Reduce costs 15%	Total Expenditure

Illustration 5.9b: Internal IT Department

Key Focus Areas	High-level Goals for Next Year	Key Metrics (KPIs)
Customer Focus	Increase internal customer satisfaction product management	Customer satisfaction index (5-scale rating)
	Resolve cases (25% faster)	Mean time to issue resolution (days)
Improve Profitability	Reduce manpower by 5%	Headcount
	Reduce capital expenses by 15%	Total Expenditure

our department (or group or function) contribute to the overall expense at the organization level?" To answer the question properly, you might find it helpful to engage a member of the finance team to discuss this with you and/ or your team; he/she can help identify the linkages and perhaps give some ideas as well.

The bigger problem that I have seen in companies, however, is that their mission, vision, strategies, and objectives are so vague that it is just not actionable and, hence, the individual departments don't know how to interpret them. For example, popular phrases such as "unique customer experience," "stakeholder alignment," and "service quality" are relatively toothless, as they can be interpreted differently by various departments and, frankly, even within departments.

After all, a "unique" customer experience may not mean the same as a "positive" one, and the value of unique differs from department to department, as does the definition of who, exactly, the "stakeholder" is at the level of "service quality."

Therefore, it is critical to develop a strategy using words that cannot be misinterpreted, and that have a laser-sharp focus on the result you are actually trying to achieve. Our business world is filled with lifeless, toothless, and relatively useless words/phrases; make sure you stay away from them. To keep yourself on track, ask yourself the questions, "Will we be able to measure it? How will our stakeholders interpret it?"

In this lap, I will introduce an approach that will not only help in linking your strategy with actions but also make it measurable as well. Illustration 5.10 shows the high-level flow required to create an effective success map.

Illustration 5.10: Success Map

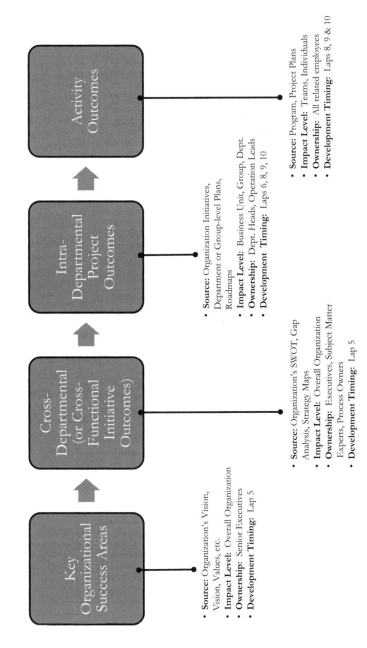

- **Source:** Organization's Vision, Vision, Values, etc.
- **Impact Level:** Overall Organization
- **Ownership:** Senior Executives
- **Development Timing:** Lap 5

- **Source:** Organization's SWOT, Gap Analysis, Strategy Maps
- **Impact Level:** Overall Organization
- **Ownership:** Executives, Subject Matter Experts, Process Owners
- **Development Timing:** Lap 5

- **Source:** Organization Initiatives, Department or Group-level Plans, Roadmaps
- **Impact Level:** Business Unit, Group, Dept.
- **Ownership:** Dept. Heads, Operation Leads
- **Development Timing:** Laps 6, 8, 9, 10

- **Source:** Program, Project Plans
- **Impact Level:** Teams, Individuals
- **Ownership:** All related employees
- **Development Timing:** Laps 8, 9 & 10

Quest Credit Union: A Success (Map) in the Making

To better illustrate a viable success map in real-time—and living color—let me walk you through an example success map of Quest Credit Union (QCU) (true name withheld). Only a part of this map will be worked on in this lap. It will take its final shape in lap ten.

At the outset, QCU Credit Union was quite clear on its mission, vision, strategy, and key objectives. In this case, the executives at QCU Credit Union had four key success areas or outcomes, namely:

1. World-class service
2. Market recognition
3. Institution growth
4. Financial stability

Without taking your vision and strategy to this level of granularity, you will not be able to measure it. You know what they say: You cannot achieve what you cannot measure. At every stage, bear in mind that we are capturing the desired outcomes, not just writing a bunch of jargons (see Illustration 5.10).

Now, to develop a laser-like focus, distill these four key areas down to the next level. We can call these "cross-functional" (or cross-group) initiatives that will help you achieve the key success areas.

Let's take these one by one, using the QCU specifics as an example:

World-class service: World-class service starts with world-class employees, which means QCU should aim to have more-than-competent employees. This then becomes the desired outcome at the second level. In other words, the outcome of the first initiative becomes, "having more-than-competent employees."

Market recognition: For QCU to be recognized in the market, it is almost a pre-requisite that the customers value their service. So the outcome of the second initiative is to make sure the customers value the service.

Institution growth: As you can appreciate, you cannot grow if the customers do not value your service—a key factor that needs to be taken seriously. QCU realizes that they have very unique products/services not offered by their competition. They need to get the word out, so there needs to be an increased awareness of services. As a result, the third initiative's outcome is to make sure that the customers are, indeed, aware of all the services offered.

Financial stability: QCU's customers expect that the place they put their hard-earned money is financially secure. Let's face it: today's customers are very cautious about where they put their money. The trust in banks is not that high—it is therefore extremely important that QCU demonstrates through action how they will govern and manage financial risks. In short, they need a system of checks and balances in place to make sure their customers' money is safe. So, "reduced financial risk" becomes the fourth initiative's outcome, as does the need for QCU to become operationally efficient so they are profitable (or, at least, not losing money). This will be the outcome of the fifth initiative.

Remember, in the first level you are trying to highlight the customer's perception of value as seen through the lens of your organization's vision and mission. This should remain constant over (at least) a two- to three-year time. The next layer defines the cross-functional (or cross-group) improvements you need to make in order to achieve success, as defined in the first layer (key success areas).

Do not list every "success area" that you can think of or cross-functional initiatives/projects that your organization may be working on—just list the most relevant and critical ones. I encourage most organizations I consult with to focus on just the areas of improvements that need to happen in the immediate future.

Focus on what's important; the initiative itself is merely a means to an end. Remember, in each of the above cases it is the "outcome" that we are after. This kind of thinking makes progress more measurable and, hence, more result-oriented. In subsequent laps, we will take this success map discussion deeper and work on the remaining layers as well as associated measurements in connection with QCU Credit Union.

Publish or Perish

Here's what's so interesting, and potentially disturbing, in most organizations. Let's say you've worked long and hard on your company's mission, vision, and value statements. But what if you were to take them away from the very team that created them? Could you realistically ask the team to reproduce them verbatim? Most people will not be able to.

The point here is that if the people who are in the trenches working on these for some time are unable to reproduce the statements verbatim, or even close to verbatim, how will others in your company, who are potentially seeing them for the first time, be able to remember them? How will customers, stakeholders, or the general public feel about them? You can imagine over time where these statements and objectives will end up. . . .

Do you think anybody will ever remember them? From my experience, the best way to make sure all employees understand and remember your mission, vision, values, and objectives is through a visual. There are several companies/people who can help you illustrate your statements in a visual manner.

The process involves bringing in these strategy illustrators as you are defining the mission, vision, values, and objectives. This way the illustrators understand the context and can come up with the most effective visual.

Once these visuals are finalized, make posters and stick them in all strategic locations within the company. For the most part, these visuals should be self-explanatory, but it may not hurt to walk each of the functional groups through the visual so they catch the nuances as well.

Change Management and Communication

Here are a couple of aspects you need to consider at this point:

1. How do we help everyone understand our mission, vision, values, and objectives? As explained above, walking the employees through a visual can be an effective approach.

2. What work effort and behaviors need to change (within each employee) so the new organizational new mission and vision can be achieved (using the values highlighted)? This effort does take time and the best approach is to train the managers to manage it (the process) appropriately in their respective teams; i.e., have it "trickle down" the chain of command (in a top-down approach).

Once you have the draft vision, mission, and value statements, validate them by using the complete list of validating questions (found in Illustration 5.4).

Example: Gaphu Solar was a medium producer of solar panels in California. They wanted to get bigger while still retaining their core company values, effectiveness of product, and customer service. How did they achieve this goal?

First they channeled their energy into creating a realistic vision statement reflective of where they wanted to go (see Figure 5.6): "Within five years, 40% of commercial properties in California will install advanced zero-maintenance solar panels to offset their carbon footprint. Gaphu Solar will own at least 25% of this market, maintaining a 10% increase in profitability over a year."

Next, the company created a mission that would help them reach their goals: "Gaphu Solar's mission is to research, develop, manufacture and deploy the most technologically advanced solar solution in the industry and a clean and reliable alternative energy source for companies and commercial property owners through research and development."

Once again, this mission statement answers the required four mission statement questions closely:

1. The reason for the organization's existence. What is it that you do? For example: Research, develop, manufacture, and deploy the most technologically advanced solar solution.

2. Who the organization serves. Who is your primary customer/client? For example: Companies and commercial properties.

3. What is your sustainable competitive differentiator? For example: Research and develop the most technologically

advanced solar panels (top 1% in the industry in Wattage/ square meter); or design, develop, manufacture, and deploy (end-to-end solution).

Similarly, the vision statement clearly defines where the company wants to be two to three years out: Gaphu Solar's vision is to design, develop, and mass produce the most technologically advanced solar panels capable of producing over 4500 Watts per square feet in three years time, which will help the company capture 25% of the commercial market while maintaining a 10% year-over-year profitability improvement.

Similarly, their vision statement highlights the following:

1. Where do you want to be two to three years from now? The most technologically advanced solar panels producing company in the industry.

2. What measurement defines the destination (time required/ allotted, degree/percentage of change, increase in dollars)? 25% of USA commercial market; 10% year over year sustained growth.

3. What is your long-term sustainable competitive differentiator? The most technologically advanced solar panels capable of producing over 4500 watts per square foot.

More important than crafting their vision, though, Gaphu Solar created a strategy built upon their mission and vision statements. This strategy clearly mapped out the company's goals in a way that is strategic and realistic, allowing the list to be attributed to the appropriate teams in the organization helping to meet such goals.

Finally, they used this strategy to inform clear objectives that became company mandates, such as "Hire top talent in sales and marketing who have extensive experience in renewable energy" and "identify locations to expand."

Rather than just write vision and mission statements in a vacuum, never to be seen again, Gaphu Solar used them as springboards to success. Already they are gaining significant market share due to their clear vision, their succinct mission, and their realistic goals, which they have been implementing ever since.

Lap 5 Key Takeaways

- ❑ Mission Statement: Says what you are doing today.

- ❑ Vision Statement: Highlights what you would like to achieve tomorrow (two to three years out).

- ❑ Value Statement: Defines the behaviors expected of the employees that will help the company achieve its vision.

- ❑ It is absolutely critical that these statements highlight what your "competitive differentiator" is. The competitive differentiator will impact your overall strategy and your objectives.

- ❑ Now that we know where our company is headed, this would be a good time to bring together a cross-functional leadership team to execute the opportunities identified in lap four.

- ❑ Combine your mission, vision, value, and objective statements into a comprehensive visual, so the all employees can understand and align with them as well as retain the information.

- ❑ "Road test" these statements with objective parties to see if they can tell what you do/what business you're in based on the statements.

- ❑ Next develop your strategic objectives using balanced scorecard methodology or a success map, or perhaps even both. Take the following into consideration when defining your strategic objectives:

  - ◆ Vision

  - ◆ Mission

  - ◆ Outcome from observations, feedback, and findings (from lap four)

  - ◆ Sustainable competitive differentiator

  - ◆ SWOT (pairing strategy) recommendations

  - ◆ "Success Map" with focus on defining:

    - • Key organizational success areas

    - • Cross-departmental/functional initiative outcomes

Lap 6

Design Your Organizational Structure

You know you have achieved a perfect design
not when you have nothing more to add,
but when you have nothing more to take away.

The structure of the organization refers to the formal way in which people and work are grouped into defined units. There is no one size fits all design. Choose a structure that aligns best with your vision and strategy. Any design you eventually choose will have its pros and cons forcing you to make trade-offs and compromises.

Many companies are eager to transform, but few experience any meaningful, measurable transformation. Why is this? How can serious, dedicated, and committed companies not achieve their transformational goals when, across the board, everyone in the organization seems to want transformation?

Vision and mission statements aren't enough; they are a critical part of the process, to be sure, but the process doesn't end there. Just as wanting to win a race doesn't magically propel us to the front of the pack, merely wanting transformation—even having a vision for what that change might look like—doesn't magically make it happen.

In fact, those companies whose organizational structures are not aligned to the vision can actually do more harm than good. That's because few organizations realize their organizational structure and lack of role clarity is in fact an inhibiting factor, and this oftentimes prevents them from achieving their vision.

On the flip side, I have seen many companies blame the organizational structure or process for many of the issues they face; when, in fact, the real issue may be a deep lack of trust in the organizational structure or, perhaps, even competency issues. I venture to say that a front-runner organization or team that has trust will achieve its goals regardless of structure or process gaps because they work through issues as they arise.

Most successful startups, in fact, do not have everything defined. What unites the individuals in the successful startup is a unified purpose; having this not only can make the startup successful, it can make each employee rich. This requires the individuals to put aside all differences and focus on achieving the overarching purpose. This is sometimes missing in relatively larger companies. Sometimes leaders are even partly to blame for unknowingly building a culture that breeds mistrust.

Here are a few other issues that can contribute to lack of trust among a leadership team and other key members of the organization:

Lack of visibility into how decisions are made: Without decision-making logic shared with the impacted team, there will be a perception that "politics" played a role in the decision-making, often leading to a sense of mistrust.

Inhibited communication: This could be due to a culture or environment in the organization that inhibits open communications. This is very similar to a marriage. It is said that the biggest issue for divorce, according to researchers, is open dialog and communications. When that is missing, friction often takes its place.

Mismatch of expectations among team members: This is often a result of poor communications as well.

Lack of leadership "maturity" within the leadership team at multiple levels: When immaturity, even irresponsibility, is allowed to flourish at multiple levels, it can often contribute to a sense of mistrust at the senior level.

Lack of competency and commitment at multiple levels: It is very important that those leading the transformation are up to the task.

Another key factor that should be taken into consideration is personality types. Some employees (based on function in the company) are historically known to have disputes and/or difficulty communicating with each other. For example, sales and marketing versus engineering, sales versus project management, finance versus marketing, etc.

In all reality, the very nature and goals of particular functions are at odds to each other; therefore, the employees working within those functions will naturally be at odds with one another. With such a generally known situation, it's best to spend energy and resources on the goals themselves and positive communication rather than trying to make two opposing functions see eye to eye on all matters.

Understanding the Purpose

We've learned how a company's vision is the state you want to be in within two to three years. The strategy is the path that will get you to that destination. Keep this timeframe in mind while crafting the organization's structure. Aligning the organizational structure with the vision is to give it wings (for better or worse), while anchoring it to the corporate strategy allows it to stay firmly rooted to the company approach itself.

Another purpose of this lap is to begin defining, but not to formally finalize, various roles and accountability at all levels. In addition to specific roles and accountability, we will seek to define high-level success metrics for each of the key roles and come up with succinct job descriptions to increase their effectiveness and ensure individual and team success.

There is also a vaguely contrarian bent to this lap, or at least the chance to play "devil's advocate" as we draft several different organizational structures. Last, it is important to highlight the change management issues that we may face moving forward in the transformation process.

The Organizational Structure: A Right-side-up Approach

You have to wonder sometimes why we do things the way we do them. Is it because it's the most effective way to do things? For the company, for the customer... for producing profits? Or is it simply because that's the way we've *always* done things?

Case in point: Why is it that we always have an organizational structure with the CEO or organizational leader predictably at the top? We all talk about the customer being the most essential element in business—after all, there is no business without customers—and this is true for non-profits as well.

Yet if this is truly the case, should we not have the roles facing the almighty customer represented at the top of our organizational structure? Shouldn't we put our money where our mouth is? And we should naturally place the supervisors supporting the customers directly below them. Then it would only make sense to place the leadership role below the customers and, finally, the CEO at the bottom of the chain. The CEO's job is not only to create the vision and set the strategy but, perhaps most importantly, to support the "organization" (the organization of the company and thereby the company as a whole) to be successful, while helping to set the vision and strategy in place (sort of like framework to a door or window).

Illustration 6.1 displays what I call the "right-side-up organizational structure." Notice, if you will, that instead of being at the bottom of this structure the customer-facing roles are at the top.

You might argue the opposite: Without the CEO, where would the company be? And, of course, you'd be entirely correct. But ask yourself this: How long would the company survive without the CEO? Probably quite some time, what with all the chain of command and other C-level employees, board members, and leadership support stepping in to split up his or her duties to make sure the company runs smoothly in his or her absence.

Now flip the script and ask yourself the opposite question: How long would the company survive without the *customers*? While there is a safety net to replicate the CEO's duties and keep the company afloat for months, maybe even years, in his or her absence, no such "cushion" exists for a company that loses its customers. (Fair warning: this right-side-up, customer-first mentality may be a tough sell to your leadership team, especially if they are not open to new ideas and/or new ways of thinking.)

The best part about the right-side-up organizational structure is that it doesn't have to be an either/or situation; you're not faced with losing your

Illustration 6.1: Right-side-up Organizational Structure

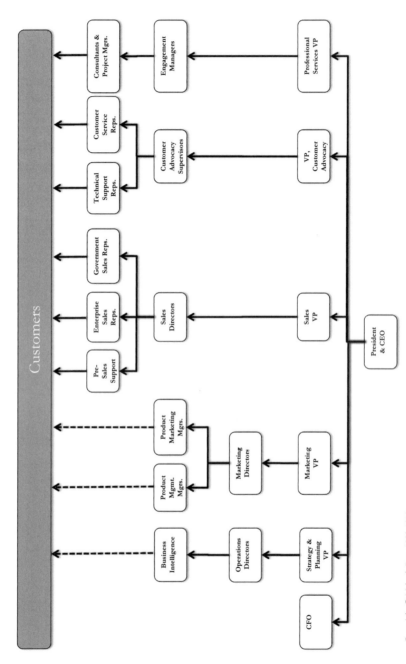

customers OR your CEO; you're simply faced with flip-flopping their order to point out which is more important to your organization.

Consulting Illustration 6.1 once more, look at how much sense this organizational style makes. You've already got your customer-facing employees, right? These include your pre-sales support staff, your enterprise sales reps, government sales reps, technical support reps, customer-service reps, and even your consultants and project managers, etc. In this organizational style, they are all still front and center with the customers, right where they should be, while their manager supports them.

Naturally, the higher-ranking the employee the higher resistance there will be for this type of organizational structure. After all, the customer service and sales reps, and the folks in R&D and marketing, won't complain about this type of structure because it actually removes barriers to their direct audience: the customers.

However, corporate America—and even corporations all over the world—is so used to the typical organizational structure, or what I call "boxology," that it is hard to change that way of thinking. I challenge you to try and change that "boxology" mindset in your organization.

If this approach is too extreme, read on.

Planning a Schedule That's Just Right: The 2- to 3-Year Time Horizon

Regardless of the organizational structure you currently have, definitely want, or are striving for, always design an organization with a two- to three-year time horizon in mind. This shouldn't be news to you; it's the same timeframe I suggested when creating your organizational vision back in lap five.

If you'll recall from that discussion, anything shorter than two to three years makes the organization unstable, and anything beyond two to three years is patently unrealistic (for the same reasons as shared in lap five). Let's take a closer look, shall we? If you're trying to design an organizational structure based on, let's say, a six-month timeline, instead of the recommended two to three years, you're basically focusing on all short-term goals with no long-term plan; it's a little like building your company on quicksand. You have to go beyond six months, even twelve months, even eighteen months (and more), to project far enough along to create realistic goals for yourself and your company. Too short a timeframe also means instability for the organization—people will constantly be thinking about "what's coming down the pike" instead of focusing on the job at hand. Transformation needs more focus, not less.

Likewise, planning too far out, say three to five years, is also too long to do your company any good. So much can happen past the three-year mark to make prudent business decisions impossible. Think of our recent financial struggles with a worldwide economy in freefall. Could any of us have predicted this economic downfall three, four, or five years ago, let alone even a year or two ago?

Now, organizational "design" is often used synonymously—and, I would add, incorrectly—to mean the same thing as organizational "structure." Organizational design includes structure, engagement, governance models, rewards, recognition, etc. Organizational structure, on the other hand, is the "boxology" I mentioned before. So in essence, organizational structure is a subset of organizational design.

If you recall, in lap four we went through the process of listing the key gaps and doing a SWOT analysis on the feedback/findings. In this lap we take on those gap issues that relate to organizational structure, as well as roles and accountability.

Traditionally, in most companies, organizational structure is crafted by the leader, with perhaps some help from HR. I do not advocate this process, as it is often impossible for one leader to understand all the inner workings of the organization (at all levels). No matter how popular it is, this approach always has problems when it comes to true adoption. And when it comes to transformation, adoption isn't just half the battle but THE battle.

Here now is an alternative approach that I have been using for years, with great success. The overall process explained below is applicable to all industries (including product- and service-based industries). It is used for non-profit organizations as well.

Before beginning any work in this area, it is important to realize that it is critical to engage key people from multiple levels of the organization to assist in crafting the organizational structure. This approach is what I refer to as a "high-engagement" approach.

The good news is that you've already laid the groundwork for this process two laps ago. As you'll recall, in lap four we pulled together a team to assist with SWOT analysis. See if the same or similar team can be pulled together for this exercise. You won't need them for very long, but you will need them (or a team similar in size and strength to them).

Depending on how we lay it out, this exercise may take anywhere from two days to two weeks. Naturally, the size and complexity of the organization plays a critical role in how long and involved the process of organizing its basic structure will take.

It is critical that all the key stakeholders/players in the organization are involved in designing (or re-designing) the structure—especially the skeptics, politically motivated, and/or passive-aggressive types who always sit on the sidelines and comment (mostly negatively) about organizational change, but do little to help initiate or fulfill it. It is important to make them feel like they are part of the solution and, in fact, their adversarial opinions and proven expertise at playing the devil's advocate may just point out the pros and cons of several alternatives that may not have been raised otherwise. This will force them into a problem-solving mode, as opposed to their just complaining and making excuses for why things are not working.

Crafting an organizational structure does not come naturally to most people, but let me assure you that by the end of this lap you will be quite good at it. In an attempt to simplify the process of designing an organizational structure, I am breaking it down into four simple steps (as shown in Figure 6.2):

Design an Organization in 4 Simple Steps

Before we get into discussing each of the following four steps, let me first give you a bird's-eye view of the entire process. The idea is to have the leader of the organization stay out of the initial work of architecting the structure. Instead, the leader develops a guideline (or criteria) that the team's proposed structure complies with. Yes, you heard right—there *will* be multiple structures proposed.

Each team comes at the problem from a different angle, making the exercise very adversarial (not always a bad thing), interesting, and comprehensive (more details on this below). The organizational leader then picks one structure and improves it by incorporating interesting elements from other structures (I call this a "cherry-picking" exercise).

You now have a draft structure to share with key stakeholders and that can be fine-tuned by more rounds of approval by the initial teams (this step can be ignored for relatively smaller organizations). The rest of the process involves developing details like job descriptions and success metrics. Now that we understand the high-level approach, let's take a look at each step and walk through the details (see Illustration 6.2).

Step 1: Develop Design Criteria and Review Gathered Information

Before you begin the design work, the core team should work with the executive sponsor to capture the "guidelines" for designing the organization. These are "non-negotiable elements" that each and every design should comply with. Refer to the design criteria throughout the design process. Here are some examples of design criteria:

Products: Create high-quality products (quality to market is key). Expand product lines. Focus on innovation through close collaboration with customers.

Services: Expanded professional services team to operate globally. The professional services team reports directly to the executive vice president.

Customer: A dedicated team to focus on customer satisfaction measurements. Marketing to expand its direct interaction via social media.

Sales and marketing: Dedicated sales team focusing on sales to government and military.

Operations: Create best-practice forums. Have dedicated team accountable for all compliance. All initiatives and projects that need over $100,000 need to be managed by the portfolio management team.

Process: Reduce time-to-problem resolution for the customer by at least 50% over the next two years. Focus on continuous improvement through lessons learned.

Next, you need to identify appropriate people in the organization to participate in this exercise. Depending on the complexity of the organization

Illustration 6.2: High-level Process for Designing an Organization

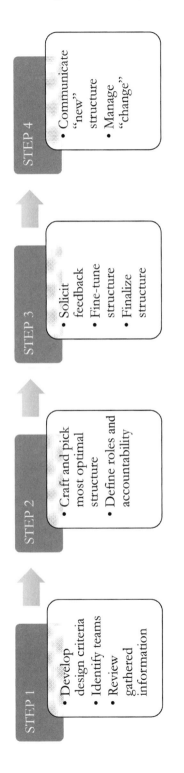

STEP 1
- Develop design criteria
- Identify teams
- Review gathered information

STEP 2
- Craft and pick most optimal structure
- Define roles and accountability

STEP 3
- Solicit feedback
- Fine-tune structure
- Finalize structure

STEP 4
- Communicate "new" structure
- Manage "change"

and the number of people on the team, consider dividing the team into three or four smaller teams (groups).

Each group has a very different objective (theme) that they will try to fulfill. Help distinguish the groups, and themes, from each other by creating an appropriate, interesting name for each of the groups. This name should reflect the themes the groups represent (see below for examples).

Here are some examples of team names (themes) I've used for organizations. I encourage you to make your own interesting themes or customize the ones below, as appropriate for your organization and its collective personality:

The sky is the limit: If budget/headcount is not a factor, how would you structure the organization? What innovative strategies can you incorporate?

Quality by design: How would you structure an organization so as to be able to focus on a "quality-to-market" mindset?

Lean, mean executing machine: How would you structure an organization so as to be able to focus on just the core value proposition, and still operate on minimal budget and headcount? Note: The goal is to minimize operating costs, thereby increasing shareholder value.

Need for speed: The primary goal of this team is to elevate the speed of execution at every step, from the designing and developing of products to closing the deal with customers and shipping the products as well as ensuring the speedy resolution of customer issues, etc.

Da Vinci: The primary charter of this team is to focus on innovation every step of the way, from business models, to products/services to processes.

Customer is king: How would you design the most customer-centric organization there is? What innovative strategies can help you add value to your customers and wow them? How can you aggressively raise the bar for product or service delivery, for example? How would you structure an organization so as to be able to focus on a "value-to-market" mindset?

United we stand: This team provides the rallying cry for proactive collaboration by breaking down the silos and seizing new growth opportunities.

The contrarian: This team acts or thinks in a way contrary to popular or accepted opinion. Their value is in questioning or second-guessing ideas in the hopes of finding what is in the best interest of the organization.

Note here that the teams are not completely interdependent of each other or acting in a vacuum. For instance, just because the "Sky is the Limit" team is charged with assessing limitless possibilities as an organizational structure, this does not necessarily mean that the team does not think of the customer when designing the organization. It's just that their focus will be to build the most ideal organization with the assumption that the budget is a non-issue. Now, you might say that this is not true to life, but that's just the point. The idea at this point is to actively apply some creative thinking, without guardrails, budgets, or gravity. We will deal with the rationalization of reality a little later.

Make sure the organization's top leader is not part of the design team. Remember, these teams are going to make a proposal to the leader, and you want him or her to be viewing these for the first time only after they're all cleaned up and "camera ready," so to speak. Having the top leader involved in the planning process dilutes the method of delivery and, potentially, its ultimate impact.

For our next step, pull all the above teams together and have them compile an "inventory of work" list. If completed correctly, this list should include all of the work that the organization does in order to complete their mission. If your new vision introduces new areas of focus that you currently do not perform, include them in the "inventory of work" list. This will serve as a checklist to make sure that every relevant work effort finds a home in the new organizational structure.

The reason why this is so important is because in architecting the organization's structure you do not want to forget any relevant components. An example is shown in Figure 6.5, what I call the "categorizing activities tool." Again, it should not be at the tactical level, nor should it be at a very high level.

I recommend a small team works on this, perhaps prior to the session, to cut the time needed for completion. The work inventories also help you categorize your work into what is critical for success and what is not so relevant anymore in your new business. (More about both of these later in this chapter.)

When crafting the work inventory, make sure to include current and future work (keep it relatively high level). In other words, not only should it include a list of all the activities within the organization, but also include any activities that need to be done in the future based on the new vision and strategy.

Next, you need a guideline/boundary for architecting the structure. These should also include your "non-negotiable" items. Here are some examples (please note that these are examples only, and should not be blindly copied as your design guideline):

1. The structure should be relatively flat, with a span of control at minimally five plus.

2. The structure should cause minimal disruption to existing contracts and/or customers.

3. Due to the critical nature of some of the existing contracts, the CEO requires the professional services organization to report directly to him.

Work with your CEO or organization leader to craft this. As mentioned earlier, unlike traditional approaches where the top leader of the organization is crafting the organization, here it's a set of key people in the organization who will be proposing few compelling structures to the CEO. The team, every team, needs boundaries within which to work. The structure being proposed by each of the teams will have to comply with these guidelines.

Now, before we get into the actual crafting of the organizational structure, we need to educate ourselves on the various organization design styles. There are a few well-known ways you can structure an organization. (Illustration 6.3 highlights the details of each.) They are:

Functional: Designed around the specialized skill/knowledge required of its members.

Geographic: Based on geographic location.

Illustration 6.3: Characteristics of Organization Types

	Type	Description	Example
1	Functional	Designed around the specialized skill/knowledge required of its members	• Engineering • Marketing • Sales • HR • Finance
2	Geographic	Based on geographic location	• US/CAN • APAC • LATAM
3	Customer	Organizing around *Customer Groups* that have specific and unique requirements	• Service Provider, Commercial, Enterprise • Internal, External • Partners
4	Technology/Product/Service	The organization may be structured around specialized technology, product family, or service Each organizational unit is fully responsible for development and distribution of the technology, product, or service	• Financial Products • Audio Products • Video Products • For Fee Services • Intranet & Desktop Services
5	Process	Organized around complete end-to-end processes that cut across several traditional functions	• Issue to resolution • Quote to cash
6	Channel	Organized around distribution channel	• Retail • Internet • VAR
7	Matrix	A matrix organization allows the organization to focus on two or more dimensions simultaneously. In a matrix relationship, a person has two bosses, each of whom represents equally important dimensions. The matrix forces a multi-dimensional world view	• Country Manager Vs. Sales Manager
8	Hybrid	This can be a combination of multiple organizational types; for example, "functional" at the first level and then one or more types of subsequent levels	• Level 2: Functional • Level 3: Geographic

Customer: Organized around *customer segments* that have specific and unique requirements.

Technology (or product or service): Organized around specialized technology, product family, or service. Each organizational unit is fully responsible for development and distribution of the technology, product, or service.

Process: Organized around complete end-to-end processes that cut across several traditional functions.

Channel: Organized around distribution channel.

Matrix: Organized to focus on two or more dimensions simultaneously. In a matrix relationship, a person has two bosses, each of whom represents equally important dimensions. The matrix forces a multi-dimensional world view.

Hybrid: Organized as a combination of multiple organizational types; for example, "functional" at the first level and one or more types of subsequent levels.

For your reference, I have shared just a few pros and cons of each of the structures in Illustration 6.4. Review them carefully, as you will be using elements of these in crafting your structure in the next step.

Step 2: Craft the Most Optimal Structure and Define Roles and Accountability

As shared earlier, depending on the complexity and size of the organization, lap one (Develop Design Criteria and Review Gathered Information) and lap two (Craft and Pick the Most Optimal Structure, Define Roles and Accountability) can be done relatively quickly; perhaps in one long day, so long as it is off site and away from daily distractions.

If you recall in the earlier step, all the teams got together to inventory the work list. Each team (as seen in Illustration 6.5) will now take the list and categorize the job duties listed there based on whether it is competitive work, necessary work, compliance work, or minimally relevant work (see below for detailed descriptions of each).

Illustration 6.4: Organization Types—Pros and Cons

Type	Pros	Cons
Function	• Relative role clarity • Increased knowledge-sharing within functions • Permits greater specialization • Best skills will be applied to organizational problems • Greater efficiency—Avoids duplication • Fosters professional identity • Offers clear career path • Easier to supervise, managers have technical expertise • Standardization of processes and procedures	• Different departments have different priorities; the customer's interest can get overlooked • Silo mentality; collaboration may be challenging • Narrow focus may sub-optimize enterprise needs • Conflict over allocation of functional resources • Integration typically occurs at high levels of the organization • Lengthy, bureaucratic communications channels • Difficult to manage diverse product and service lines
Geographic	• Relatively better geographic accountability • Distribution costs optimized • Ability to respond to uniqueness of geographies (local focus) • Improved communications within geographies	• Consistent use of process tools and methodology may be an issue • May not serve global customer well • Redundancy of resources possible • Broad knowledge base expected of the employees • Technical expertise may not be shared • Causes confusion in managerial hierarchies
Customer	• Responsive to customers' needs • Strong customer satisfaction emphasis • Ability to build depth in relationships • Increased accountability for performance • Healthy competition amongst customer groups	• Redundancy of resources possible • New product development could be completely around customer opinion • Broad knowledge base required • Technical expertise may not be shared • Possibility of excessive customization and logistics complexity
Technology/ Product/ Service	• Increased accountability for product/service success • More rapid product/service dev. cycles • Focus allows for "state-of-the-art" research • P&L responsibility for each product is located at the division level with a general manager	• Sharing of specialized expertise is difficult • Redundancy of resources possible • Broad knowledge base required • Unhealthy competition amongst product groups
Process	• Optimizes organizational resources • Minimizes conflicts amongst functions • Improved focus on continuous process improvement	• Vertical silos may be replaced with horizontal silos • Difficult to implement • Less direct accountability
Channel	• Similar to "Customer"	• Similar to "Customer"
Matrix	• Mirrors the reality and complexity of the client world • Enables more flexible utilization of technical depth • Forces employees to adopt a multifunctional perspective • Enhances collaboration (if architected and implemented well)	• Dual reporting relationships can cause conflict • Confusion around roles and accountability • Engagement and governance (decision-making) can be complex • Various groups may have conflicting priorities

Illustration 6.5: Work Inventory Categorization

Work Inventory	Strategic Or Competitive Work	Necessary Work	Compliant Work	Minimally Relevant
1 • <Enter work item>	Mark "X" where appropriate	Mark "X" where appropriate	Mark "X" where appropriate	Mark "X" where appropriate
2				

While working on this exercise, it is important to align with the overall strategy defined in laps four and five. Look through the lens of the team's theme. If done right, each team will differ in what constitutes, for example, "competitive work." This exercise can also help you determine, at a high level, your resource requirements. You tend to be more accurate when you go through this prioritization exercise.

Here is a high-level definition of each of the four categories:

Competitive Work

- ❑ This work makes our strategy happen directly.
- ❑ This work gives our organization a competitive advantage and helps sustain it.
- ❑ Example: Researching and developing new products, managing partner relationship, employee selection and retention.

Necessary Work

- ❑ This work is necessary to business, but not critical.
- ❑ Examples: accounting, general council, building management, and so on.

Compliance Work

- ❑ This work is done in order to maintain regulatory compliance.
- ❑ Examples: various health or legal protocols. This could be work related to FCC, FDA, or OSHA compliance, ISO-related activities, etc.

Minimally Relevant Work

- ❑ This work is no longer relevant, or losing relevance, especially with your new vision and strategy.
- ❑ Example: activities related to products or services that may be discontinued.

While there are no specific industry standards on record, from my personal experience the work inventory breaks down as follows. Again, to highlight, there is no right or wrong answer here and every company is different, so do not use these percentages as strict rules but merely guidelines:

- ❑ Competitive work activities: 35%
- ❑ Necessary work activities: 40%
- ❑ Compliance work activities: 20%
- ❑ Minimally relevant work activities: 5%

Here are some thoughts that I have compiled that may help you craft a more effective organizational structure:

- ❑ Consider categorizing the work inventory based on alignment to the strategy or mission, not the work itself.
- ❑ The grouping, location, and resourcing of work should be driven by the greatest competitive impact and cost impact.
- ❑ Structure the organization around primarily competitive work.
- ❑ Consider outsourcing necessary work.
- ❑ Eliminate minimally relevant (non-value-added) work.
- ❑ It is highly recommended that you never outsource competitive work.
- ❑ Optimize synergies between work groups by combining similar/like functions and eliminating duplication/waste.
- ❑ Do not lose sight of the fact that all structures being proposed must meet clearly defined design criteria.
- ❑ Remember, all work is not strategically equal, except in organizations that don't have strategies.

Last, it is important that you craft the structure based on "business need," not "people need." What's the difference? For instance, the CEO may know an individual very well and want to appoint him to a position, possibly a high-level position, even if there is no justifiable business need for such a position. It could be his brother-in-law, stepson, a friend of a friend, or his accountant, who may or may not be qualified for this position. I am sure you can recall numerous examples in your organization when this has happened, right? This should be avoided at ALL costs (for obvious reasons).

In brainstorming design options, make sure you do not lose sight of the design criteria. Also, up front, before you begin to design, consider identifying those gaps highlighted in lap four that can potentially be addressed through an optimal organization design.

Review the pros and cons of some of the design types you may consider. Once you have a draft design, spend enough time discussing the pros and cons of the design you just put together.

Make sure you think through how cross-departmental or cross-functional decisions (governance) get made. Clarify with subject matter experts how the end-to-end processes might work in the new design, and then optimize as appropriate.

Determine how you can leverage the SWOT analysis (strength, weakness, opportunity, and threats) work from lap four and see if you can turn any of your weaknesses in to strengths through an effective organizational structure. See if you can leverage your opportunities better through an effective organizational structure. Make sure to align with the strategy you crafted in laps four and five—this is the single most important aspect you will need to keep in mind.

Draw your recommended structure down to three or four levels below the organization leader (CEO or GM), depending on the size and complexity of the organization. Going any deeper into the design would be premature. Each of the respective leaders chosen (more on this in lap seven) will design their respective organizations as appropriate, making sure to align with their "parent" organization (sort of like a trickle-down effect). At each level in the design process, highlight the roles/functions and associated roles description and success metric (see Illustration 6.6).

Be sure to highlight the various reasons for your design selection and the most interesting aspects of the design. During the presentation process (see below), it can be easy to miss the forest for the trees, so highlighting *why* you chose a certain design option helps you focus on priorities when presentation time comes. Last, catalog the following:

1. Pros and cons (see Illustration 6.7)
2. Risk and mitigation (see Illustration 6.8)

Illustration 6.6: Roles, Accountability and Success Metrics

Level	Role/Function	Role Description	Success Metric
L1			
L1			
L1			
L2			
L2			
L2			
L3			
L3			
L3			
L3			
L3			

3. Change-management issues you foresee, if the design is adopted (see Illustration 6.9)

Now get all the teams together and have them present to each other and the organizational leader. Give each team precisely twenty minutes to state their case. (No more, maybe less—if they are unable to make their case in twenty minutes, they may not have thought through it well enough). If, however, there are any questions that the organization leader or other team members may have, be flexible and provide an additional ten minutes for a brief but informative Q&A.

Transformation is hard work, so grab some levity and laughter when you can get it! For instance, there is no reason this part of the process shouldn't be fun and engaging. To that end, the presentation moderator should make it like a competition of sorts. Again, you can give interesting prizes to the team whose design is chosen—movie tickets, dinner for two, gift cards, a weekend getaway, etc.

If you do not have a big budget for prizes, it can even be something as simple as a brown bag lunch with the senior-most person in the company. Imagine being able to have the organization leader's (or even CEO's) undivided attention for an hour or so—an opportunity that you may not get otherwise—to get your questions answered about the future direction of the company. See what works for you and provide gifts according to your budget, not necessarily your wish list.

If the atmosphere is competitive and the ideas are engaging, you may want to moderate the session in a way so that teams challenge each other on the structure being proposed. Competitiveness often brings out the best in people, and by having to "defend" their structural ideas some teams could rise to the occasion and make a surprisingly strong case that sways the CEO.

Here are some tips for presenting your structure to other teams:

Present with conviction: Be humble enough to accept aspects that you have not incorporated in the design because you did not have the time or did not have enough data. Highlight the human aspect of how the company might "look" based on your structural ideas. Don't be afraid to admit "we don't have all the answers." This is not about coming to the table with a ready-made answer but, instead, it's about proposing an idea and opening up

Illustration 6.7: Capture Pros and Cons of the Organization Design

Pros	Relevance to Desired Objectives

Cons	Relevance to Desired Objectives

Illustration 6.8: Design Risks and Mitigation

#	Design Risks	Implication	Mitigation

Illustration 6.9: Issues that May Require Change Management

Change Management Issue	Entity/Person related to issue	How it will be handled	Owner	Suggested timeframe to be solved by

the floor to troubleshoot it before going live. Be sure to engage the audience in a dialog on any issue that you were, perhaps, struggling with in the design phase.

Give each group a name. For example, "Marketing" (if it is function-based) or "Issue-to-Resolution" (if it is process-based). Do not personalize them; i.e., refer to them as "John's organization" or "Nancy's group." This can cause internal, even unconscious, prejudice among the other groups or attendees. Besides, it is wrong to assume John or Nancy or anyone else involved in the presentation teams is the best person to lead those organizations in the future. Giving a group an individual's name sets the wrong tone!

Always have an open mind when it comes to feedback being given by members of other teams. It's important to create an atmosphere in which no one participating in this process is present just to hurt someone else or tear down others' ideas; this is all for the greater good of the company, and sometimes an objective opinion from someone who is hearing this material for the first time—or from a different perspective—can lead to intriguing discoveries that benefit you all.

Be sensitive to non-team members' roles in the organization. Remember, people can become defensive if they perceive—through your teams' presentation—that they may not have a place in the organization. A good moderator should be able to manage the emotions if it gets out of control.

As mentioned earlier, depending on the organization leader's management style and personal preference, have him/her pick the most appropriate structure after all the presentations are done. It is beneficial, I think, for all those teams involved—and everyone for whom the restructuring will have a direct impact—to have the leader explain why he/she picked the chosen structure. Also, if there are structural elements proposed by other teams that sound like a good idea, he or she should feel free to "cherry pick" these ideas and incorporate them into the chosen structure to make it the best possible solution.

Oftentimes the organization leader may want a day or two to think through and process all that's been presented—that's okay. In this case, schedule another meeting to share the decision and/or the reasons for the decision.

I also recommend doing what I call a "break the model" exercise. This exercise may need a moderator. As its very name suggests, the idea here is to try and break the model; i.e., the organizational structure that you have just assembled. We are actively trying to "break" the model to see if it holds up.

Have the teams identify critical things that they currently do or engage in and see how it plays out in the new organizational structure. It could be, perhaps, a process you currently use with the organization for customer escalations or how certain key decisions are made in the new structure. The idea is not to work on the process or governance now, as those will be dealt with in lap nine.

Once everyone is satisfied with the structure, make sure to update the roles, role descriptions, success metrics, and pros and cons based on the "new," updated structure.

Step 3: Fine-tune and Finalize

We've gotten the internal feedback from a variety of teams, departments, and even high-level employees, now it's time for some external feedback. In this step, the organizational leader can share the design with key stakeholders outside the organization. Depending on their feedback, the organization can be further fine-tuned. This is obviously only applicable for relatively large companies with multiple business units. For smaller organizations, this step can be safely skipped.

Step 4: Communicate the Final Structure

We now have an organizational design that has a better chance for organizational adoption due to the high-engagement model used in developing it. We now need to communicate it to the entire organization. How many people, what departments, divisions, etc., does that encompass?

Here are some of the entities you need to communicate to:

❑ Leadership team (if everyone did not participate in the above exercise)

❑ Employees

❑ Stakeholders

❑ Key customers (large customers)

❑ Key partners

At this point we are just communicating the organizational structure, not who leads each of the boxes—this will happen in lap seven (which, incidentally, needs to be completed in no more than one to two weeks).

Remember, the timing of this communication is important. It's important to remember that these exercises are not occurring in a vacuum, there will be a real impact on the company, and, as a result, on company employees. Even in the largest of companies, employee scuttlebutt is such that your people will know "something is going on."

If you delay communication (see my Case Study, below), employees will become very anxious and worried about their future, as well as that of the company's, which will impact the current and future productivity levels. If you communicate too early, there will be a long gap between the "structure" announcement and the leadership announcements—this will, again, make people very uneasy. Remember, you promised the employees that they would be kept in the loop throughout the journey—you need to stay true to that conviction, particularly as these laps begin impacting employees' jobs in a very real way.

Also, make sure you give employees a date by when all organizational decisions (leaders, teams, etc.) will be finalized and communicated. Here is a more detailed breakdown of whom to communicate with, and how:

Employees: Here is an example of an actual letter I crafted for one of the employee groups at a Fortune 100 company recently:

Building a Customer-Relevant Organization Through Improved Internal and External Partnerships

Dear All,

Many of you know that I embarked my organization on a transformational journey about three months ago through "Project Asteroid." The purpose was to raise the bar for ourselves and build a more customer-relevant organization through tighter external and internal partnerships.

We initiated our journey by interviewing our customers, partners, and stakeholders, and carefully analyzing their needs. This has helped us crisply define our vision and strategy, supporting the vision and strategy of our parent organization.

Today I am happy to share with you that we have taken another step in further aligning our organizational structure with Worldwide Sales. This will not only help us serve our customers better but will also help us stay true to our CEO's vision of being globally consistent while maintaining local relevance. 2010 will be a year of strengthening our internal and external partnerships.

Here is our organizational structure reporting to me (L2 level):

Service Delivery: The Service Delivery functions will now report centrally to a single leader. This includes XXX, YYY, and AAA functions in east, central, and west regions. The structure will closely align with BBB Markets. The MY delivery organization will also include service creation, field liaison, and complex-deals support.

Business Operations: This critical operations role will now include managing alliances for the channel and will continue to report to me directly.

Global Support: This will continue to be a critical organization. The Global Support leadership team will be expanded with the addition of the 2nd Director role. In addition, there will be a new role created to lead the "service capability readiness" function.

Service Marketing: This function will continue to report to me as well. In addition, each of my direct reports, once chosen, will further design their respective organizations and share the L3 structure and beyond in the next two to three weeks.

Our vision is to accelerate customer and partner success in their own competitive environments by effectively driving innovative service delivery that focuses on our customer's infrastructure. Our organization will provide a comprehensive service-delivery environment that proactively ensures network reliability and optimization at all times. This proactive and predictive mindset will drive the innovative services, further enabling accelerated customer success. Our globalization engine will be a competitive advantage, helping us achieve this vision.

With each step we take and each change we make, we continue to sharpen our focus and provide more value to our company and the customers who buy our products and services.

I look forward to your continued support.

Warm Regards,

Joseph Teller
Vice President (Service Delivery)

Don't forget to thank the teams for their effort and creative thinking. I would even go so far as to encourage the CEO to send out personal "thank you" cards to show appreciation for employee effort on the company's behalf.

Stakeholders: Make sure you tie in the organizational structure with the feedback you received from the stakeholders; i.e., "close the loop." This may necessitate feedback from customizing messages for each of the stakeholders based on their initial feedback in lap three.

Customers: You may ask yourself, "Why should we communicate these upcoming organizational changes with our customer(s)?" I agree that you do not *have* to. However, if you have large customers that are your bread and butter, here is an opportunity for you to build trust by opening and sharing the details of the organization prior to any press release or notice to the general public. Everyone wants to feel like they're part of the "inner circle," so why not capitalize on that very human emotion with large, game-changing customers?

Partners: Follow the same protocol you used for the customers.

Change Management and Communication

Positioning this exercise properly will go a long way toward making it both more effective for you and more enjoyable for the participants. Specifically, I suggest that you position this exercise as a privilege being given to the participants—they should not misuse the exercise but, in fact, make full use of the opportunity. Confront anxiety (as a result of uncertainty) head on. The more open you are with people, the more trust you build.

Throughout the exercise do not use any names of people against any roles/functions. No function or role should be off limits. Be aware there may be a tendency for the leadership team to influence "waivers." Here the CEO should stay firm if he/she wants to include all functions/roles. The more restriction (or waivers) there are in design criteria, the less optimal the resulting structure will be.

Remember, communication is key to this step, and not only communication internally but externally as well. You can't deny that rumors will run rampant, nor should you. Be open with your employees and your stakeholders as well (see step four, above), not only now but throughout the transformation process.

Transparency about this restructuring is not a weakness to be avoided but an opportunity not to be missed. Finally, consider leveraging "change ambassadors" to get deeper buy-in from respective constituents.

Case Study: Timing Really IS Everything

This is a story about why it's so important to communicate with your employees during the transformation process; because even when the process itself is going smoothly (as it did in the company you're about to meet), if employees outside the "inner circle" aren't kept apprised of the situation, uncertainty and "information anxiety" can alter bottom-line productivity, and cost you plenty.

Case in point: there is a midsize sports equipment manufacturer in the Pacific Northwest that has been in existence for over fifty years and which has a brand that is well-recognized by most fitness enthusiasts and athletes.

The company has grown tremendously over the years, not only in size but in consumer offerings. They have diversified into many areas beyond sports equipment, including nutritional supplements, sports apparel, and even training programs.

As a result of the down-turn in the economy, their sales of mid- to low-end sports gear was not selling that well. However, their custom equipment designed for top athletes actually picked up.

Why? It turns out that nobody except this company offered a custom solution for A-list athletes. So despite the economic downturn they seemed to have leveraged their strengths to take advantage of an opportunity they saw several years ago, and it seemed to have paid off. However, with regard to the mid- to low-end equipment, they were competing against some of the cheaper, Chinese-manufactured brands.

Clearly, the company was top-heavy with its one success story but struggling toward the middle- and bottom-end of its once-competitive lines. Now, equipped with a renewed vision and a well thought-through strategy, the company was off to do an organizational transformation in an attempt to better align their organization to their strategy.

Many of the leaders in the organization felt threatened that their positions may be lost, and hence lobbied strongly on why their organization should be exempt from participating in the organizational transformation. However, the CEO (thankfully) was unmoved and the right structure was architected.

That was the good news; the bad news came when the restructuring was unveiled, for while the communication was done, it was not quite done at the right time. For one reason or another, the CEO wanted to hold off on any announcement until the leadership team was identified, which took over two months!

Two months may not seem long in black and white, on paper, but in the meantime anxiety set in with the employees, hampering bottom-line productivity. Most front-line employees were uncertain, anxious, and far from focused on their day-to-day job duties.

Again, the transformation occurred, the restructuring was successful, and today the company is much stronger and profitable because of it, but during those sixty days when the employees experienced a definite lack of communication, not only was goodwill for the CEO and other C-level leaders lost amongst the employees but actual profitability was lost as well.

Lap 6 Key Takeaways

- ❑ The purpose of this lap is to craft the most optimal organizational structure that aligns with the vision and the strategy.

- ❑ Begin defining (but not finalizing) roles and accountability at all levels.

- ❑ Define high-level success metrics for each of the key roles and come up with succinct job descriptions.

- ❑ Identify overall pros and cons as well as risks of the structure being proposed.

❑ Highlight the change-management issues that may be faced.

❑ The right-side-up organizational structure has the customer at the top of the "food chain" and the CEO at the bottom.

❑ Aim to design the organizational structure within two to three years—same timeframe as your vision.

❑ In lap four we pulled together a team to assist with SWOT analysis. See if the same or similar team can be pulled together for this exercise.

❑ This design exercise, depending on how you lay it out, may take anywhere from two days to two weeks. Size and complexity of the organization largely determines how long the process takes.

❑ It is critical that all key stakeholders/players in the organization are involved, especially the skeptic, politically motivated, and/or passive-aggressive types. It is important to make them feel like they are part of the solution.

❑ Here are four key steps to design a most optimal organization:

1. Develop design criteria and review gathered information

2. Craft the most optimal structure and define roles and accountability

3. Fine-tune and finalize

4. Communicate the final structure

❑ The final design or "structure" of the organization should clearly define all hierarchies, roles, and objectives within the company. Definitions before the transformation may be similar but different, so good communication to all stakeholders, both internally and externally, is key.

Lap 7

Assess the Competency of Leaders and Employees

An A-rated team can make even a C-rated idea or product successful.
On the contrary, a C-rated team can drive an A-rated idea
or product straight into the ground.

What good is a well-structured organization if it is not led by competent people? Competency assessment is critical to ensure the right people are leading the right teams in the right way, all the time.

Before we begin the assessment process, we should be clear on *exactly* why we want to do competency assessment in the first place: Is it to select the best individuals for leadership positions? Or is it to develop existing leaders into those areas where the organization has existing gaps?

In an ideal scenario, of course, it would be *both*. Research has shown that selection of the right leadership team yields better results than developing existing leaders. While the statement cannot be generalized, there are many reasons for this, including perhaps because not all skills can be developed.

Warning: lap seven is not for "chickens." Many leaders tend to take a shortcut by either not doing any assessment at all or by assessing only for development, rather than for competency. These leaders may not have the stomach to take on this discussion of "selection."

After all, convincing the leadership team (who, let's face it, may have been around for a long time) to go through a selection process will doubtless face opposition. Taking a shortcut will come back and haunt the decision-makers, however; and as a result, I cannot emphasize enough the importance of this decisive step.

In an ideal environment, of course, the assessment should not stop with the top leaders but, in fact, be done through several levels within the company, depending on the organizational structure. This lap will help you follow these steps so that your competency assessment is not only comprehensive, but also effective.

Purposeful Competency Assessment

Now that we have an organizational structure in place (see lap six), the next step is to assign the right people for the right jobs. As one might imagine, this is a critical step when it comes to assigning roles. Now that you've worked so hard to find an organizational structure that fits your business model, you wouldn't just hand over the keys to anyone would you?

The proper fit is vital to the success of your transformation efforts; key people are critical before, during, and well after the transformation, so don't take this step lightly. This lap can either make or break the transformation you are hoping to achieve. You can have the best vision and strategy in place, but if you don't have the right people for the key positions, the organization is bound to fail.

Many companies feel they can "fudge" a little on this step because they've worked hard to create a solid foundation for the ongoing success of the company transformation. Additionally, they may feel they already have good people working right where they belong. That may very well be true, but a new organizational structure often demands new skill sets, new competencies, and potentially even new players to ensure that it succeeds.

Don't undo all your hard work up to now by going along with the flow or by succumbing to upper-level pressures. When it comes to filling new job requirements, first complete a full competency assessment on both new and old employees alike.

Now, I'm not implying that this will be an easy step, particularly for those employees, many of them senior, who have been around for some time and may see anything with the word "competency" in it as a threat.

But, again, I am saying this is a vital step in the process, and one you can't overlook—or go without.

You may recall how, back in lap five, we started to architect a "success map" for a fictional credit union. One of the cross-functional initiatives that came out of that exercise was "to develop competent employees." The focus of this lap will be to break that process down even further, as shown in Illustration 7.1. (Some of these aspects may be touched on again in lap nine.)

A Candid Approach to Competency Assessment

Taking the organization through a competency assessment can be very politically charged. Throughout my consulting practice, I have seen many executives who initially sign up to take on this exercise, but succumb to pressure from other leaders and quickly change their minds. Over the years I have seen the same executives fail as a result of the temptation to skip this lap entirely.

The big question my clients continually ask is: "Do we do the assessment for only the new positions identified, or should it be done for *all* the positions?" It's a good question and, of course, the natural, human inclination is to do as little competency assessment as possible, especially considering the political ramifications involved.

In response, however, I say that this depends on how comfortable the leader is with the existing team. If you were a leader, wouldn't you take this opportunity to clear out "dead wood" and start with the most suitable people at the top and hold them accountable with clear success metrics?

Let's face it; you are doing this transformation because things are perhaps not going that well in your company. Taking a shortcut on this lap, in particular, or not taking it seriously, can keep things going not so well.

Let's say you've just bought a Ferrari, only this isn't any old Ferrari; this particular sports car has been custom-designed to race in the Indy 500 and features all kinds of bells and whistles that only an experienced racecar driver can fully access. You wouldn't let just anyone drive it, would you? What if they didn't have the right experience or, for that matter, any experience? Your sleek, beautiful sports car could be ruined simply because you were being

Illustration 7.1: Example QCU Success Map

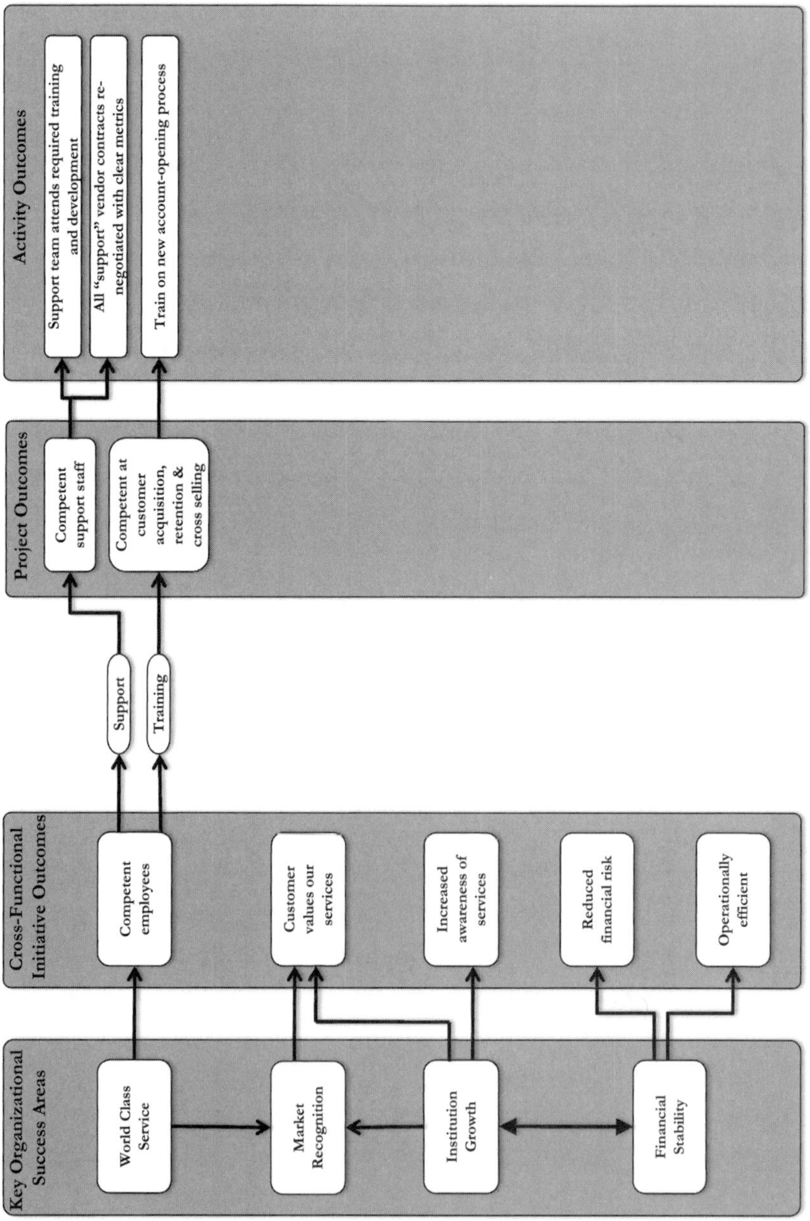

polite or allowing for the status quo to exist when more appropriate drivers (employees) were readily available.

The answer in this case is pretty clear: you'd hand the keys over to the expert, right? Well, the same goes for your company. Thanks to this transformation effort, you are attempting to transform this company into a fine-tuned, money-making machine. ·

So . . . don't you want the right people to "drive" it? Before getting into the assessment aspect, one of the first questions you need to ask yourself is, "Why does the company want to do this assessment?"

Is it for selection, development, or both? If it's for **selection**, you need to know how to recruit for, locate, scout, and interview potential talent with specific criteria in mind for the position you're hoping to fill. If it's for **development**, you want to learn how to do the same within your company.

To answer the above question, it's critical to understand the implications of each route. To assist you, I recommend you read a very good book, *First, Break all the Rules*, written by Marcus Buckingham and Curt Coffman. If you're talking about a comprehensive analysis of good leaders, here is the place to start. The authors interviewed over 80,000 managers from over 400 companies in what was hailed as the largest such study of its kind.

The authors discovered that not only do the greatest managers differ in sex, age, and race, but they also employed different leadership styles and focused on different goals. However, despite their differences, great managers share one common trait: They do not hesitate to break every rule held sacred by conventional wisdom.

They do not believe that, even with enough training, a person can achieve anything he sets his mind to. They do not try to help people overcome weakness. They consistently disregard the golden rule. And, yes, they even play favorites! (The book explains why. I encourage you to read the book and see if you agree with their findings.)

When I read the book it was like a sudden revelation; I thought everybody felt, lead, lived, and breathed this way! I have always led by instinct, as have most of my clients. From my further experience, though, I believe there are *some* key traits that cannot be learned and *some* that can be learned.

This is where doing a competency assessment for both selection and development helps you find out which type of employee you're dealing with, and who will ultimately be the best fit for key positions.

Adopting the Best Competency Model for Your Company

There are many competency models out there. If your organization does not have a model that it already uses, I encourage you to assess and adopt an appropriate competency model that works best for your organization. Many of these models are based on scientific research. Using such models ensures that you are utilizing quality definitions and that the competencies demonstrate a high degree of specificity (which is crucial to success).

Keep in mind, however, that you have no more than two to three weeks to complete this critical step—from the time the organizational structure is communicated to the powers that be. So be cognizant of the time and money you put into this exercise. While it would be great to put as much time and money into this step as possible, I am aware that you have a company to run and you want this to enhance your organization, not derail it!

Once you commit to this step fully, it's very tempting to get carried away with getting it done perfectly, but in doing so you will be perceived as "dragging the process along" and may even run the risk of losing the wind behind your sails in your transformational journey. Remember, you still have three more laps to go, so pace yourself. (After all, you don't want the teams "worn out" before they start on laps eight–ten.)

Top hiring managers understand the importance of talent management in unlocking and sustaining a competitive edge. Finding the right person to fit the right job, however, is a challenging task, and most hiring managers have felt the pain of making a bad hire. The costs can be enormous, both personally and professionally.

The key to talent management begins with hiring the right people. However, before the organization searches for candidates to fill a job, the organization must know what is needed to be successful in that job.

We have defined our strategy in laps four and five. We have crafted our organization's structure in lap six. These three previous laps are key in defining what is needed to be successful in each of the positions needed to staff your new organizational structure.

A way to start building this knowledge database is by using the duly filled Illustration 6.6 as a starting point. While the design recommendation exercise highlighted the description of the job, now is a good time to craft the competencies for each of the roles. Remember, it is critical that these competencies be linked to the organization's business goals and objectives.

There are hundreds of definitions for a "competency" and, frankly, most are poor. To be specific, a "competency" is best defined as, "an identifiable characteristic expected of an individual that contributes to organizational success."

Identifying and defining the core competencies necessary to be successful in a job is much easier said than done. Few organizations truly understand the "science" of competency modeling, let alone do it well. An effective competency model is developed by carefully analyzing the critical components, both technical and behavioral, that are required to be successful in any particular job.

Competencies fall into either of two categories:

1. Technical competencies: Technical competencies refer to the skills and knowledge necessary to be successful in a given job (i.e., knowledge of accounting principles, computer skills, etc.).

2. Behavioral competencies: Behavioral competencies refer to specific behaviors necessary to be successful in a given job (i.e., delegation, communication, etc.).

Competency Assessment: 12 Simple Steps for Success

The most effective competency models are developed by first examining the outcomes expected for success in a given job. Once the outcomes have been clearly defined, then the organization can better analyze the behaviors needed to achieve the outcomes.

Below is a step-by-step process for successfully completing a competency assessment for your organization.

1. Create a Job List of all the Roles

Depending on how complex or large the organization is, consider peeling the onion back one layer at a time. Analyze each role one level at a time, or consider working on high-impact jobs, or positions, within your organization first and then moving on to do the others.

As you examine the "layers" of your existing organization more closely, the roles will become clearer, as will the job responsibilities for each role. Being clear on the role will help you develop or select key players appropriately.

2. Define Performance Expectations

For each role or position you identify, further determine the outcomes expected as a result of successful performance within this position. These are the success metrics as indicated in the exercise you completed on page 184, which should be linked directly to organizational strategy and objectives.

3. Identify Technical and Behavioral Competencies

Next, using the role descriptions you worked up and filled in for that same exercise as a starting point, identify the technical and behavioral competencies necessary to achieve the desired outcomes. At this point, this is just a draft; you can finalize the competencies after you have selected the model in the next couple of steps.

4. Define Competency Model

If your organization does not already have a model, do not bother creating one from scratch—it takes considerable time and expertise to put one of these together, and you have plenty else to do to keep you busy. No need to reinvent the wheel when you're looking for a full-fledged competency model to adopt. Instead, just go to the Internet and search "competency model." You will find plenty of models out there. Choose the one that is most appropriate for you, keeping the above guidelines in mind. To save you some time, check out: www.careeronestop.org/competencymodel/pyramid_definition.aspx.

I've found, for many clients, this is a good place to start. By way of a little background information, look into Career One Stop, which is sponsored by the US Department of Labor, Employment and Training Administration. So not only can you trust the information here, but this site also allows you to customize the model based on your industry *and* your business goals and objectives.

Remember, good competency models will contain definitions and behavioral elements that are highly specific and well defined. If a competency model is based on scientific research, the vendor can provide you with the corresponding articles.

5. Highlight Traits or Attributes that Align to Each of the Roles

Once you pick out a well-defined model, the next step is to highlight traits or attributes that align to each of the roles. (The above site can help you with this step.) For instance, as highlighted above, Career One Stop has three consecutive "tiers" built specifically around occupation-related traits or attributes. As they explain it:

> "The competencies on Tiers 6, 7, and 8 are grouped and referred to as Occupational Competencies. Occupational competency models are frequently developed to define performance in a workplace, to design competency-based curriculum, or to articulate the requirements for an occupational credential such as a license or certification." (www.CareerOneStop. org)

So dig deeper for each role and specifically highlight those traits or attributes you deem necessary for each of the roles.

6. Use Critical Data Points for Assessment

There are many data points you can leverage to assess the competency of an individual for a particular role. Which ones you pick depend on many factors, including availability of time and resources, neither of which is very plentiful these days.

However, logically speaking, the more data points you use for assessment, the more accurate the results. Remember, you have less than two to three weeks after the announcement of the organizational structure to complete the assessment and announce the positions (at least the critical ones).

To make the best use of this brief time, here are some guidelines on a few common data points:

Review credentials: These are quite straightforward. As mentioned earlier, there are two credentials to concern yourself with: technical and behavioral. Depending on the technical complexity of your particular function, there are many accredited and industry-specific certifications such as Project Management Institute's PMP certification or the Six Sigma "Black Belt" certification from Motorola, etc. Such trusted criteria can test a candidate's technical aspects within a narrow field of accuracy. So, for instance, can a particular employee run a specific software program or piece of hardware that is mission-critical to the role you're trying to fill? There are also many online assessment tools that the candidates can be requested to take as part of the initial assessment. On the behavioral side, study the candidate closely for past experience that proves he or she can adapt behaviorally to the role in question. For instance, can she/he communicate? Delegate? Strategize? Identify problems? Past performance and strong referrals should be good indicators of these behavioral benchmarks.

Conduct interviews: In my honest opinion, data gathered through interviews can give you some valuable insights about a person, provided multiple people conduct the interviews. The following people can complete the interviews:

> **Manager**: This is critical and will also help the hiring manager assess chemistry and culture fit.
>
> **Stakeholder**: These can be peers or groups that the individual will be working with very closely. Giving the stakeholders an opportunity to conduct the interviews helps build trust. Besides, since they have participated and helped select the individual, in all likelihood they will support the chosen individual. If time is a factor, consider panel interviews which, if done well, can be quick and effective.
>
> **Third-party individuals:** You may consider bringing in a consultant to assist with the interviews or, if you do not have the budget for this, get someone outside your group (such as a trained HR person) to assist in this process. This works just as well, as long as

the interviewer does not know any of the candidates being presented. The intent is to get an unbiased perspective on the candidates. This is also important to save you time and energy, and helps in setting the right perception. Let this expert do what he or she does best and save you time that can better be spent elsewhere.

Panels or groups: You can interview by panel, quickly and efficiently, if you plan properly. Most likely you want to schedule a half-day for this. Next, schedule a conference room and have a team of trusted interviewers work from a set list of questions. Once the interviews are done, everyone can get together and engage in a round table discussion to reveal opinions/assessments.

Assess personality (or strengths): You may have heard and/or even used many of the more common and respected personality or strength assessments (see below), some of which can be taken online while others need to be performed by certified professionals. From my experience, they only serve as an additional data point, but a good one nevertheless. None of these tests are comprehensive, covering all aspects. Please note that most of these tests are self-administered, so there may be a "fudge" factor—and this is particularly true for those tests that ask direct questions. Here are some well-known personality tests that you may want to do more research on:

- ❑ Myers Briggs Type Indicator (MTBI)
- ❑ Herrmann Brain Dominance Instrument (HBDI)
- ❑ 16 Personality Factor (16PF)
- ❑ Dominance, Influence, Steadiness and Conscientiousness Method (DISC)
- ❑ Method Teaming
- ❑ Strength Finder

For you to choose which of the tests might be right for you, you need to consider the following:

- ❏ What was the original purpose of the tool? Was it developed for clinical use, training, and development or business?

- ❏ Does it measure simple behavioral styles or more complex personality traits and business competencies?

- ❏ Is it relevant in today's business?

- ❏ Does it require expert interpretation or extensive training to understand?

- ❏ Is it self-administered, where the honesty and integrity of people taking the test is assumed, or is it administered by a third party (typically an expert), who can make a more accurate, unbiased assessment?

- ❏ Does it have both cognitive and personality tests in the same assessment, with a combined reporting mechanism?

- ❏ Is it quick, as most organizations are only looking for assessments that do not take more than an hour to assess and report?

- ❏ Does the reporting include benchmarking?

- ❏ Is it cost-effective? These can be expensive, so get your money's worth.

7. Identify and Interview

We are circling the bottom of the selection funnel now, so it is time to get specific, identify and make lists, and begin the formal interviewing process. First, make a list of the names of candidates being assessed for each of the roles. Next, schedule interviews as appropriate.

8. Begin Conducting Assessments

Review the competencies being assessed and the list of people being assessed for a given position with the hiring manager and fine-tune, as appropriate. These assessments will be critical in matching the right people with the right roles.

9. Test for "Chemistry," Review Results with Hiring Manager, and Finalize

In case there are multiple people being assessed for a given position, review the results with the hiring manager to see who might be the right fit. There are, of course, other aspects that may need to be assessed before offering anyone the job; for example, "chemistry" with the hiring manager and the rest of the organization, past performance, technical competencies, etc. This issue of chemistry, in particular, is what I refer to as an invisible factor. For instance, they might "fit" perfectly well based on quantitative scores, but if they don't "fit" with the rest of the team, weigh that heavily against the skills and be realistic about how well this person is going to be able to perform his or her duties without the full support—be it conscious or subconscious—of the rest of the team.

Finally, it is critical that planning and rollout align, that the people assessing for the position are in line with the people hiring for the position, so that the efforts go smoothly and begin seamlessly. To that end, make sure to choose appropriate candidates in consultation with the hiring manager.

10. Develop a Learning and Development Roadmap

Have the HR person work with each of the chosen candidates to develop a learning and development roadmap so as to foster growth in the core competencies necessary for success.

11. Institute Performance Management and Developmental Processes Around the Competency Model

It is critical to have a firm grasp on the competency model that best fits your organization prior to filling any of the roles that surround it. Entice potential candidates deemed worthy of filling such roles to improve in the areas identified by tying them to their MBOs (management by objective). This will help focus on the desired results.

12. Integrate the Competency Model

Take the time to integrate your competency model to the succession planning process. This should help you identify and develop candidates for succession into your critical jobs.

Finalize the Competency Assessment Process

Once the key leadership positions are assessed and individuals are identified, it is time to proceed deeper into the organization, engaging respective leaders in building their sub-organizations. It is important that they are part of the selection process. After all, they are the ones accountable for their respective sub-organizations.

Remember, it's not just weighing the individual "as is," but seeing where you are in the transformational journey to see which individual might "fit" best based on all the data you've gathered throughout this process.

Finally, continue the process until all the roles are completed. If you are constrained by time and resources, then you can limit the assessment to the most critical and/or senior positions.

Change Management and Communication

Keep in mind that if everyone is going to go through the assessment (and I do mean *everyone*, key people included), then this means people will have to **re-apply for their existing positions**. Understandably so, this may not go very well with many of the company's established leaders. That said, the CEO or the organizational leader needs to handle this re-application process with care (see this chapter's Case Study as a true "study" in how to handle this process).

If you are constrained by time and resources, then you can limit the assessment to the most critical and/or senior positions. If this is the case, make it clear up front which positions need assessment. Regardless of who or how many candidates you assess, keep in mind that people—many of them key people—are anxiously awaiting a "verdict," and this is why it is key to complete this process in no more than two to three weeks.

Speaking of anxiety, this is where communication can become your ally. Transparency is important, especially at this critical stage. Therefore, communicate the overall plan of action to everyone who will go over the assessment so they understand the process, desired outcome, and timeframe. It is critical that everyone understand how decisions will be made. You should also involve general counsel and HR folks to make sure there are no potential legal issues in a long-time veteran potentially losing his or her position during this admittedly controversial process.

Case Study: A Lesson in Why Change Comes from the Top

"Sheryl" is a business-unit general manager at a major telecommunications company. Not long ago, Sheryl was taking her organization through a transformational journey. As expected, when she came to lap seven, the discussions around assessment and who the right people might be for the right jobs became very political and the situation became quite intense.

Fortunately, Sheryl handled the situation with poise; she called her entire leadership team for a meeting and informed them that, in no uncertain terms, *everyone* had to go through the assessment process—with *no* exceptions. Naturally, to back up her firm grip on the situation, she explained why this was critical for the organization.

However, she did something that most leaders are very hesitant to do. Sheryl raised her hand and said that she would be going through the assessment for her own job as well. This executive team scoffed, at first.

"If I do not qualify," she added resolutely, "I will resign."

No one was scoffing after that rather bold announcement.

As you might imagine, this was a daring move for Sheryl to make. The fact that she might actually lose her job, willingly, after going through the assessment process and being found, essentially, "unfit" for her current role in the restructuring process was not only a leap of faith in Sheryl's abilities but a vote of confidence for the validity of the process itself. This immediately put an end to the "lobbying" being done by the leadership; they got the message that Sheryl was dead serious about this.

Fortunately, this case study has a happy ending! Not only did Sheryl get re-selected for the job, she was from that moment forward very well respected by her team, her peers, and the top management in the company. She eventually received numerous accolades for the successful transformation of her organization.

Let Sheryl's story be a lesson in commitment. The only way to see a successful transformation through to fruition is to be 100% committed to the process, even to the point of being reassigned, restructured—or replaced. You are making this transformation for a specific reason, and your belief in the process is critical to seeing it succeed.

Lap 7 Key Takeaways

❑ Now that we have an organizational structure, the next step is to assign the right people for the jobs. This is a critical step when it comes to assigning roles. You would not just hand over the "keys" to anyone, would you?

❑ You can have the best vision and strategy in place, but if you do not have the right people for the key positions, the organization is bound to fail.

❑ Do not take this lap lightly, as this can either make or break the transformation you are hoping to achieve.

❑ Taking the organization through a competency assessment can be very politically charged. Be prepared to deal with this constructively.

❑ Before getting into the assessment aspect one of the first questions to ask yourself is, Why does the company want to do this assessment? Is it for selection, development, or both?

❑ There are many competency models out there. If your organization does not have a model that it already uses, I encourage you to assess and adopt an appropriate competency model that works best for your organization.

❑ Top hiring managers understand the importance of talent management, and their ability to unlock and sustain a competitive edge. Finding the right person to fit the right job is a challenging task, and most hiring managers have felt the pain of making a bad hire. The costs can be enormous both personally and professionally.

❑ The key to talent management begins with hiring the right people. However, before the organization searches for candidates to fill a job, the organization must know what is needed (what traits and skills) to be successful in that job.

❑ The most effective competency models are developed by first examining the outcomes expected for success in a given job. Once the outcomes have been clearly defined, then the organization can analyze the behaviors needed to achieve the outcomes.

❑ If you are constrained by time and resources, then you can limit the assessment to the most critical and or senior positions. If this is the case, make it clear up front which positions will need assessment.

❑ Identifying and defining key roles within the newly structured organization and assessing people to fulfill those roles needs to be done in no more than two to three weeks. People will be anxiously awaiting announcements.

Lap 8

Transform Products and Services

Innovation is the ability to see change as an opportunity—not a threat.

In this lap, I will share with you some approaches that can help you transform your products and services. The assumption is that you have already determined your company's overall vision and strategy (including market focus). In lap two, if you recall, you developed a report of how your current products help job performers in getting their job done (JTBD). You observed their behavior as well as captured their opinions. You noted, through deep analysis, what works well and where there are opportunities for improvement.

In lap four, if you recall, you worked on building your strategy, and you weighed the pros and cons of new products versus new markets (Illustration 4.7). If the company is planning on getting into new markets or new JTBD, then I would highly recommend conducting new ethnography studies at this point. Whether you are considering revamping your entire product/service line or just enhancing your current line, this lap will give you some "how-to" ideas.

To understand transformation on its fundamental level, it is critical that we remember this is not merely a "cosmetic move," but that change—true change—must happen where it matters most: in producing better products and/or services in a way that laps the competition and makes your company the front runner in its own industry.

To force change you must first ask yourself a series of probing questions based on all we've discovered so far during the transformation process. Note that many of these questions are dependent on your "new" vision and strategy.

- ❑ What markets should we enter that will help us achieve our business goals? If you recall, we answered this question in lap four. However, we will revisit and validate it in this lap.

- ❑ What JTBDs are we focusing on? Who are the job performers we are trying to target?

- ❑ How do job performers get the job done currently?

- ❑ Are the job performers able to effectively and efficiently get the job done with the current solutions?

- ❑ Is there room to improve the job performer's experience of getting the job done? (speed, accuracy, ease of use, reliability etc.)

- ❑ Can any of our current products/services assist in getting job done in related or new markets? What changes do we need to make to our existing products?

- ❑ Are there new jobs that we are getting done for existing markets?

- ❑ Can you define the new products/services in details?

- ❑ What is your competitive differentiator?

- ❑ What minimum revenue and margin expectations do we have for the new products? I strongly recommend you put together a compelling business plan (no more than a ten-slide Power Point).

- ❑ Do we have a clearly defined new product development life cycle? (Different from ones used for mature products). If it does not exist, I suggest adopting well-defined methodologies like "Discovery Driven Planning" or "D4". Make sure that management buys into the methodology. Use appropriate change-management techniques to ensure adoption.

Based on the strategy you developed in laps four and five as well as answers to the above questions, you may have to revamp your products and services completely in order to become a front runner in the industry. In other cases, the analysis may lead to the fine-tuning of existing products and services in conjunction with development of just a few new products/ services.

Taking the above into consideration, this lap guides you through a series of mini-steps to define the future state of products and services, including elements of segmentation, targeting, and positioning. What should your investment ratio between improving existing products versus building new ones be? This lap offers guidelines that can help you make this difficult decision. Do not underestimate the work involved here. If done right, the rewards can be huge.

Finding Purpose in Your Products and Services

Innovation isn't just a state of mind; it's a state of being. The best companies, the top dogs, the front runners, are always finding ways to innovate, change, keep peace, and outpace the competition; even companies that use price as a "differentiator" need to innovate to bring down price.

What is the process for innovation? How do you know if you have successfully innovated? Innovation is very tricky. Why? Because, at its heart, innovation is all about change, and if you've been doing these laps successively, you've seen how companies big and small, how leaders brave and petty, are all, at heart, reluctant to change. (Remember, this work should only begin after key members of the senior leadership and product/service management teams have been identified.)

This lap offers a true system for innovation; a proven way to turn the fear of change into a quantitative measure of *how* to change. Companies welcome systems because they make life easier. This lap may not make your work life easier, but it will make change easier; easier to sell change to your leadership/board, easier to sell change to your managers, easier to sell change to your team(s), and, as a result, easier to sell change to your customers.

A Systematic—but CREATIVE—Approach to Innovation

Let's talk about innovation a bit before we get into any other details of how, precisely, to be innovative. Take a careful look at Illustration 8.1. R.B Tucker calls this a "balanced innovation portfolio." You will notice that "innovation" is broken down into three groups:

        1.) Products/Services

        2.) Process

        3.) Business Model

In your organization, you may have noticed that you generally have more product/service and process innovations than business model innovations. What would a business model innovation look like? Let's look at one such example: the music industry.

Specifically, let's compare the way music used to be sold (up until the early '80s and late '90s) through brick and mortar stores versus how music is increasingly being delivered over the past few years, from buying an entire CD to downloading individual mp3s. In the past several years, in fact, many companies have even let you listen to unlimited music for a small monthly fee.

This new way of buying, downloading, listening to, and even personalizing music completely revolutionized the music industry's business model. Record companies, recording artists, and brick and mortar retailers that didn't innovate couldn't keep up; soon stories of music stores closing shop for good dominated the industry publications.

Case in point: Music First Record Stores, who had just as many brick and mortar retailers as Sound Notez but a more innovative home office, saw the future and figured out a way to respond. They capitalized on their brand name and shifted their energies to the download service. While companies like Napster.com, Limewire.com, and eMusic.com started offering downloads for sale, Music First did so, too, but with a more "record store" feel to their websites.

Illustration 8.1: Balanced Innovation Portfolio

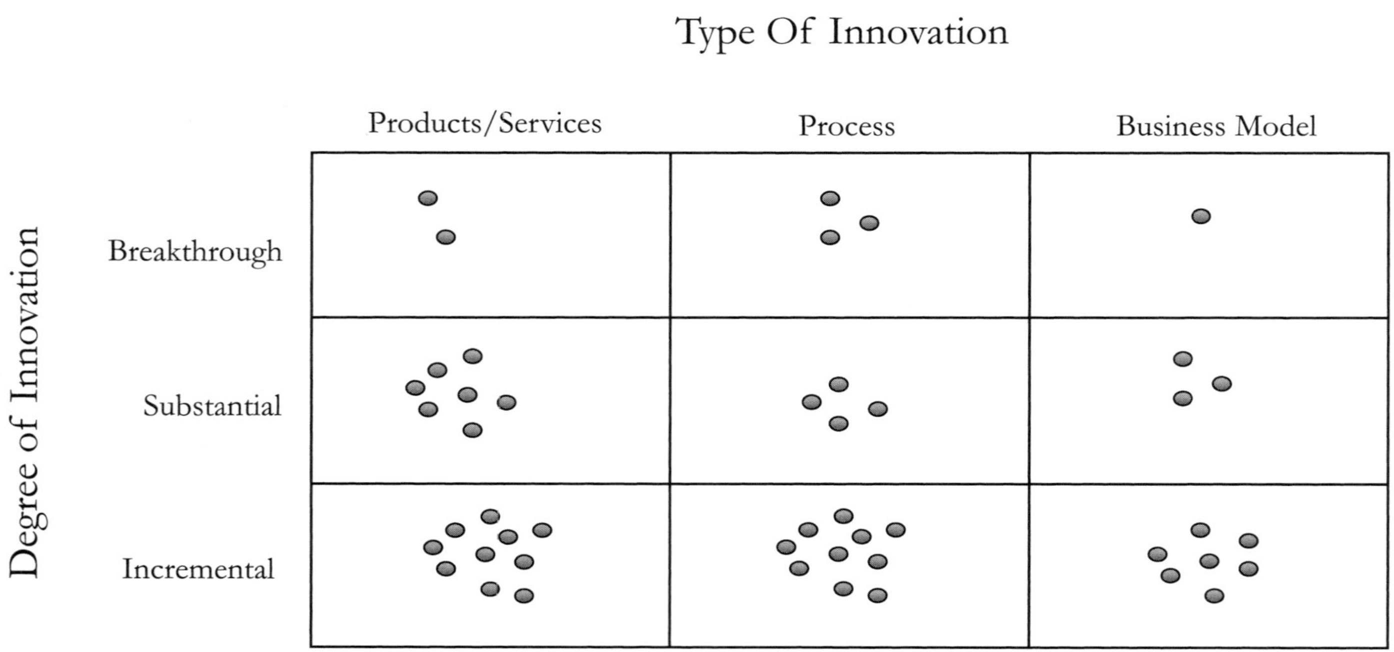

Type Of Innovation

Products/Services · Process · Business Model

Breakthrough · Substantial · Incremental

Degree of Innovation

Adopted from R.B Tucker: Driving Growth Through Innovation

They adopted an Amazon.com-style model, where fans could write reviews, rate album releases, publish personalized playlists that listeners could download, etc., which made website users a part of the online family, thereby producing more and more interest in their branded website. They were still in the music store business, but their storefront had shifted from brick and mortar to the Digital Age. As a result, Music First might have closed down most of their real-time stores, but successfully made the transition to online sales.

How did all this happen? Simply by being innovative.

When it Comes to Innovation, Consider the JTBD (Job to be Done)

As shared with you in lap two, products or services exist because there is a human need that is being fulfilled. The company that fulfills this need through appropriate products and or service delivered in the most effective way will get the attention of the customer. The question you have to ask yourself is, "How well does your product or service help customers with that job they need or want done?"

In the Music First example from above, consumers had a simple job to be done: buy music. Rather than make that job easier, Sound Notez made it harder; Music First made it easier. Which company do you more closely resemble: Sound Notez or Music First? Or, in a real-life example that is still being played out, do you more resemble a Tower Record Store or an iTunes?

Remember the "milkshake" example regarding Dr. Clayton Christensen's JTBD (see lap two)? What does this say about customer loyalty? How about branding, product placement, or even advertising? If you're an innovator who has always taken the time to understand the customer's need and has put the customer's needs at the forefront of your company-wide, decision-making process, you probably already have an eye on the JTBD and are in line with this concept; but if your company has shifted focus for whatever reason over the years, or even recently, it could be time to turn up the innovation notch.

The tricky part, however, is that sometimes a solution for the JTBD— or a family of JTBDs—does not exist, or the current solution may be sub-optimal. First, finding these are not easy, but when you do, there is tremendous opportunity for innovation. Here are some great examples of how companies have developed industry-shaping solutions using the JTBD concept (see Illustration 8.2a).

Like much-printed matter in the Digital Age, greeting-card companies faced a huge challenge as the cost of postage went up, consumers went green, and greeting-card sales went down. Who changed, grew, or innovated to succeed? Those companies that recognized the job to be done—convey greetings—went back to the drawing board and decided to turn the Digital Age to their advantage by creating what we now call eCards.

More established companies like Hallmark and American Greetings adapted by folding in eCard divisions to their already successful print greeting cards, while new technology opened the market door for companies like Blue Mountain Greetings and even Yahoo! Greetings.

As consumers, we will likely never know the length, time, energy, or cost involved in shifting from a predominance of printed greeting cards to branching out into the eCard market and, frankly, as consumers we never should. When you or I go to send a card, we simply have a need to fill, a job to be done; and the fulfillment of that need is all we care about.

Brand loyalty is one thing, but if I have a choice between two companies and only one of them helps me get the job done in the most effective (and costly) way, I will forsake the bigger brand for the newest rival.

The internet has impacted almost all industries, and the most innovative companies have managed to respond with new ways of doing things. Banks responded to customer needs by making online banking both affordable and convenient. Companies like Facebook and Twitter have responded to society's need to share photos, experiences, thoughts, and messages through social media. GPS has sprung up to replace static road maps or big, bulky printed atlases with up-to-the-minute navigational systems, while film and flash bulbs have taken a backseat to digital cameras and online photo-sharing sites.

What does the future hold? Front runners and top innovators know that the only way is to be in the forefront of developing industry-shaping platforms, products, and services. Consider the following very common, very lucrative job to be done—washing dirty clothes.

Illustration 8.2a: Job to be Done

Customer: Job to be Done	Old Solution	Innovated Solution
Conveying greetings	Greeting Cards	eCards
Invitations	Printed invitations or emails	evites
Keeping in touch with friends and family	Emails and phone calls	Social media
Ingest medicine	Pills and shots	Inhale, skin patches
Paying bills	Mail checks	Pay online
Keeping in touch with friends	Emails, phone calls	Social media
Finding best direction from point "A" to point "B"	Static maps	GPS system with traffic
Capture photos and share them with friends and family	Take photo, develop film, send prints to friends and family	Take photo, share photos online

What's the solution? Two companies think they have the answer: the first is a company that is working on developing a better detergent, while the second is working on a washing machine that doesn't need detergent at all. Whose solution will capture more market share and be more profitable? The simple answer is: whichever company can better fulfill the outcome expectations for itself and its customers.

For this exact reason it is critical to understand how job performers measure success (see illustration 8.2b). Keep in mind that you may come up with an approach to either reduce or change the steps involved in completing the job so as to improve the overall experience. Still, knowing how job performers measure success can help you focus on the right areas and come up with better products and services.

8 Ideas on Innovation (From Front Runners Far and Wide)

What do front runners think about innovation or, for that matter, the future? Here are some additional thoughts that I would like to share from my experience, a few of which may be contrary to conventional thinking:

1. **Companies spend too much time reading market-research data:** This is like looking at the review mirror while driving a car and expecting to make the first turnoff. Most of the data in these reports are too old to be of any use. And remember, your competition has access to it as well, so where is the differentiation? If we want to develop an exciting new product, we don't look for it in market research, no matter how good the research papers.

2. **The best place to start is with your existing markets and products:** Here's the reasoning: if your current product has been around for a while, then it has stood the test of time and perhaps even has a brand that everyone recognizes. Granted, the sales may drop off over the years, but if the product is still selling it has several features and aspects that your customers obviously care about. This recognition is critical to making the new products successful, as well as to leverage features that have made the current product successful while coming out with new and exciting ones that customers want/need. This is the reason fast food chains like McDonalds, Chipotle Mexican Grill and Subway have not gone away. They have fine-

Illustration 8.2b: Steps Involved In Getting The Job Done

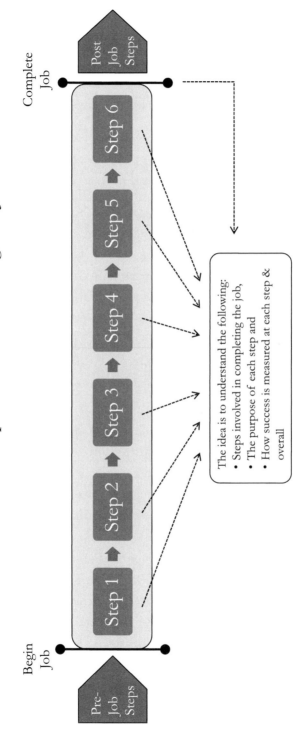

The idea is to understand the following:
- Steps involved in completing the job,
- The purpose of each step and
- How success is measured at each step & overall

tuned their current product offering, adapting to the rapidly changing needs of consumers and capitalizing on their existing brand.

3. Put "like with like." If a company is good at doing one thing and has brand recognition around it, would you dare try to get into completely unrelated markets? If Proctor & Gamble made cars, would you buy them? If Microsoft made planes, would you fly in them? However, if Nike made nutritional bars . . . well then, you would buy it, right? But isn't it the same thing as Microsoft making a plane? No, not really, because Nike making sports bars is vaguely related to their current market and product offerings— i.e., sports sneakers, sports apparel, etc. It just "fits," whereas Microsoft and plane manufacturing are apples and oranges. Nike has a brand that fulfills a need—they are associated with taking care of athlete's needs. Don't get me wrong, there are a number of brands that have crossed over to very different markets and not only survived but done well, for example Mitsubishi TVs and Mitsubishi Cars. These products have nothing in common except the brand name Mitsubishi, and yet they succeeded. There will always be exceptions, but in general it holds true that you should put "like with like." In other words, even when trying something brand new, it is important to still stick to what you do best—and everyone recognizes you for.

4. Base your innovation on facts, not opinions: Should we base our innovation efforts purely around customers' opinions? As shared with you in earlier laps, observing and taking notes on customers' behavior is probably more important than gathering their opinion for developing the right products. Don't ask the customers what they want; instead ask them what job are they trying to accomplish and observe the steps they are taking to getting the job done. Also, it is important to note that customers do not always know the boundaries of product/service innovation. You need to be able to predict their needs and, in fact, invent what gets their job done in the most effective and efficient way, meeting all their success criteria. Remember, your competition is reaching out to customers as well, so you have to stay ahead of the curve in order not to follow along in their wake.

5. When it comes to creative thinking, set limits and parameters: In other words, prime the pump, so to say: Most of us agree that creative thinking sets the foundation for innovation. To be able to think creatively, though, we need to erase all we know about the existing situation and try to think it over from scratch. But there's one problem: it's almost impossible to do this. Ask any inventor and they'll tell you that a blank page is a sure recipe for a creative "block." On the other hand, if we continued to think in the same way we have always thought, we will eventually reach the same ideas. And if we started from scratch, we'll get a creative block. This is where having some level of constraint helps you focus better. It's a little like having guardrails for your creativity; rather than being "all over the place," now you have some definite parameters within which, or around which, to be creative. Let me illustrate through an example: If somebody walked up to you and asked you to develop a new form of camping gear "from scratch," could you do it? Close your eyes . . . go ahead . . . and creatively think! Could you come up with any ideas? Would it be easier if you were asked to design a specific form of camping gear, say, a portable appliance to cook eggs? Now you have some guardrails on your creative thinking; suddenly you have something to focus all that creativity on. This illustrates the point that we need to have some boundaries for effective creative thinking.

6. Creative thinking does not necessarily have to come only from your R&D teams: In fact, it can come from any of the team members from any of the functions. I encourage bringing together cross-functional teams during the ideation phase (more on this later).

7. The bigger the pain you are solving, the better the payoff: This is provided that you have, in fact, solved the problem in the best possible way. If the pain is not big, then the solution becomes "a nice to have" rather than "a need to have," and it therefore becomes a riskier proposition to sell.

8. Make innovation part of the organization's DNA: Look to innovate not just products/services but also processes and, perhaps, even the business model. In fact, I think there is room for innovation in every function of the business, including operations.

The 5 Steps for Developing Innovative Products/Services

Want to learn more about how to be innovative? Let me take you through five logical steps that will help you develop innovative products and services (Illustration 8.3).

For those who are familiar with other models like the Discovery Driven Planning, D4 model (Define-Discover-Develop-Demonstrate), Six Sigma, SRI, TRIZ, Agile, GEM, etc., you will see that our approach here aligns quite naturally on most of the aspects of those proven models. Again, feel free to leverage and customize, as appropriate.

The important thing is not to stick blindly with one model or another or to feel apprehensive about spinning two models into one to fit your particular needs. My model, your model, four steps, five steps, D4, or Six Sigma—consider all of it a pool from which to draw just enough water to fit your specific needs.

1. Identify the Pain

As shared with you earlier, one of the first things you need to do when trying to innovate is to decide which markets will help you achieve your business goals (for example 20% revenue and margin growth, etc.). Remember how we defined market in lap four: it is a group of people with similar JTBD.

Next you decide on what jobs you are helping your customers get done in the chosen markets. As shown in illustration 8.2, capture the steps customers use to get their job done along with success measures. Illustrations 8.4, 8.5a and 8.5b and 8.6 show approaches on how you can "peel the onion" layer by layer in identifying the pain.

The above exercises allow for targeting your efforts and make them more actionable. Solving these problems can help you come to solutions that lead to innovation. It can also help capture boundaries and shed some light on the direction to take.

The idea here is to first capture outcome expectations, as we know them through the eyes of the job performer. We then run "value analysis" based on key aspects of the product or service. You may even plot competitors' products/services so as to give you better comparison on where you stand and what your key differentiator may be.

Illustration 8.3: Overall Process for Transforming Products and Services

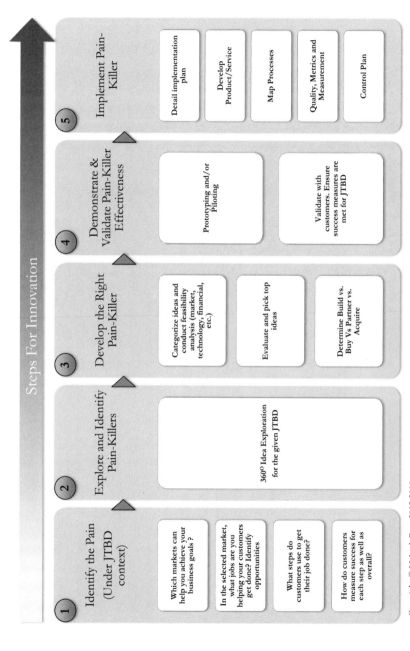

Steps For Innovation

1 Identify the Pain (Under JTBD context)
- Which markets can help you achieve your business goals?
- In the selected market, what jobs are you helping your customers get done? Identify opportunities
- What steps do customers use to get their job done?
- How do customers measure success for each step as well as overall?

2 Explore and Identify Pain-Killers
- 360° Idea Exploration for the given JTBD

3 Develop the Right Pain-Killer
- Categorize ideas and conduct feasibility analysis (market, technology, financial, etc.)
- Evaluate and pick top ideas
- Determine Build vs. Buy Vs Partner vs. Acquire

4 Demonstrate & Validate Pain-Killer Effectiveness
- Prototyping and/or Piloting
- Validate with customers. Ensure success measures are met for JTBD

5 Implement Pain-Killer
- Detail implementation plan
- Develop Product/Service
- Map Processes
- Quality, Metrics and Measurement
- Control Plan

Illustration 8.4: Outcome Expectations

JTBD: Be able to easily capture videos and photos and share with family and friends

	Customer	Organization
Desired	• Ease of image capture • Ease of image sharing • Capture anywhere, by anyone, anytime • Ruggedness • Ability to capture images in low light conditions • High storage capacity • Resolution size • Display size	• High margins • Revenue growth • Customer loyalty • Steady demand • Product differentiator
Undesired	• High battery consumption • High cost of using the product • Poor image quality • Reliability issues	• High cost of goods • Supply shortage • Lack of reliability of parts • Product liability/lawsuits • High complexity for manufacture

• Improve the ease of image capture
• Improve the ease of image sharing
• Improve ability to capture anywhere, by anyone, anytime
• Maximize ruggedness
• Improve ability to capture images in low-light conditions
• Increase data storage capacity
• Increase resolution size
• Improve display quality
• Lower battery consumption
• Lower cost of usage (low maintenance)
• Improve image quality
• Reduce any reliability issues

• Improve margins
• Increase revenue
• Improve customer loyalty
• Improve steady demand
• Improve product differentiator
• Lower cost of goods
• Minimize supply shortage issues
• Maximize product reliability
• Minimize product liability/law suites
• Minimize complexity for manufacturing

Illustration 8.5a: Prioritization of Expectations (Measures)

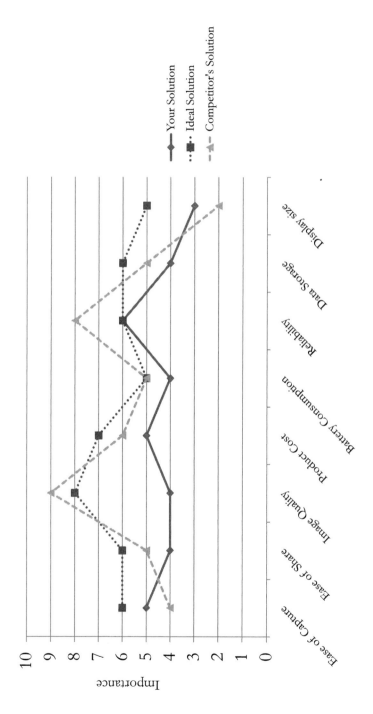

Illustration 8.5b: Success Measure Plot Across Job Performers (Sampling) Satisfaction vs. Criticality

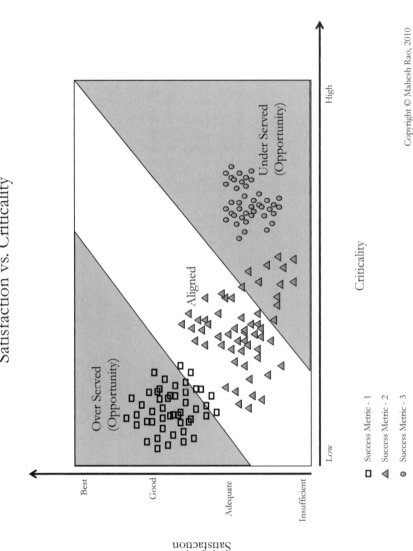

Copyright © Mahesh Rao, 2010

Illustration 8.6: Critical Reasoning

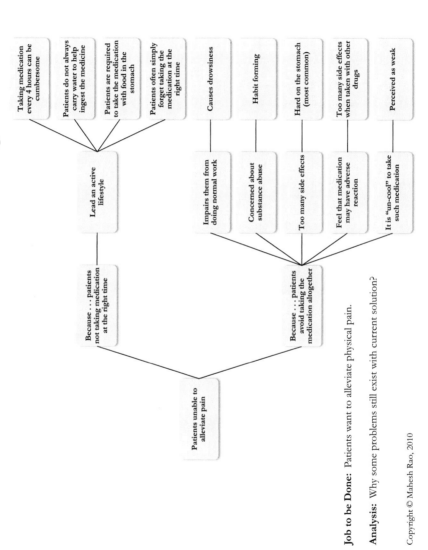

Job to be Done: Patients want to alleviate physical pain.

Analysis: Why some problems still exist with current solution?

Keep in mind we are just using this as a starting point. Especially if you are entering a new market or focusing on a new JTBD, you will need to spend enough time on this step so as to help you focus better during the ideation or "Explore and Identify Pain-Killers" step (step two).

2. Explore and Identify Possible Pain-Killers

The key to successful innovation is to capitalize on an opportunity by fulfilling an unmet customer expectation in a way nobody else has done before. Finding this is far from easy because at the core of most opportunities lies a difficult problem; i.e., there's a reason no one has done it before—it's hard! Great news, though! You began laying the foundation in lap two when you conducted the ethnography study.

Customers, for instance, do not want to spend time vacuuming their home; this is not what most people consider an "interesting" chore. However, this was certainly an "interesting" opportunity for iRobot, the makers of robotic vacuum cleaners. They used robots with sensor technology to automate cleaning of floors despite obstructions (furniture).

The age-old dilemma of finding interesting solutions to non-interesting problems is not a new one. In fact, I distinctly recall having the following conversation with my then boss at a former company nearly two decades ago.

I remember my boss said this to me one day, "Mahesh, think outside the box."

My (admittedly frustrated) response was, "How on earth can I think out of the box when I don't have a clue where the box is? How can I think differently when all my life I've thought in a certain way? How is it possible to expose hidden assumptions if they're hidden? How can I think differently if I do not know what the baseline is?"

I asked these questions very innocently, as I was eager to learn. After all, this was my first job after getting my undergraduate degree. My peers thought I was crazy for speaking this way, but my boss appreciated the points I was making. Unfortunately, he did not have any answers. The senior leadership, in the meantime, quickly recognized my thinking style and took some big chances. In turn, they took me through a fast-track promotion process to put me in charge of research and development of some key product lines.

Only several years later did I come to know that I was spot on in my thinking—it took a genius like Altschuller (creator of the TRIZ method, see below) to discover that creative ideas have . . . a box of their own! The only thing is that you are in the box with clear guidelines, not otherwise. So now when someone tells you to "think outside the box" you can safely say, "I need a box to think in!" Remember the camping gear example from page 227.

Identifying trends: Innovation exercises for the future front runner. Trend prediction is a powerful, knowledge-based technique that extrapolates how current systems will evolve in the future. With this information, you can plan your innovation. There are many ways you can predict trends in the industry. There are many researchers who have done extensive work around this ideology. The one that is most notable is what's known as the TRIZ Method. In fact, the theory of inventor's problem solving (TRIZ) is both scientific and practical.

For those interested in learning more about the TRIZ Method, there are plenty of websites that offer a lot of information about the methodology. The basic idea behind trend prediction is that evolution is not random but, instead, follows certain patterns and stages that can be predicted. If you know these patterns and stages, then you can solve difficult innovation problems on behalf of your company.

We all know the classic S curve as it applies to business entities—conception, birth, growth, maturity, retirement, and decay. Each S curve moves slowly from conception to birth, then rapidly from birth to maturity, then slowly again from maturity to retirement. After this, the value seems to taper off (decays in value). There are numerous examples of one S curve eclipsing another, each employing new technology or processes along the way (see Illustration 8.7). Think about the portable music industry, for instance.

It's funny to see the evolution of portable music in movies. In the early 1980s people carrying large boom boxes, then in the later '80s people carried Walkmans, and in recent years people carry mp3 players. You can see multiple S curves in how each new form of technology eclipsed the other.

Here are some ways to get your creative juices flowing: Remember the Product/Service Opportunity Matrix (Illustration 4.7)? Well, we will

Illustration 8.7: Classic S-Curve Generations

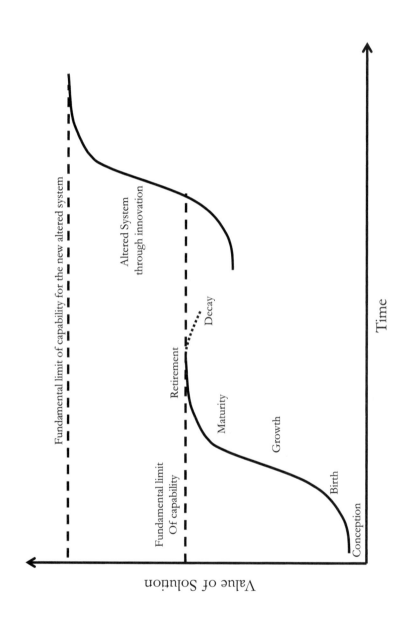

sort of be getting back to it now as this will help us explore the various opportunities and assess in a logical way what might work best for us. The only difference now you will be working on a JTBD opportunity matrix (see illustration 8.8).

In order to illustrate the idea, lets take the example of iRobot, the company that develops robotic vacuum cleaners. If you are unfamiliar, they are most famous for their "Roomba" product, which was their first consumer product way back in 2002. Let's first understand what iRobot was trying to get done for the consumer. It is "keeping floors clean." Their initial target market for this product was "consumers" like you and me.

How were consumers cleaning their floors prior to the introduction of their product? At a high level, most consumers would have done the following to get their job done:

1. Identify the area to be vacuumed
2. Setup the vacuum cleaner (make sure canister/bag is empty, plug into power socket etc.)
3. Vacuum the floor in the identified area
4. Store the vacuum back in its place

If it were a wooden floor they would perform the following additional tasks:

5. Pick up the mop
6. Rinse the mop prior to use
7. Prepare a wood-friendly, mild soap solution in a bucket
8. Dip the mop in the bucket, and then wring the mop to remove excess soap solution
9. Mop the entire floor surface area
10. Rinse the mop thoroughly
11. Replace the dirty water in the bucket with clean water
12. Dip the mop in the bucket, and then wring the mop to remove excess water
13. Mop the entire surface area to remove any soap residue that may be left on the floor
14. Leave the surface to dry

Illustration 8.8: JTBD Opportunity Matrix

Job To Be Done

	Current	Related	Unrelated
Current	Roomba	Scooba	**Rain gutter cleaner**
Related	**Commercial Roomba**	**Commercial Scooba**	**Robotic public swimming pool cleaner**
Unrelated	**Roomba for aircraft**	**Commercial window cleaner**	**Robotic solders for war**

Markets

As you can see there are many steps involved. The company initially decided to tackle vacuuming the floor with their Roomba product. As part of their growth strategy, they then decided to introduce a "related product" for the same market segment, namely, "consumers," to assist in getting more aspects of the same job, done (see Illustration 8.8). They introduced a product called "Scooba" which took care of customers' floor mopping needs as well. Then they added a scheduling and automatic recharging capability to their robots so they could pretty much work unattended. With these two products, the consumers' job of keeping their floors clean is completely taken care of with little intervention except for emptying the dirt from the canister in the case of Roomba or draining "dirty" water or adding fresh water and detergent to the Scooba tank.

Both the above products were a great hit in the market and paved the way for a new industry to be born. With this success under their belt, iRobot decided to venture into new products with the same "consumers" they had developed a brand with.

We all know how much time and effort goes into cleaning rainwater gutters. If you are like me, you would probably procrastinate or completely avoid doing this unless and until there is serious damage to your home. Well, our friends at iRobot came up with an effective way to get this "gutter-cleaning" job done. Remember, in this case it is the same market segment ("consumers") but a completely unrelated product.

iRobot then decided to expand its market beyond "consumer." With the highly successful Roomba product, they tried to make a more rugged version for the "commercial" market segment, which included small to medium size offices, hotels, etc. All they had to do in this case was redesign the existing product to include a higher battery capacity and a larger bin or canister to collect more dust, as well as "up" the power of the motor.

Similarly, they could come up with a commercial version of the Scooba as well. Through research, iRobot found out that public swimming pools (falls under the "commercial" market segment) had a crying need for active pool cleaners. To address this need they were able to come up with a brand new suite of products to clean pools.

If they ever wanted to get into a brand new market segment leveraging their mega hit product concept Roomba, they could consider coming up with a floor cleaner for the commercial aircrafts in between flights. Now we all know that the airline industry can use some help in this area! If iRobot did decide to go in this direction, they would have to develop a new sales channel, and their marketing efforts would be quite different. The Scooba concept on the other hand could be leveraged to clean the "outside" part of windows for multi-story buildings.

iRobot over the years has also branched off into completely unrelated markets with completely unrelated products with their "ground and maritime" robots for industrial and military purposes. They also offer customer-designed robots for specific needs. Many people, in fact, do not realize that iRobot started their company developing industrial grade robots in the early '90s. One such example is Genghis, a robot designed for space exploration. They also developed Ariel, a robot that detects and eliminates mines in surf zones. I, however, decided to turn the "opportunity matrix" in this example upside down, just to make it more interesting and easier to understand.

Also, please keep in mind that we are looking at the rear-view mirror in this case to illustrate how iRobot may have worked on their "opportunity matrix." In your case, however, you will need to gather and list ideas for each of the nine blocks. This is not as easy as it might seem. No matter what, though, do not lose sight of the job you will assist the job performers in getting done. It is pivotal to understand this for your success.

3. Pick and Develop the Right Pain-killer

Once you have taken the time to fill the matrix (illustration 8.8) with possible ideas, the next step is to assess these opportunities and pick and choose the best ones based on several key criteria. The worksheet (Illustration 8.9) will help you assess each opportunity in an objective way. The opportunities with the highest points should be the ones considered.

Here are some questions you may want to consider thinking through (Many of these questions may have been answered in laps four and five):

- ❏ Is there any intellectual property that you will need to protect?
- ❏ Are you depending on anybody else's intellectual property? Will you be potentially infringing upon anybody else's IP?

Illustration 8.9: Opportunity Assessment

Assessment Criteria	Rating (See below)	Evidence/Comments
Alignment with Business: • Mission, Vision and Strategy • Business goals and targets		
Skills to Execute: • Degree to which capabilities are being leveraged • The teams have the knowledge and expertise required		
Build Vs buy Vs Partner Vs M&A • We have alignment on execution strategy		
Ability to Impact Customer's JTBD: • Is the proposed solution better than the current alternative? • The solution has been confirmed and validated for effectiveness • The risk associated with customer "switching" is relatively low • It is relatively easy to "switch"		
Market Landscape: • The market size is big enough to warrant attention • The competitive landscape looks favorable • We have a clear competitive advantage		
Ability to Impact Financials: • Funding available relative to funding required • Net Present Value (expected) • Product/service profitability • Breakeven		
Others: • •		
TOTAL SCORE		

Rating guidelines:

4—Let's go ahead with this opportunity immediately – we know enough already, the risk is low and the time is right

3—This opportunity is good but we need to do some more research before we can invest resources into this opportunity

2—This opportunity isn't very strong, but still holds some promise; no action needs to be taken for now

1—This opportunity isn't worth pursuing at all – let's not waste any more time on it

❑ What will be the impact on current initiatives and projects?

❑ Does technology exist to develop such product/service?

❑ Decide how best to achieve your product vision: Build vs. buy, vs. partner vs. acquire, etc.

❑ If you are deciding to build, how long does it take to develop? What might the roadmap look like?

❑ How do you propose to develop the product? Acquire technology? Build solo? Partner (and if so, with whom)?

❑ How will this product be marketed/sold? Channels?

❑ What impact will it have on existing customer support?

❑ Do any of the new functions (sales, customer service, etc.) need training? If yes, what will be the time and/or cost to do so?

❑ What impact, if any, will it have on your internal/external process?

❑ Will there be any changes to current manufacturing processes/ techniques involved?

❑ What does the financial analysis of the product/service tell you?

❑ How does this new product/service align with the brand image (public perception) of the company?

❑ What are the risks for the customer?

❑ What are the risks associated with the product/service?

❑ What are the risks associated with not developing the product/ service?

❑ Are there any dependencies or unknowns?

❑ What assumptions are you making (other than the ones mentioned above)?

Once the subject matter experts (SMEs) have analyzed the above sets of criteria and engaged in the corresponding Q&A, they report their findings, and that report must be thoroughly reviewed by the leadership team (CEO or business unit leader and his/her direct reports).

I encourage the leaders to challenge these findings through appropriate (and respectfully probing) questions—they should demonstrate professionalism and not have any pre-conceived notions. The leaders should also take the opportunity to provide constructive feedback and guidance to SMEs and help to pick the top ideas.

4. Demonstrate and Validate Pain-Killer Effectiveness

Once you have picked out the top contenders for new and/or improved products/services, you need to validate them with the customers to see which design they feel most comfortable with and if the chosen design needs any further tweaking.

Depending on the product or service being explored, a "rapid, high definition prototyping" technique can be used to demonstrate the product to the customers. This could either be a computer-generated, 3D-modeling enhancement of the product or some sort of animation of the services being offered. In the case of software, this could be a demonstrable user interface that captures the business logic and illustrates the user experience. It's important to render an as-close-to-physically-possible prototype. Keep in mind the prototype needs to be comprehensive and realistic enough so the engineering teams can take this and develop a product without a 200-plus page requirements document. Leverage social media to identify just the right mix of people—blending existing customers and future targeted customers— to see if any potential conflicts arise. Depending on the complexity of the product/service you have in mind, you could do a "webinar" or invite them over to a specific location for an in-person focus group. See what gets you the most accurate results and is most cost effective for your organization.

If your organization does not have the expertise to put on such data-gathering sessions, there are companies that can assist you. Working with an outside source can help you with anonymity as well. (Alternatively, you can apply many of the guidelines I put in place in previous laps for running your own focus groups.)

Be sure to avoid sharing any key information about potential products/ services through social media. Once the information is on the Internet, you can't control it and your competition may have access to it. We tend to think of social media as a "warm and fuzzy" place to interact with our customers but, in fact, our competition sees it as a great way to "cherry pick" our ideas and try to beat us to market!

Based on the feedback and any further analysis done internally, you will finally define the final product. Now the task at hand is to share the design with the development teams (may not be applicable for some services) to enhance implementation.

Counter to the conventional practice, I personally do not see a lot of value in developing BRDs (Business Requirement Documents), or PRDs (Product Requirement Documents) as they are called in some companies. These are documents typically written by product management teams for the development/design teams and are typically several hundred pages thick and take forever to write. It also takes considerable time for the development team to: actively read; seek clarification, where necessary; and then translate it into a technical framework. There is also room for misinterpretation and error.

A better practice is to develop a high-definition prototype that explains the "form, fit, and function" of the product you are trying to build. From my experience, this prototype considerably reduces the time it takes to get the product to the market, with fewer glitches along the way. Like all approaches, this approach also has its pros and cons but, overall, I have found that it helps build a better product faster with minimal glitches.

By now if the product management team has not formalized a product/service development plan, this is a good time to start putting it together. I highly encourage engaging other departments/groups within the organizations to define the product in a high-engagement format (discussed in previous laps). This is critical to success (see illustration 8.10).

5. Implement Pain Killer

The last step to implementing innovation is developing the product or service. Now it's time to revisit the product plan to make sure all aspects are covered. The intent of this step is to develop a thorough and comprehensive development and commercialization plan. Please keep in mind that such a plan does not exist in a vacuum or at the sole discretion of one department but, instead, spans across multiple disciplines.

At this point you should have a fairly thorough idea about how the end product will look and how it is meant to work in the customers'

Illustration 8.10: Product/Service Management—High Engagement Model

Department/ Group	Few of the Reasons for Early Engagement	Recommended Time to Engage				
		Identify Pain	Explore & Identify Pain Killers	Develop Right Pain-Killer	Demonstrate & Validate Pain-Killer Effectiveness	Implement Pain Killer
Product Marketing (+ Marcomm)	• Protect and maintain brand • Assist with segmentation, targeting, positioning • Participate in competitive analysis discussions • Recommend product pricing based on value • Assist in elevating customer experience • Work with sales teams in coming up with a strategy for generating buzz, which includes a communications plan (leverage social media to create the desired viral effect)		X	X	X	X
Product Development	• Better understanding of the product being proposed • Advise on technical feasibility, time lines, risks		X	X	X	X
Manufacturing & Supply Chain	• Advise on manufacturability of the product • Component availability issues • Prepare and optimize supply chain				X	X
Customer Service	• Potential customer service issues and suggest remedies • Prepare and train customer services teams			X	X	X
Professional Services	• Understand product/services being offered • Provide internal and external training prior to launch			X	X	X
Sales	• Provide any insights based on their interaction with customers or knowledge about their needs • Any information on competition • Salability of products/services with insights on pricing		X (if possess information)	X	X	X
Finance	• Detail financial analysis and viability • Assist with product pricing and elasticity calculations			X	X	X
HR	• Assist with appropriate talent acquisition			X	X	X

environment. What are all the aspects that need to be worked on to make this a world-class product or service? To make this exercise worthwhile, you must extensively mitigate/minimize risks and recheck assumptions so that there are no surprises just before implementation.

Since there are a lot of touch points and hand-offs along the way to market, I highly recommend using a SIPOC tool (which you are quite familiar with by now since you have used it in previous laps) to define function engagements. If additional levels of role clarity are required, you may want to consider using a simple RACI tool.

As you will surely agree, many teams "touch" the quality element in a product or service being delivered. This includes the partners and the channel. A cross-functional team should be put together to define the intended quality and customer experience guidelines, as well as success metrics and measures.

Do yourself and the cross-functional teams a favor by not developing a thick "bible" that nobody ever actually refers to. Instead, have a simple and accessible compilation of key elements being measured with acceptable tolerances as well as targets. Make sure to clearly define which teams are responsible for each of these and how and when they will be monitored, measured, and reported.

Don't let this part of the process exist in a vacuum. Instead, have an all-hands (entire company) pep rally/town hall meeting to share the information with the rest of the organization prior to the launch. And make it a "launch" in every sense of the word; get excited about it by getting your people excited about it. After all, their enthusiasm will filter down to all levels of the product's ultimate success—or failure.

If you are concerned about information leaks prior to actual release date, leave yourself fewer windows of opportunity by doing it at least a day prior to the launch. Apart from the obvious advantages, the employees will enjoy the sense of ownership and belonging that such an all-inclusive meeting fosters.

Leverage the opportunity to rally them around the transformation. In addition to getting them excited, this will get you more tail wind to push the product even more successfully. Have the CEO or the senior-most leader of the organization deliver the inspirational and spirited message to the masses, and I guarantee you will see the fruits of your labor pay off in untold enthusiasm.

A quick note on product pricing: There are many interesting product pricing strategies and, frankly, there are many factors that go into determining the right pricing for products and services. However, this topic is beyond the scope of this book. Please do visit my website www.BeFrontRunner.com to drop me a line, and I would be happy to share my thoughts with you.

Closed-loop Corrective Action

It is absolutely critical to make sure there is a closed-loop corrective action process defined before full implementation mode. This is part of organization's continuous improvement cycle. I recommend a small cross-functional task force team to lead and monitor issues and resolve them on a real-time basis.

Many companies fail to make this process repeatable, so every time they come out with a new product or service, they do not learn from previous mistakes. They also panic when "unforeseen" issues come up, making it a less-than-optimal work environment. Besides, it will have a negative impact on the overall user's experience as well.

Let's face it, all new product service launches have unforeseen glitches or "issues." However, what is critical is the magnitude and time to resolution. With a repeatable, well thought-through plan of action around a new product/service launch, you minimize the impact to the user experience, thereby improving the brand image.

Remember, a pleasant experience—despite a few minor issues—can convert a previously loyal customer into a "committed evangelist." I have worked with many world-renowned organizations all over the world that have seen this trend—and benefited from it—firsthand.

One company that has made this thinking part of their DNA is Cisco. And the individual behind making this part of Cisco's culture is Joe Pinto, Senior VP, who heads the Technical Services Division and with whom I have had the pleasure of working on several successful endeavors. When it comes to front runners, few outpace Cisco; and this committed evangelism to their products and services is partly to "blame."

Green Thinking

As we all know, our environment is in peril. Whether you do so out of a deep personal belief in creating a better world around you or in reaction to your brand perception on the open market, it is important to participate in what I call "green thinking."

At every step of your innovation process, think of how you can embed green thinking. Ask yourself the following questions:

1. Overall, does your product satisfy the customers' job in an environmentally friendly way?

2. What environmentally friendly approaches are being considered to build and manufacture similar products?

3. Is your product packaging environmentally friendly? Have you been able to considerably reduce packaging material without compromising quality?

4. Is your product easy to recycle? What steps are you taking to encourage customers to recycle?

5. Do you have "green" guidelines for your vendors and partners?

6. Are you highlighting and marketing the "green" features in your products and services?

Change Management and Communication

While product management teams naturally take a lead role in this lap, they cannot do it alone; effective collaboration with other departments is almost a pre-requisite for success (see Illustration 8.10). To consider rewarding participation on all levels, consider setting a "bonus program" for those who proactively collaborate for success. Up the stakes for top collaborators— give them something handsome (airline tickets, a three-night stay at a local resort, etc.)! For those organizations with smaller budgets, give appropriate gifts (movie tickets, gift cards, free dinner coupons, etc.). Most importantly, communicate this bonus program up front so that everyone is encouraged to actively participate in making it a success from day one. Depending on the complexity of the project and their engagement level, make sure to involve external partners and channels at the appropriate time.

Lap 8 Key Takeaways

- ❑ The purpose of this lap is to help define or refine your product line so that it better aligns with the new vision and strategy.

- ❑ To understand transformation on a fundamental level, it is critical that we remember this is not merely a "cosmetic move," but that change—true change—must happen where it matters most: in producing better products and/or services in a way that laps the competition and makes us the front runner in our own industry.

- ❑ Do you need to innovate? The answer is always "yes." Innovation isn't just a state of mind; it's a state of being.

- ❑ Three types of innovation:

  1. Products/Services

  2. Process

  3. Business Model

- ❑ Products or services exist because there is a human need to fulfill (JTBD). The company that fulfills this need through appropriate products and or service in the most effective way will gain customers.

- ❑ The best place to start is your existing products.

- ❑ Use an "opportunity matrix" to decide future product/service direction. Make sure it aligns with the vision and overall strategy of the company.

- ❑ You must predict customer needs and, in fact, invent what they want.

- ❑ Implement boundaries for effective creative thinking. Creative thinking does not necessarily have to come only from your R&D teams.

- ❑ The bigger the pain you are solving, the better the payoff.

- ❑ Make innovation part of organization's DNA.

❑   5 Steps to developing innovative products/services:

- ◆ Identify the pain

- ◆ Explore and identify pain killers

- ◆ Develop the right pain killer based on three separate criteria

- ◆ Demonstrate and validate pain-killer effectiveness

- ◆ Implement the pain killer

Lap 9

Transform Functions

*Running a successful business can be compared to an orchestra playing
a composition—you need to play with your mind and heart . . . be able
to feel it. The song sheet (strategy) needs to indicate who plays what
and when. The various instruments are like various departments—
they need to play in unison for the melody to come through.*

So far we have crafted the "new" vision, designed an organization
structure to align with the vision, chosen competent leaders to lead the
respective organizations, and transformed our products/services. Now,
it's time to optimize the rest of the organization; i.e., each of the functions.
In this lap we will be taking each of the functions/groups through a mini-
transformational journey of their own.

Depending on the data gathered and the gaps identified in laps two
through four, there will naturally be areas of improvement for some very
specific functions in your company, like sales, marketing, manufacturing,
customer support, shipping, etc.

Who will lead these functional transformations? It will be the "new"
leaders selected based on competency assessment. They will take on the
task of developing their respective vision, strategy, and execution planning,
taking into consideration the previously identified gaps and aligning their
functional vision with that of the overall organization's.

The Purpose of Transforming Functions/Groups

Now that we have an organizational structure that aligns with the organization's vision and a strategy, as well as individuals to lead each of the groups or functions, our next goal is to transform each of the key functions and make them work in unison. So the purpose of this lap is also to define an engagement and governance model both individually for each of the functions and, collectively, as an organization.

There is likely to be "blowback" during this critical phase, but it is imperative that our core charter team learns to deal with such setbacks effectively so that, in effect, the entire organization can benefit from the transformation that's occurring.

Where might this blowback come from? We all know that change is difficult, but as we reach a critical phase of the transformation process now we're going to be dealing with people's daily lives; not just the key leaders who have been ingrained throughout the transformative process, but individual workers in their own little space.

We all know how organizations work in "silos." Take, for instance, the gap that nearly always seems to exist between marketing and sales. Here is marketing working on a new ad campaign designed to increase sales, but they're doing it way over there, in their little silo, with no direct contact with the sales people of whom their campaign is about to impact.

When the work is done, marketing basically "tosses it over the wall" to the sales department. In an ideal world, marketing and sales teams need to collaborate to effectively sell to the customers. In this very common scenario there is no well-thought "handoff" during which some interaction helps both departments understand their roles. The lack of interaction contributes to frustration between departments. It is critical to understand that transforming each of the functions just in itself is not enough. We need to be able to define how each of these transformed functions engage with each other (internal process) and how they make decisions, especially the ones that are cross-functional in nature. This is the kind of fundamental, functional, and cross-functional transformation we'll be talking about in this section.

A New Approach for Transforming Function

As you may or may not realize by this point, the silo method—workers in various departments toiling in isolation and merely "tossing assignments over the wall" to other departments/silos—is not the most effective way of running a company, let alone transforming one. Now the time has come for us to transform the way each of the key functions work within their respective groups and with other groups.

In this lap you'll get some tools to define and articulate your vision, strategy, objectives, processes, roles, and accountability (at all levels). You may already be familiar with many of these tools. I have explained how some of the others should be used to increase not only your familiarity with them, but also their effectiveness.

Before we get into each of the functions and highlight specific aspects that need to be considered for transformation, let me take a few minutes to highlight common actions that apply to all the groups and functions, regardless of how small or large they are. I cannot emphasize enough the importance of completing this review step before moving forward:

Make a Genuine Attempt to Understand and Internalize the Functional Gaps Previously Identified

If you recall, in lap four we identified a list of gaps that may exist in your company. Now it is time to pick out those gaps from the "master list" that pertain to each of the functions or groups. Knowing the gaps is one thing; eradicating them is another. To accomplish this task, each of the groups within the organization should take on the action of doing further root cause analysis before working on appropriate solutions (see Illustration 4.6).

While it is good to focus on the prioritized gaps (review lap four), do not lose sight of the relatively lower priority gaps as well. Oftentimes you may be able to knock off some of the lower priority gaps along with the high priority ones with the same set of solutions.

Remember, there are always gaps that span across multiple groups; in such cases, the group that can make maximum impact should take on as the lead team working with a cross-functional team to eradicate/resolve the gap.

Tying into the Organization's Vision, Strategy and Objectives

Remember the vision, strategy, and objectives we worked on for the entire organization? It's now time to put those into action. Illustration 9.1 explains how the objectives should align not just between departments who work closely together but with the overall organization as well.

Develop the vision, strategy, and objectives for each of the functions, making sure you align them to the overall organization's vision, strategy, and objectives. To ensure that this alignment occurs, work from the top down. Start by asking yourself the following questions:

❑ For the entire organization to achieve the stated vision, what do we (as a function/group—for example, marketing, sales, etc.) have to do?

❑ How does the group's strategy align with the overall organization's strategy?

❑ What objectives should the group work toward to achieve the overall objectives?

❑ What initiatives and projects need to be initiated at the group level to achieve the group's objectives?

Develop an Engagement Model

With the key objectives now identified, it is time to identify objective and operational linkages (see Illustration 9.2). First, list out all the key groups or departments within your organization (for example: marketing, sales, product management, support, manufacturing, etc.). Next, ask yourself the question: What information do I have that may be of relevance to each of the other groups? Similarly, what information might the other groups have that might be of relevance for your group?

Please do not leave out any of the groups. You may struggle a bit in filling in Illustration 9.2, especially for some of the groups you rarely interface with like HR or finance. However, with a bit of creative thinking you will be amazed at what you may be able to do for the other groups and vice versa. This is an exercise that each group must do independently. Create such a table for each group that you interface with.

Illustration 9.1: Alignment of Objectives

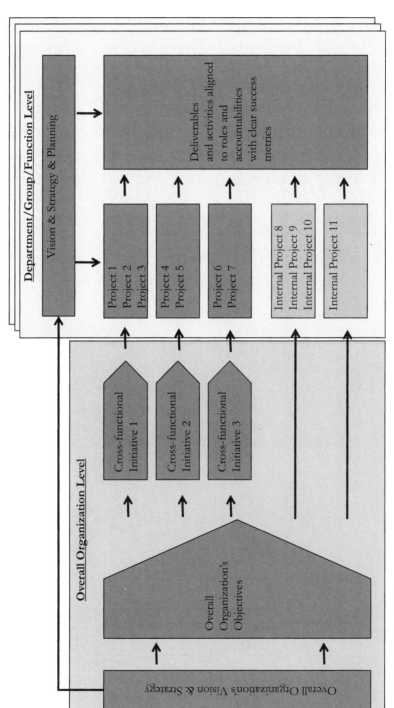

Illustration 9.2: Identifying Links with Other Groups

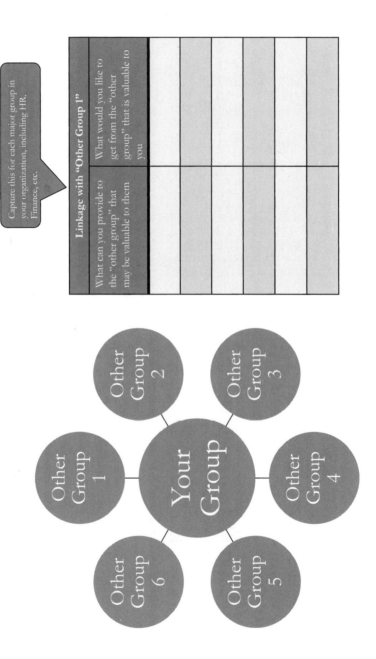

Next, the transformation core team gathers all this information and compiles a master spreadsheet, as shown in Illustration 9.3. Once completed, share this spreadsheet with all the groups. As you can appreciate, this can be of tremendous value to each of the groups. Each of the groups can then work with each other to define the engagement model, as shown in Illustration 9.4.

Now identify and work on key end-to-end processes for the entire organization. I cannot emphasize enough the importance of doing this. If there are people in the core team that have process re-engineering or operations management experience, they can assist in crafting and mapping the key end-to-end processes for the entire organization, giving a top-down view.

Leverage group-level engagement via a framework provided by each of the groups; and then fine-tune these as you begin to build the end-to-end map. Wherever there is a hand-off across groups, articulate the details of the hand-off (see an example in Illustration 9.5).

Linkages, or how each of the groups engage each other and make critical decisions, are as vital to a company as its products or services—and gives your organization a competitive advantage over the others. For example, most computer manufacturers can build high-quality, affordable computers but, to date, only Dell has been able to uniquely integrate the end-to-end process from manufacturing to selling and support in a way that greatly satisfies customers.

Likewise, Apple has a very unique end-to-end process that allows customers to buy software for their iPhones and iPads directly from developers. This keeps the cost low, while allowing for greater choices and open competition. So again, it's not just the activities that need to be performed but the linkages that make them so effective.

Some of these activities clearly add more value to the customer than others. Those that do not add much value can be potentially outsourced. However, as I said before, the power of end-to-end process mapping and analysis is not so much listing the activities that should be performed and understanding which ones add value to the customer; it is more about understanding the linkages between the activities.

Illustration 9.3: Value Matrix

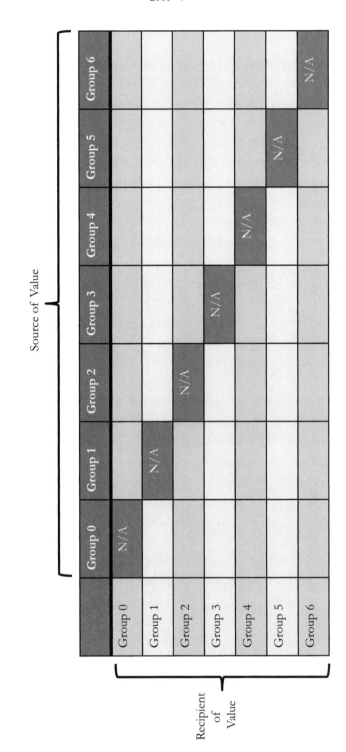

Illustration 9.4: Group-level Engagement Framework

Supplier	Input	Time	Metric	Process	Output	Customer	Metric	Time	Decisions
Who is the Supplier?	What are they supplying?	When are they supplying (time/frequency)?	How is success measured (up until this point)?	What do you do with it within your group?	What are you supplying?	To whom are you supplying?	How is success measured (up until this point)?	When are you supplying (time/frequency)?	What key decisions need to be made along the way? How are these decisions made and who makes them?

Illustration 9.5: SIPOC for Computer Repair Department

Supplier	Input	Time	Metric	Process	Output	Customer	Time	Metric
Support Team	Case Number	Every time a case is opened	# of cases opened	Open repair ticket	Update repair status against case	Customer	Every time the repair case is closed	# of successful repairs
Computer Parts Distributors	Computer Parts			Repair of computers	Computer repair Ship computer back to customer red			Average time for repair
								# of repairs per technician

Process flow:

Customer drops off computer → Assign technician → Inspect Computer → Estimate repair costs & time → Get customer approval → Order parts → Install parts → Test → Customer picks up computer

Enabler								
OEM's Warranty (if applicable)								

Because of the cross-functional nature of "end-to-end" processes, one of the biggest challenges is how decisions get made. This is particularly important, because a wrong decision, or even changes made in one end of the process, can impact other groups. For this reason, care should be taken to make sure that a small cross-functional team owns and manages key end-to-end processes, similar to a board in a startup. (More on boards and councils later in this lap.)

Develop a Plan of Action

As you can see, transformation can't take place in one silo without affecting the others; change will ripple along the value chain, affecting everyone in its path. Taking all of the above into consideration, it is important to develop a plan of action to facilitate functional change.

This sort of a plan has a dual purpose: 1.) It serves as a reference document for the internal teams within the group, and 2.) It serves as a good communications tool for communicating with others outside each of the groups. Here are some of the key components of the plan:

High-level executive summary: This should highlight the overall plan in multiple bullet points.

Current state of business: This should highlight the current state of the business (you get this from lap four). Make sure to include key (performance) metrics, compare and contrast with the competition, list all perceived business challenges, identify key gaps related to the function, and identify the key marketing-related gaps the company should plug.

Future state of business: Based upon the overall organization's key objectives (see lap four), what are the key objectives of each group? Based upon the above overall organization's objectives, what key strategic initiatives need to be put in place for each group? What key capabilities will you achieve with the above strategic initiatives? What will be the impact on the group as a result of the changes in product and/or market mix (discussed on lap eight)?

End-to-end processes: What end-to-end processes does this group touch or is it part of? What value does the function/group add in each of the above end-to-end processes? Who plays what role within the group in each of the end-to-end processes?

In order for you to accomplish everything in the plan, who will be working on what? What will the organizational structure look like? When working on the strategic initiatives, how will the team engage with others in the organization? How will cross-functional decisions be handled?

Financial impact: Show the implications of spending and how the business will hit the objective. Show budget highlights (you do not have to share the detailed budget slide with other groups in the organization, if you so prefer).

Risks and mitigation: What are the key risks and how can they be mitigated?

Timelines: What does the group's execution roadmap look like? In the above roadmap, highlight linkages to other key initiatives driven by other functional groups.

The next steps: The leader of the group should take the time to share what the next steps are for everyone in the organization. This is critical for success.

In the sections that follow, I will be sharing thoughts and ideas on specific areas within each of the groups/departments/functions to transform:

Marketing (Product Marketing, Corporate Marketing, etc.)

As we all know, marketing is an extremely important aspect of any company's transformational success. But if it's true that any one department considers themselves "an island unto oneself," it is often marketing. This is probably because most of their work is creative, and "marketing types" tend to be clique-ish, while the rest of the company needs more uniformity of process to function well together.

But in this transformational process it will be very important for marketing to play a major role; here's how:

Turning Explorers Into Evangelists: The Philosophy of "Inbound Marketing"

I am sure you will agree with me when I say that the business environment around us has changed. Customers have changed the way they buy products and services. What's more, the culture around how consumers make their buying decisions has changed fundamentally, in large part thanks to consumer conversation—and empowerment—through social media. Unless you adapt, and quickly, you lose your market share and revenue, and you eventually perish.

Over the past several decades, companies like IBM, Nike, Proctor & Gamble, Pepsi, and Coca-Cola have drenched us with their advertisements and effectively pushed their way into getting a piece of our wallets.

The fundamental objective of a marketing team is to spread the word about the organization's products and services. However, not every company has the nine-figure marketing budgets of a Nike or a Pepsi—in fact, most companies don't. How will the rest of us compete? In the coming years, companies will leverage social media to feel the pulse of their customers and market their products to them (see Illustration 9.6).

Oftentimes people don't just stumble upon your website—they usually are "exploring" the web for some information, and they find your website via Google or some other search engine. After keying in a search term, be it "gardening tools" or "tax preparation software" or "install your own cabinetry," consumers (potential customers) are taken to a webpage that most closely matches what they are looking for. This could be a page with information about your product, service, expert reviews, blogs, articles, etc. So the explorers who are investigating the Internet need to be brought into your website—they now become "visitors" to your site. In other words, you want to convert explorers to visitors.

The idea is to convert people from explorers to visitors, from visitors to leads, and move them up gradually, one stage at a time. Not every explorer will become a lead; not every visitor will become an opportunity. However, with persistence and calculation more people than ever before can be converted; it takes a well thought-through strategy to do this.

Once you have these people on your site, you need to convert them to qualified leads and paying customers. It does not stop there, though;

Illustration 9.6: Philosophy of Inbound Marketing

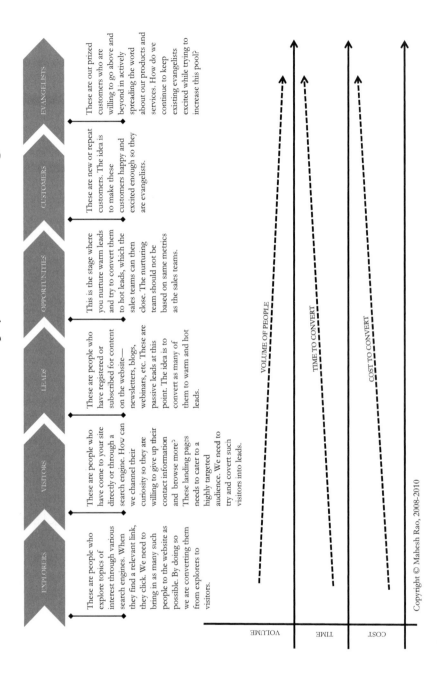

EXPLORERS

These are people who explore topics of interest through various search engines. When they find a relevant link, they click. We need to bring in as many such people to the website as possible. By doing so we are converting them from explorers to visitors.

VISITORS

These are people who have come to your site directly or through a search engine. How can we channel their curiosity so they are willing to give up their contact information and browse more? These landing pages needs to cater to a highly targeted audience. We need to try and covert such visitors into leads.

LEADS

These are people who have registered or subscribed for content on the website—newsletters, blogs, webinars, etc. These are passive leads at this point. The idea is to convert as many of them to warm and hot leads.

OPPORTUNITIES

This is the stage where you nurture warm leads and try to convert them to hot leads, which the sales teams can then close. The nurturing team should not be based on same metrics as the sales teams.

CUSTOMERS

These are new or repeat customers. The idea is to make these customers happy and excited enough so they are evangelists.

EVANGELISTS

These are our prized customers who are willing to go above and beyond in actively spreading the word about our products and services. How do we continue to keep existing evangelists excited while trying to increase this pool?

VOLUME OF PEOPLE

TIME TO CONVERT

COST TO CONVERT

VOLUME

TIME

COST

successful companies want to move these customers (who are generally passive) into active evangelists. What better vehicle is there to "spread the word" than your current customers actively marketing your products and services? You want more than just customers; you want active evangelists.

Consider a company like Disney; they are not just interested in one-time customers: nearly every piece of advertising, promotion, or literature is invested in creating evangelists. Watching a Disney movie, buying a Mickey Mouse doll, or going to a resort is not just a consumer experience but an indoctrination into the "Disney way." This is why people willingly wear Mickey Mouse shirts and tout the Disney experience. Disney marketers are masters at turning explorers into evangelists. Why? Because they make it a major priority, even adjusting their value chain accordingly.

Apple makes a similar investment in turning their explorers into evangelists; few consumers are as vocal about their support of a product, service, or company as "Apple fans." Try converting an Apple user into a PC user and you'll find out firsthand what it's like to come face-to-face with a corporate evangelist!

So the philosophy of inbound marketing is not just about "snagging customers" in as few clicks as possible, but is instead about taking a very thoughtful, thorough, and calculated approach to gradually turning explorers into evangelists by leveraging social media. At every step of this process there is a clear action that we want the people to take—subscribing to your email newsletter, registering on your website, taking a poll, or adding your blog to their RSS reader.

Make sure not to design a sales-centric website, as people visiting your website are in different stages in their sales cycle. Some are very early and may take three months or more to buy, whereas others may be almost ready to sign up as a customer. Do not forget existing customers. You need to continue to engage them as well. Remember, in the inbound marketing cycle we don't just need them to buy from us, we need to convert them into evangelists as well. It's important to provide a variety of different ways for visitors to move up the "inbound marketing" value chain.

It's better to provide them with options to engage them at whatever level they are comfortable with, be it providing their name and email address to more information about them and the products they use. Remember, asking them to fill in a long form too early in the process—or even ever—will overwhelm them, and they might go away. As an alternative, consider collecting information on one to two questions every few times they come in. (Remember how every few weeks Netflix asks whether a DVD has been returned or how the picture quality was?) It is critical to gently nurture those who are not yet ready to provide all the information at once.

Another critical area to keep in mind is that you want people to come in to your website through the major search engines, as this will improve your site ranking. There are many good books that can help you on this topic.

The bottom line is that an inbound marketing approach will help you focus on how to engage current customers—and potential customers—regardless of where they are in the cycle. Oftentimes companies spend way too much time in converting leads to customers when they actually should be spending more time increasing the number of visitors in the first place, which if you are targeting right should bring in more leads and eventually convert those leads to more customers.

If your company develops multiple products/services, I encourage you to have multiple Facebook and Twitter sites—each attracting its own highly targeted audience. Once people visit these various social media sites, the idea is to get them back to a very specific landing page on your site that caters to the targeted audience, depending on their personal preferences.

Consider having multiple landing pages depending on what stage of the buying process they are in. To better cater to their specific needs, people later in the cycle will see a page with a different call to action than those who are early in the cycle. In general, make sure these landing pages are simple, highlighting the call to action while removing any distractions from the website. It's important to get the right information to the right people at the right time.

Make sure your marketing team is made up of people who are familiar with social media (and in fact have huge followings—this shows that they know how to get people's attention), who are frequent bloggers, and/or proficient in web analytics. Many companies who are pulling their "ecosystem" together—potential customers, regular customers, partners, employees, etc.—have roles like "community managers" to manage ecosystems and micro ecosystems.

Also, I highly recommend you leverage the information you gathered from the ethnography studies to design your positioning and advertisement campaigns. Remember, if the opinions of customers and their influencers are different from the needs you observed through ethnography, then fine-tune your campaign to address this gap.

Marketing Plans

Now and then executives invite me to discuss their company's business and marketing strategies. Many of them even share with me their "inch-thick" marketing plans and claim that they are "well put together." If they are that good, I often wonder, then why do they want to talk to me in the first place? While these are pretty looking documents, sometimes as thick as a textbook and loaded with high-quality graphics, they are often filled with little substance.

I have led large marketing operations for complex products/services, so believe me when I say that most marketing plans should never be more than ten to fifteen Power Point slides. Anything more makes it hard to communicate and comprehend, and harder still to execute. I must, however, confess that some really complex marketing plans may take up more than fifteen slides. (To develop a marketing plan, use the template shared earlier on in this chapter, see page 261.)

Sales

Since people have changed the way they buy products and services, the old "brute force" selling technique is not as effective anymore. New times call for new methods, not just in your marketing department but in sales as well. For you as a sales person to be effective in this new age, you have to equip yourself with some new skills. Economies and market trends may change, but responding to the change profitably is your responsibility.

When economies change, CEOs, senior executives, and buyers all hunker down to chant the same mantra over and over again: "We have to cut our expenses across the board. You have to make do with what we have in terms of resources." With this reactionary philosophy in mind, the sales people are often pressed to pick up the phone and start "cold calling," trying to reach people with whom they have not built trust/relationship.

In such a scenario, more is not always more. Now more than ever, potential buyers are getting more and more sophisticated and have the tools to avoid such "cold" calls altogether. Companies struggle to meet revenue projections and sales people wonder if they should be moving on to greener pastures. Meanwhile, businesses continue to stagnate and decline. What's the solution?

There are two schools of thought that most sales leaders have in difficult times:

1. "The sky is falling, everything is falling apart and no matter how hard we try nothing is going to work. Don't bother selling anything; nobody is buying!"

2. "Times are really not that tough; it's just a perception. You just need to work a little harder and we should be able to hit the numbers."

Reality, though, is quite different. Tough times offer unique opportunities for smart sales people to make more sales than they have ever done before. (Remember the front runners mantra: change is opportunity!) If done right, they could position themselves quite well so that when the cycle changes, they are extremely successful.

The key to succeeding with such opportunities is to master the art of adaptation, so that no matter the market condition, you thrive. Panicking at one flux or change in the cycle makes no sense, particularly not when you understand the business cycle from top to bottom.

Dr. Clement Juglar (1819–1905) was the first to come up with the idea of a four-part business cycle:

1. Expansion
2. Peak
3. Contraction
4. Trough or Recession

During trough times, or even a recession, many people steer away from sales jobs, leaving the market ripe for top sales people. The ones that continue to be in sales give up selling and do nothing until the market recovers. However, this can go on only so long—after a while they get "hungry" and try different techniques to sell solutions to customers that will eventually move the market to the "expansion" phase.

Sharp sales people ask their clients what they can do to help, and then begin working aggressively with their respective organizations to try and deliver. These clients are more likely to return with a purchase order.

The time between recession and expansion is time for top sales people to work smart and make their mark. They must focus on expanding their network and building relationships. When the business cycle reaches the expansion phase, that is when everyone tries to get in, but the smart people have already made inroads and established their position, so they are in a much better place to take advantage of increased opportunity.

Over the years I have known some of the best sales people in the country's top companies; folks who can pretty much sell anything to anyone in any market condition. One of the key attributes that separate the "men from boys," so to speak, is their ability to focus on what brings results.

For example, a good friend of mine—we'll call him Scott—heads the sales division for the western region of a Fortune 200 organization. I have known Scott for over twenty-five years now, and he has consistently managed to exceed expectations, even through some of the toughest recessions we've endured. One of the key reasons for Scott's success is what I call "smart working," rather than just "hard working."

Scott agrees that top sales people need to have the right focus, attitude, and adaptation. Apart from those traits, he also believes that one of the biggest reasons for sales people not hitting their quota is not because of the economy, but because they have been spending more time doing "busy work" or "low-value activities" rather than smart work.

These activities include sending out "thank you" emails, setting up meetings, managing calendars, prospecting research, gathering competitive data, updating customer relationship management (CRM), getting on the phone with your organization's customer service team to resolve issues your customer is having, filling in expense reports, formatting documents for customers (e.g., converting a document to a .pdf), etc.

Some of these "busy work" activities may also include personal activities like scheduling doctors' appointments, taking a computer class at the local community college, etc. According to Scott, people who had the highest job satisfaction were those who did little of the "low-value activities" and more activities with high value.

But there is a disconnect here; some of those low-value tasks are required per your job description. Not every sales person, few in fact, will have an administrative person to handle such tasks, so what do you do? Thanks to modern technology you can now outsource much of this busy work, such as scheduling, "thank you" emails, conference calls, etc. In fact, there are many companies that do this for a low fee. For example, take a look at sites like www.AskSunday.com and www.TasksEveryday.com.

I am not endorsing these sites, but simply making you aware that such services exist. In order to address the high-value activities that will make your job more rewarding and profitable, you may want to dump all the low-value activities over to them. This will allow you to spend more time on activities that can help generate sales. As a side benefit, you will be spending more time with family and loved ones as well. You will be happier as a person, and that personal satisfaction will be reflected in the quality of your job.

Scott also emphasizes that when the economy is tough, your customers are also laying off employees, as their needs are changing as well. Either you can spend a ton of time talking to people who are shaky on the job front or focus on identifying people who are committed to adding value to their organizations and have the authority to make key decisions. Sales in this sense is not a numbers game; it is meeting more of the right people (at the right time) and being able to understand their needs and being able to help them out by offering solutions through your company's products and services.

Another key trait of a successful sales person is his/her ability to learn as much as possible about their customers. They ask such probing questions about their customers as:

❑ What is the customer's vision and strategy for the current fiscal year?

❑ What are their key objectives?

❏ What problems are they facing in delivering to their customers (if your customer is not the end user)?

❏ How are your customers being perceived in the market? (Social media can give you some idea of their perception in the marketplace.)

❏ What are their top challenges?

❏ If they currently use your competitor's product, what do they think of it?

❏ What problems are they facing with it?

It's amazing how savvy salespeople get this kind of information from various people they know within the company. When the time comes for them to talk to the decision makers, they know exactly what to pitch, how to pitch, even when to pitch, all based on this resourceful information-gathering activity. It is all about linking a pain killer (your company solution) with pain (what a customer is looking for).

In my opinion, it is critical for salespeople to be Internet savvy; that they understand how inbound marketing works. They should be astute at having large followers in various social media circles and have the art to influence them. In other words, they need to have a personal brand. If they do not have one, they should work toward building it. Leverage tools like Facebook, LinkedIn, and Twitter to stay in touch with your clients/constituents.

Leverage technologies such as blogs, v-logs, podcasts, webinars, and other online presentation tools to share information and improve collaboration with clients and community. You should brand yourself as the "authority" in whatever line of business you are in. The key thing to remember from this discussion is that when you see people talking about your products or services, you want to follow to see what is being said.

"Ah, easier said than done," you say? Well, nowadays you can do this very thing by typing your company, products, or service in search engines at www.twitter.com or www.monitter.com. You must have a pulse on the market and so you can position your sales appropriately.

Remember, salespeople can never be successful working in isolation within the company. Companies are bound to fail if the company culture encourages such an environment.

Another key aspect to remember is that most salespeople are compensated on sales closures, which does not encourage nurturing deals that take longer than a few months. They are not being compensated for it. Turning warm leads to customers (or even continuing to keep them warm), as discussed earlier, does take patience and perseverance. Consider having a few people in the organization who are compensated for this type of nurturing. Align the compensation to match the metrics.

Make sure the sales team aligns with the new strategy and objectives of the overall organization. If the organization has made a decision to specifically target a customer segment, then the sales team will need to change its focus as well to better align with the overall organization's focus.

Product/Service Management and Engineering

If your organization produces products, you will agree with me that product management is probably one of the most important functions within the organization. Many organizations place product management under engineering or marketing.

I do not recommend such a structure, because engineering organizations are typically focused on building the product right, not necessarily defining the right product, which is the work of product management. From my experience, when product/service management is reporting into marketing departments, their product/service innovation is limited and sometimes even too tied to customers' needs.

While this might sound good, remember what I shared with you in lap eight: It is important to take the time to understand what job we are helping customers get done. The idea is to innovate your products and services so you can help the customer get the job done better, faster, cheaper. This gives you a competitive advantage. That is why I encourage organizations to have product management as a separate organization; this way it is on par with engineering and marketing teams.

In many of the companies I've worked with, product management never even comes in contact with customers. This can be a problem, especially since their charter is to define and design products/services. Well, how can you do that without interfacing with customers?

In most companies, product/service management and finance teams barely talk to each other. In many, they may not even know each other! From my experience, the product management teams should work very closely in evaluating the financial aspects of the product/service.

Provide guidance on the subjects of buy versus build versus partner. The finance teams may be able to give guidance on terms of partnerships (if any). They can even help build a business case for any new ideas you may have. Maintaining a great relationship can help you considerably.

As stated earlier, I cannot emphasize enough the importance of product management teams being social-media savvy. This is perhaps the best way to keep your finger on the pulse of your customer base and understand what the target market is looking for, as well as what they feel about your existing products and services. You should be able to leverage social media to pick and choose the right feature set, for example. It is a key data point.

If you do not already have one, consider defining a new product introduction (NPI) process. NPI is a process that starts with product discovery and goes all the way through product development, testing, and finally delivery. There needs to be clarity around which teams are engaged when.

For example, in the case of a software company, product management should own activities through the definition stage, and then development takes over all the way until delivery. The deployment will be owned by the professional services organization. In all cases, at all stages, the handoff needs to be crisp and clear. A detailed SIPOC or something similar to Illustration 9.4 can help, as can the addition of a RACI. Also, it is critical that once the product is in the development stage there should be no temptation to modify the product definition. All teams in the value chain should discourage any product modification requests, no matter where the request is coming from.

To assist you in this process, here are some guidelines for defining the team's guiding principles:

Product principles: These are guiding principles that define what the team stands for; what is strategic versus what is tactical. These guiding principles are not specific to any product or service being developed. Instead, they are principals that guide you on what your beliefs are and where to focus your efforts and, perhaps, the value system within the team. If done right, a good set of product principles serves as the foundation for inspiring products. They serve as a clear statement of what the customer, partners, suppliers—and even everyone in the value chain within the organization—can expect from your team. It defines your team's product philosophy. When defining these, do not make them very generic like "build reliable products" but, instead, get very specific, such as stating "increase product durability by 25% over the next six quarters," etc.

Design Principles: These principles, on the other hand, highlight best practices that your team will be using in defining and designing products.

Both of the above need to be documented and, more importantly, put into practice. Formation without execution is folly. These principles, when practiced, will allow new members joining the team to quickly understand and work with the rest of the team better. Most importantly, however, it will help rest of the teams in the value chain—namely, engineering, professional services, and others—to understand how to engage with the product management team.

Product/Service Governance

I highly encourage the product management team employ a governance model for critical decisions. This team is always under the spotlight, with people second-guessing their decisions and, in addition, is under constant political hits from pretty much all parts of the organization. Also, this is accentuated if the product/service management team has a matrixed structure. We will talk more on governance and engagement models later on in this lap.

At many successful companies, like Cisco, there are in fact multiple product councils—perhaps one for every segment that they cover. Alternatively, for companies that have complex product/services, you could have one council but have multiple boards, each one representing a different market segment/product line.

This is a cross-functional team led by the leader of product management. The intent is to have this team lead and make decisions pertaining to products/services. It is important to pick and choose the right roles. Again, depending on the company and product/service you offer, membership for this team could consist of leaders such as GM or CEO, VP of Product Management, VP of Engineering, VP of Marketing, VP of Customer Service, etc.

The team can meet monthly and should be facilitated by the product management leader. Define the charter of the council (purpose, members, how are they elected etc.) and its mode of operation. Communicate to everyone in the organization so that everyone is clear not only on the purpose for the committee, but also on how decisions get made (i.e., how the detailed process flows).

Product/Service Advisory Board

Consider developing an advisory board consisting of some industry experts and subject matter experts to facilitate new products/services and/or enhance existing ones. The members could change depending on the requirements; i.e., new product launch that falls under one expert's purview but not another's, etc.

The purpose of this board is to solicit advice from experts without having to actually hire them. These experts are interested in helping you because they get to add it to their profile. Besides, it is a networking opportunity. These members are compensated a nominal sum for each meeting in stocks or kind; meanwhile, this interaction is also developing a type of "brain trust" they can then utilize to solicit other work or opportunities.

Don't forget to develop a charter that defines the purpose and the roles each board member will play, the time expectations, what's in it for them, etc. Share this very clearly with them up front and have them sign a legal document (as appropriate). You may want to consult your legal counsel first; this may be needed to protect the company's interest since sensitive information may potentially be shared with them from time to time.

User Community Board

Imagine a group of your customers—real people who actually use and endorse your products and services—advising you on new and existing products in a legitimate and credible position. These are your select customers who are, in fact, "evangelists." You can not only consult these marquee customers as references, but you can run ideas by them and help solicit input on new products/services you are planning to introduce.

Having a list of "marquee customers" as references is one of the most important things you can do, yet most companies don't have these! Make sure to have customers on the board, representing all segments in which your company has products.

Again, don't forget to develop a charter that defines the purpose and roles the members of this user community board play, the time expectations, what's in it for them, etc. Share this very clearly with them and, again, have them sign a legal document (as appropriate). This user community board offers a variety of benefits to both you and the customers who join.

Benefits to those who join:

❑ They get the satisfaction of being revered by the company as VIC (very important customers)—i.e., they are always treated special.

❑ Have the ability to speak directly to the senior management.

❑ Get an opportunity to hear about products and even provide feedback prior to the rest of the market.

❑ Favorable pricing on products.

❑ Receive products sooner than the rest of the market.

❑ Gain deep understanding of products/services.

Benefits to your organization:

❑ Access to users and customers who can vouch for the products/services (reference).

❑ They can be evangelists who will spread the message about your products and services.

❑ Ability to develop case studies that cite these customers' success stories.

It is important to make sure that you do not pay these people to be on the board. This would position the relationship very differently. Where might you find these very important customers? Enlist the help of the sales teams in identifying such customers. Keep rotating names in any reference being made (i.e., you don't want to use the same name again and again).

The Design-to-development Hand-off

Now let's talk a bit about the design-to-development hand-off. In most cases, product managers "hand off" the design to the engineering team for them to develop. How does it work in your organization? Is it effective? In many companies I see, the product managers craft product-requirement documents, business-requirement documents (BRD), etc. Many of these can grow to inch-thick documents that few people, if ever, actually digest.

From my experience, working on an accurate or high-fidelity prototype will help you get a realistic representation of the proposed user experience. Avoid paper prototypes. There are many tools available that are not expensive and can simulate your product very effectively, much more so than a document or simple artist's rendering.

If done right, this prototype should represent all the features of the proposed product. In my opinion, this is the best way to get everything right before you actually develop the product. This is true for both software and hardware products. The engineering or development team will love it, while the support team can provide active feedback so as to reduce support calls, and the professional services teams will have a better idea of what's coming down the pipeline.

Last, in many companies there isn't a clear way of improving products— i.e., closed-loop, corrective action that is based on input from customers, support staff, professional services teams, as well as sales and other teams. It is critical when defining end-to-end processes to capture and highlight how the closed-loop, corrective-action process works and who owns it.

Customer Support

In most companies the customer support organization is designed to be a reactive component. They are the problem fixers who swoop in once the product is already in the customers' hands. In my opinion, this positioning is wrong. They need to be a proactive organization, not a reactive one; i.e., they need to be involved in active "fire prevention" versus just putting out the fire after it's already started.

How can they be a proactive organization, you ask? Well, first, by making sure that the support team is engaged sooner in the product development cycle. This helps in two ways:

1. They are going to be better prepared to deal with support issues when the product is released, since they understand the product better from its inception moving forward.

2. An equally important aspect to consider is that the support team can actually improve the product quality and reduce support calls by helping to identify potential issues and even offering advice on how they may be resolved. This is truly proactive support from a valuable team, wouldn't you say? Unfortunately, very few companies consider support teams as anything but an afterthought. As we have just seen, however, the support team can be an invaluable asset for the organization.

I strongly believe that social media is the best thing that ever happened to organizations. You need to leverage it to your advantage (you have heard this from me numerous times by now). But there is a good reason for that; in almost every branch of your organization, there is a way to leverage social media to your benefit.

The support staff, for example, can do some research on social media sites to see what customers are potentially saying about your products in real time and prepare an appropriate remedial action. For instance, if a feature you and your company were really excited about seems to be upsetting or alienating customers, what can you do to remedy that—and quickly? Unless someone on the support staff is following social media closely, you might not even know the situation exists until too late.

Also, if you are a company that sells components of a subsystem to OEMs (original equipment manufacturers) then you can stay ahead of the curve by researching what people are saying about your component. For example, if you supply displays to computer manufacturers, what are people saying about the display relative to the entire product? There is so much data available—we just need to be proactive in identifying critical data and leveraging the knowledge gained to your advantage.

Another problem most organizations have is a missing feedback loop from the support desk back to the product design desk. There is very valuable data you might be missing—or not getting enough of—if social media isn't playing a prominent role in the loop. For example:

- ❑ How is the product being used by customers?
- ❑ What job is the customer trying to get done?
- ❑ What other products/services do customers use to complete their job?
- ❑ What features do they most like?
- ❑ And don't like?
- ❑ What features would they like to see?
- ❑ Is it compatible with other products that customers often use it with?

If only companies were to mine this valuable data and feed it back to product design as part of a "lessons learned" cycle, they could improve their product by leaps and bounds.

Many companies sell their product through distribution channels and, as a result, may not have a direct link with the customer. This is, in fact, a "missing" link you definitely want to bridge. When customers call the support desk, this is a tremendous opportunity to get more information about them and their views on the product or competitors' products, the features they would like to see, etc. Not leveraging this "touch point" is a lost opportunity. For this to happen, there needs to be a major culture shift in how product management and support engage with each other.

Consider rewarding support teams for gathering as much information as possible about the customer and similarly rewarding product management teams for building products that require reduced support. Making this touch point a priority increases the odds of your people making it a habitual behavior. These results are measurable and can potentially be linked to their MBOs.

Imagine instead of putting more and more people into support organizations to fix problems, spending more time proactively preventing problems in the first case. Again, do not forget to have a "support plan" in place based on a template shared earlier in the chapter.

Strategy and Planning

Most companies that have a separate strategy and planning organization are either too weak or too strong. There needs to be a healthy balance—strategy and planning should play the role of a catalyst and provide overall structure and guidance on how various groups need to engage with each other. They should also interface with key leaders in developing a vision and an overarching strategy as well as key objective for the overall organization.

Most importantly, make sure that all organizations are aligned to this strategy and key objectives. Apart from working with finance on an overall budget and defining a two- to three-year plan as well as fiscal planning and investment focus, they need to also manage overall risk.

Remember, strategy and planning groups are typically considered "overhead" by most employees; so be sensitive to this tendency and keep the team lean but effective. In fact, the strategy and planning team will be more effective if they leverage and engage other teams within the organization.

This will mean the people leading this team should be able to thrive on cross-functional collaboration. As one might imagine, the more the team interacts with others and proves its efficacy, the less likely others will be able to view it as "overhead."

Human Resources and Legal

Over time, the human resources department has become, perhaps, one of the least evolved groups in any organization. In most organizations that I visit, they are relatively "passive"—they come into the picture only when a group has an opening.

What more active role should they be playing? Well, in my opinion, they should position themselves as a "business partner"—one that will help the business succeed. After all, to say that HR is less evolved does not imply that they are not in a position to evolve; these are highly-trained individuals with a variety of expertise to offer the company.

Okay, what does this entail? This means that they need to partner with the business to identify and work on the following questions:

- ❑ Do we have the right leadership and teams with the right competency?

- ❑ How do the changes in vision and strategy impact the competency?

- ❑ What new skills and competencies are expected of the employees?

- ❑ What should the change management strategy and roadmap look like for the entire organization? (HR needs to work with management)

- ❑ What new training programs need to be in place to get the employees to the desired state?

- ❑ How and from where should we find top talent?

- ❑ Actively network through social media and identify and maintain relationships with top talent in the industry—even if there are no positions currently open.

- ❑ What changes in behavior are required in the company to achieve the new vision?

- ❑ What change management strategies need to be put in place?

- ❑ Develop MBOs (or similar best practices) and align them to key execution of key objectives/success metrics.

- ❑ Keep an eye out on the competition—for example, finding job openings on competitors' websites may shed light on their direction and overall strategy.

- ❑ Sharing this level of information with businesses can be invaluable.

❏ Develop and nurture a group of change agents throughout the company that can help make major cultural or behavior changes—in other words, help manage change.

With respect to legal function, in the new organization the legal department needs to work on a lightweight yet effective "social media governance model." The idea is to come up with some key "enforceable" policies for how employees engage and use social media—what type of information can be shared and what should not be shared.

Again, just developing these policies won't help—adoption is key to success. Don't put policies in place that are not enforceable or too complicated. Whatever you do, don't discourage social media interaction. In fact, we need employees to promote products/services—but not at the expense of sharing valuable intellectual property.

Finance

Finance can play a very critical role in helping companies focus on what is important. They often have a wealth of information that is under-leveraged. For example, product management can work with the finance teams to help calculate product costs, craft financial "what-if" scenarios, detail breakeven analysis, and even price products.

Similarly, other groups can benefit from their expertise as well. I encourage finance teams to open up and engage with other teams in a more collaborative style. They need to demonstrate more value than just number crunching. An appropriately designed MBO can encourage them to do so.

Quality

Let us pause here to discuss the irony of having a "separate department" devoted solely to quality. I have never understood why many organizations have "quality" as a separate group, especially since there are quality elements in every function or group within the organization. Worse yet, if you have this separate department define the overall "quality," it dilutes the accountability of each of the departments to proactively do their bit.

Everyone has a role to play when it comes to quality. Hence, in my honest opinion, this should be a cross-functional team in the form of a board or council that should promote quality in every department. Having a separate department for quality gives the subconscious notion that quality is only important to that department. It also implies that not every department needs to have quality assurance, as it will all get "cleaned up later in quality." Quality should be a part of every department, in every company, and if it isn't, no separate department can help.

Governance Models

Depending on the size of the organization, complexity of products/services, geographies covered, and culture of the organization, decision-making becomes more and more challenging. With most organizations working in a matrixed environment these days, having a well-defined governance model becomes a pre-requisite for efficient and effective operations. So the question we need to answer becomes: How do we make decisions across the organization so we can all contribute to building the best products for our customers and in turn add shareholder value?

Some companies, like Cisco, have boards and councils to help make these decisions. Of course, these councils are only as good as the people running them. If you have a cross-functional team of leaders working together to make decisions, you need to have a structure in place that will allow for effective monitoring and decision-making. Here are some of the questions you need to answer before that happens:

- ❑ What is the (primary and secondary) purpose of the board/council?
- ❑ What kind of decisions get made by this body?
- ❑ Who gets impacted by decisions made in this board/council?
- ❑ What roles in the organization need to be in the board/council?
- ❑ How does the information flow into the body?
- ❑ How do the decisions that get made get communicated?
- ❑ How frequently does the board/council meet?

❑   How are the meetings facilitated?

Change Management and Communication

Communication is key to succeeding when it comes to transforming key functions in your organization. The importance of objective-based communication can't be stressed enough. In other words, when communicating with each other, teams need to be cognizant of their recipients' needs.

Marketing needs to know how sales is going to interpret their new campaign, rather than just creating a clever campaign for cleverness' sake. Likewise, sales needs to communicate challenges with marketing to help begin the new campaign on the right foot.

Relevance is key for effective communications. If what you are communicating is not of any relevance to the recipient, you will not be able to engage them in a way you would like to. Hence it is critical to tie your communication to the recipient's key objectives. Take the time to understand their key objectives and make the connection.

People are busier and time is more valuable than ever. With multiple active communication threads across multiple groups within the organization, it just gets more and more difficult to schedule, reschedule, postpone, and re-postpone and have follow up meetings over and over again. One way to facilitate communication is to encourage each group to build and actively participate in group- or department-level wikis and blogs, v-logs, etc. This allows any team in any department to see what any other team is doing.

It is also a fun and creative way for teams to communicate with each other, particularly younger hires that have grown up communicating this way. Try this out and you will see how this drastically reduces the time you spend in meetings while significantly increasing cross-functional collaboration. For those of you who think putting together an internal site with these features costs a lot of money, think again. There are readymade website templates from companies, like Wordpress (www.wordpress.org) and Joomla (www.joomla.com), that are cost-effective, user-friendly, and quick to build.

Collaboration is hard to come by; this we know. So how do we encourage people to collaborate more often, and make it more fun? One way is to have cross-functional team contests that encourage collaboration. Teams can work together in concert to win a joint goal, such as tickets to a sporting event, a paid holiday, or other perks. This encourages collaboration. It is also important to switch the teams up regularly so that every team has the opportunity to work with every other team and truly promote the idea of cross-communication.

There's no reason communication can't be fun. In fact, the more enjoyable it is, the more often it will happen! To that end, consider having brown bag sessions to encourage employees to share their area of expertise with everyone. These don't have to be every day, or even every week, but should be regular happenings in an informal setting where folks from different teams can really learn from and experience sharing with each other.

When discussing the importance of collaboration with executives and middle management of organizations, I am often asked how to balance engagement through collaboration and coaching versus command and control. This is a very good question. Illustration 9.7 illustrates how to do the balancing act throughout the journey from vision to execution. You will notice that you engage people in the cycle up front and in a collaborative manner; and once joint decisions are made, you move into command and control mode for those aspects. It is important to make sure everyone in the organization understands this.

Finally, consider leveraging "change ambassadors" to manage change. If they are not change management experts, they can get guidance from the "change management lead" (identified up front for the entire organization). Also, the "change management lead" choreographs "change" across the entire organization through the help of the "change ambassadors."

Illustration 9.7: Collaboration vs. Command Control

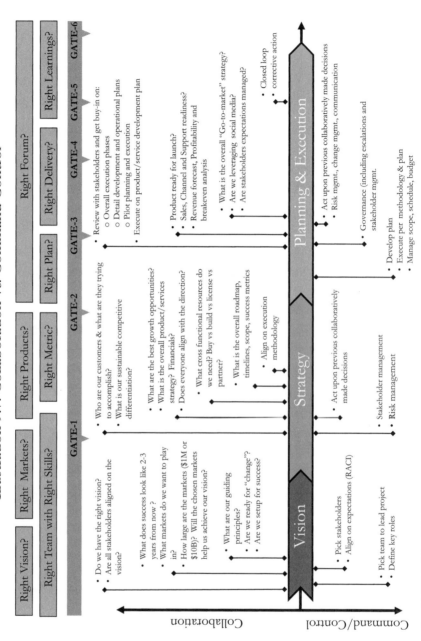

Case Study: High-Engagement Model in Action

"Tom" was the CEO of a mid-sized manufacturer of industrial-grade motors. Recently, Tom invited me to assist him with his company's transformation effort—specifically, the transformation of his company's culture and people's behavior in that culture. Tom had hired some of the best people in the industry and hoped that this elite "team" might collaborate with much effectiveness. Instead, the concept of teamwork seemed to be a foreign one to these high-performers. Now each of the separate groups, like marketing, sales, product management, manufacturing, purchasing, etc., worked in silos with little cross-collaboration.

I was told that in the past Tom had tried numerous tactics and even brought in outside consultants to help make these teams collaborate better, but until now all such efforts had been in vain. I have seen this to be a common problem in many companies. Solving this problem is not easy and it does take time. We are talking about a major shift in culture here, one that involves the entire company. Before agreeing to work on this project, I made sure that Tom was genuinely committed to removing these silos and promoting cross-collaboration among his various high-performing teams.

Once I was convinced that Tom was on board, I next reached out to each of the groups or department leaders to get a feel for whether or not they saw the "problem" and how receptive of "change" they would be.

In this case, the people I spoke to shared their opinions candidly. I later facilitated a group or department-level, all-hands meeting without the respective leaders in attendance. This idea was to probe deeper into the organization in such a way as the participants didn't feel "allegiance" to a certain leader and thus hold their tongue. What I found was amazing.

Once I had all the data, I summarized the findings, and then shared the findings with Tom. Once Tom understood the level of change needed for his transformation to be successful, it was time for me to share the findings with everyone in the organization. I didn't want to just share the findings with those in some briefing or inch-thick report. Instead, I wanted them to be aware and actively acknowledge the problem. To make it less daunting, I wanted to do this in a fun sort of way.

So here is what I did: I picked a few smart people from each of the groups and invited them to a meeting. I explained the concept of role-playing and asked them if they would be willing to participate—everyone showed interest; good news so far!

Next I asked them to exchange their roles with people in other groups that they would like most to communicate with. In other words, one person in marketing plays the role of a sales person while the other marketing person played the role of a product management person and so on. Likewise, the sales people played the role of marketing and support, etc. (Are you with me so far?)

These are the people who actively felt the pain of collaborating with each other, so they were all keen in demonstrating the behavior of other groups (not specific people, mind you). Once the roles were finalized, I shared the findings with them—which they acknowledged were spot on!

I gave them a day to come up with the script (for the skit) on their own and requested them not to share it with anyone yet. Here were the top four reasons why the teams in this case were not collaborating (in no particular order):

1. The company never operated in an "end-to-end value chain" fashion. Each team was measured on just their deliverables—they were not responsible for each other's success. Once done, they would toss their work "over the wall" for other teams to work on. (Does this sound familiar?)

2. Whatever little cross-communication happened, it was not based on mutual objectives. In other words, the initiator

never took the time to tailor and tie the communication to the recipient group's core objectives. So since the content was not relevant, the recipient groups really did not care about the messaging.

3. Over time there was loss of trust amongst the leadership team. This trend showed itself in the meetings that their teams were in. This behavior hence trickled down; they felt that they had their boss's permission to speak out against other teams in the open.

4. Since there was no formal engagement or governance model, leadership teams and their respective organizations made decisions without realizing the impact up and down streams. As a result, people were frustrated with the impact these unilateral decisions had on their work. Over time, this led to distrust and territorialism.

An all-hands style meeting was arranged for the next day; the plan was to have the teams enact their skits. I was stunned by how realistic they played the roles of each other. They were similarly stunned by how much each of them learned about the other through this exercise. The interesting thing was they introduced humor into it to make it very entertaining.

At the end of the all-hands meeting, Tom and I facilitated an interactive session where the teams got a chance to share their thoughts and views. Most commented to the effect of: "We know we are in this mess, but how can we correct it?"

"Halleluiah," I said to myself. "Finally I have been able to move them from an awareness state to understanding state (See Illustration 4.11)." Now, it would have been easy for me to come up with a solution to recommend, but I wanted to take this up a notch and move them to the "desire" state. I gave each of them the exercise of coming up with solutions in a couple of day's time. I shared with them that Tom might be giving out prizes for those who come up with great suggestions. There was enough motivation/incentive for the teams to think.

The next day the teams were back with a lot of suggestions, and I had quite a few of my own as well. In the end, we reviewed and prioritized the list based on size of impact, time to resolve, etc. Even though there were some skeptics, most people had moved to the buy-in state. Here are just a few novel ideas that made it to the list as a result of this exercise:

Make core objectives transparent; make sure each group's objectives tie to the overall vision and strategy of the company. This will help everyone engage each other in a more productive fashion (relevance-based communication).

Take the time to map out end-to-end value chains and understand the roles and accountability of each of the groups (use SIPOCs and RACIs, where necessary).

Put in place a lightweight governance model and communicate it to everyone. There were posters pinned on the walls that depicted the model. Employees did not have to second-guess how decisions were being made any more. Similar engagement models were shared on how each group would engage with each other.

Use interactive communication tools. To increase transparency, blogs and wikis (at group, function, and department levels) were created so anyone interested could go in and get more information on what the other groups were doing and perhaps even get answers to questions via blogs, as opposed to having multiple meetings with multiple people just to find the right person who could answer the questions.

Introduce brown-bag lunch sessions where specific topics would be chosen to help educate the entire organization about what each of the teams were working on and the challenges. This helped the teams appreciate each other's challenges and issues in each group and helped appreciate their point of view.

Offer incentives. Each team voted for the collaborative team awards in various categories. The prize? Well, let's say I had convinced Tom to buy a few weeks of time-share for employees! Everyone loved the idea, to say the least, since they could choose the destination of their choice. Furthermore, at the leadership level, each executive had bonuses aligned to supporting each other (through MBOs, etc.).

Encourage cross-team interaction. In an attempt for the teams to get to know each other better, it was recommended to start private-interest groups (leveraging social media) where people who had common interests like music, photography, art, wine, sports, etc., got together. The "common thread" helped bring many of them closer. People like to be appreciated for their talents outside work. Research has shown that this level of engagement builds trust. Their art was displayed in the front lobby, music played in break rooms, etc., so there was appreciation. There were articles written on an employee (internal) website that highlighted their charitable work, etc. Furthermore, the organization encouraged employees to "rotate" among different groups. This allowed for cross-pollination of talent (and respect).

Fortunately, this story has a happy ending. Almost a year later an employee survey was done and the results were clearly much better. The employee morale was way higher, with a mean value of nine out of ten (ten being the highest), and as a result the teams were more productive.

The results showed in the profit margin as well. The company, which was otherwise almost stagnant in the past, grew by over 50% in revenues and profits within one year of transformation. Needless to say, the teams had moved over time to the committed state. As a result, Tom was extremely happy with the transformation, and so were all of the employees.

Lap 9 Key Takeaways

❑ So far we have crafted the "new" vision, designed an organization structure to align with the vision, chosen competent leaders to lead the respective organizations, and transformed our products/services. Now, we will be taking each of the functions/groups through a mini-transformational journey of their own. This effort will be led by the "new" leaders of each group.

❑ Make a genuine attempt to understand and internalize the functional gaps.

❑ The vision, strategy, and objectives we worked on for the entire organization will now be put into action. Illustration 9.1 explains how the objectives should align not just between departments who work closely together but with the overall organization as well.

❑ With the key objectives now identified, it is time to identify objective and operational linkages (see Illustration 9.2). This is done by first listing all of the key groups or departments within your organization (for example, marketing, sales, product management, support, manufacturing, etc.). Ask yourself the question: What information do I have that may be of relevance to each of the other groups? Similarly, what information might the other groups have that might be of relevance for my group? Please do not leave out any of the groups.

❑ Once each group defines this, a group-level engagement model is put together (see Illustration 9.4).

❑ Next, identify and work on the end-to-end processes for the entire organization. This is critical for success. It is highly recommended that people in the core team with process re-engineering or operations management experience take on the task of crafting and mapping the key end-to-end processes for the entire organization, giving a top-down view. Leverage the group-level engagement frameworks provided by each of the groups and fine-tune these as you begin to build the end-to-end map.

❑ Companies with matrix structures should consider boards and councils to help make these decisions. Of course, these councils are only as good as the people running them. If you are having a cross-functional team of leaders working together to make decisions, you need to have a structure in place that will allow for effective monitoring and decision-making.

❑ Relevance is key for effective communications. If what you are communicating is not of any relevance to the recipient, you will not be able to engage that person in a way you would like to. Hence it is critical to tie your communication to the recipient's key objectives. Take the time to understand their key objectives and make the connection.

❑ One way to facilitate communication is to encourage each group to build and actively participate in group- or department-level wikis and blogs, v-logs, etc. This allows any team in any department to see what any other team is doing.

Lap 10

Define Measures and Roadmaps

What gets measured gets done. What gets rewarded gets repeated.

The main goal of this transformation, from the bottom to the top, is now, will be, and always was one very specific thing: success. Being a front runner is all about leading the pack, not racing to catch up or even running in the opposite direction. Accordingly, everything we have done so far will not mean much if we do not have clearly and commonly understood metrics for what that success will look like when we finally get there.

Many of the previous steps work on respective metrics, but this step will pull it all together and highlight all the interdependencies. When we move the needle (key metric) in one part of the organization, what will its impact be in other parts of the organization and vice versa? If not done right, "good" work being done in one part of the organization can be negated by work done by another part of the organization.

This tenth, and final, lap will help you leverage some of the best practices I've developed over the years to help you arrive at key success metrics, and put in place reward systems so people can be rewarded for achieving specific goals assigned to them. Success can be chaotic—and even short-lived—if not managed, measured, and controlled properly. If there are areas where certain solutions that were proposed and being worked on were not working, then go through the steps highlighted in the book to get things back on track. Special attention should be given to high-risk areas.

Being a front runner can be challenging; after all, there is always another company, or companies, nipping at our heels as we lead the pack. Strong employee managers and leadership can help keep us out in the front by continually adopting the ten steps discovered in this book.

The Purpose of Measures and Roadmaps

Every journey needs two things: a measure of how far you want to go and a roadmap to take you there. Our journey of transformation also requires measurements and a roadmap, but is a little more specific. In this lap, we will come away with the following line items:

- ❑ Identify and finalize metrics and related targets and goals
- ❑ Develop a common execution roadmap (capability roadmap)
- ❑ Develop a change management roadmap
- ❑ Develop reward systems

Our Approach to Lap 10

Whenever a CEO or CFO is inevitably asked the question, "How is the company doing?" the answer is usually with reference to the financial state. However, when the same question is asked by the CEO to the line of business and functional leaders there are many aspects that go into the equation, including status of initiatives, processes, etc. It is often not that easy to answer due to the complex set interrelationships and dependencies. So how to answer this question, other than in financial terms? After all, more than mere money goes into a company's success, let alone transformation. Metrics are needed, now more than ever.

If tracked regularly, well-defined metrics can shed valuable insights at all levels within the organization and instill business discipline. If done right, metrics help monitor progress toward goals and expose gaps or issues. It is a feedback mechanism we need in order to keep success, or failure, in check.

Of course, not all metrics are created equal, and the quality of measurement is only as good as the results being measured. If the form of measurement is not well thought-through, it can lead to more confusion and, in fact, even take you down the wrong path. So, before venturing out and putting a measurement system in place, organizations should really understand the following three questions:

1. What should be measured?
2. Why should it be measured?
3. How should it be measured (including frequency)?

The 3 Types of Metrics

Broadly speaking, metrics can be divided into three distinct types:

1. Strategic metrics: Strategic metrics have a direct linkage with the vision and strategy of the overall organization. These are usually what the CEO and CFO of the organization share with the rest of the world. While most of these metrics remain constant, some may change depending on the twelve- to eighteen-month strategy plan. They usually include financial measures as well as high-level, customer-related metrics, such as customer loyalty or retention. They may also include key competitive metrics like market share, etc.

2. Performance or process metrics: Performance or process metrics are metrics that are the next level down, and they are measured value contributions to the strategic results desired. Examples of these include mean time to resolution, time to market, etc.

3. Operational metrics: Operational metrics measure the day-to-day tactical operations of the business. They are specific to a business process and provide insight to rank and files within the organization. Operational metrics include such things as number of support calls (per product, perhaps), number of days in inventory, number of clicks on the website, etc.

Techniques

Over the years there have been many approaches and techniques for measuring business and transformational success shared by many measurement gurus. One of the most famous techniques that many companies still use is the balanced scorecard, developed by Dr. Robert S. Kaplan and David P. Norton.

As discussed in lap five, they published their work in early '90s and published their first book in 1996. Indeed, they had come up with a way to tie all the metrics together.

Thanks to the pioneering work of individuals like Dr. Robert S. Kaplan and David P. Norton, more and more companies are convinced of the need to measure regularly and properly.

While most business owners don't disagree on the need for regular and proper measurement, there still seems to be a decided lack of clarity on what the right metrics are and how to most effectively measure them. To provide clarity around this issue, here are some simple guidelines that you may want to keep in mind when it comes to settling on metrics for your transformational success:

Don't measure everything: Measure only what you care about and, frankly, are actually planning to do something about. Don't measure something for the sake of it or because you have always measured it in the past. If you cannot understand the relationship between what you measure with what you are trying to achieve, then think twice.

Work backward: Start with the desired results and then work your way toward identifying the right measures to get you there. If closely monitored, these will help you get to the outcome you are looking for.

Move the needle: Remember that sometimes you do not have complete control over all the measures. That's fine, as long as you have the ability to influence the "needle" where you want it to go.

Assume that your measures will conflict with each other. Successful leadership is always a balancing act—time to market versus quality to market, cycle time versus quality, profit versus customer value, etc. Management is about balancing the conflicts that are important. So if your measures are not in conflict, you are perhaps missing the key linkages.

Be a change agent: For the company to be really successful, you need every employee to think and act on measurements. It is frankly a "culture shift" in many companies. Sometimes you do have to "sell" the idea if your people are too resistant. If your employees are not big into measurements, bring in some experts to help you "market" the idea through appropriate change-management tactics. Do not move forward without everyone buying into the concept and then understanding the measures that relate to the work they do. Most companies fail because they do not take time for doing this up front; employee engagement can make or break the success of this step.

Corporations do not run on autopilot: Actually, the same can be said for measurements. Don't bother setting up your metrics and measurements if you are not willing to do the ongoing work with rigor and passion.

Make sure your measurements are globally consistent, and yet locally relevant: This applies to global companies. While the metrics have a consistent definition, they should allow for flexibility in setting different targets for different regions. For example, emerging countries may have a lower—or even higher—growth rate than mature countries. This should be tied to the overall strategy, specifically relating to growth.

Root cause analysis: If some of your measurements are not moving as smoothly as you'd like, do a root cause analysis based on data, not on emotions. A Six-Sigma approach of using fish-bone analysis is advisable (shown in earlier laps).

Do not position this as a framework to "hunt" people down: In putting a metrics and measurement system in place, employees may feel quite uncomfortable. They sometimes perceive the exercise to be a finger-pointing effort that might ultimately lead to them losing their job. The executives should take care to position this more as an opportunity for improvement that will be dealt with positive reinforcement. Remember, in many cases the measurements may trend downward due to reasons beyond employees' control. Meetings to monitor measurements should be facilitated with appropriate care. The same goes for how the results are reported.

Collaborate with transparency: You will never achieve your desired goals without a collaborative spirit and a transparent environment. Humility, trust, and listening skills play a key part in achieving quantifiable metrics. Consider informal sessions to share accomplishments, issues, and challenges at multiple levels.

Make it habitual: Measurement is not a tool or a one-time event. Instead, it needs to be a way of life at your company and for your people.

Make it informal: It's easy to get caught up in the data you're collecting at the expense of the people you're collecting it from. To keep your people in perspective, consider informal sessions to share accomplishments, issues, challenges, and dependencies at multiple levels. Keep in mind that not everyone is an expert on measurements, so try to have a small team of support staff to answer any questions people may have.

Measurement ambassadors: Consider identifying "measurement ambassadors" or "metrics ambassadors" who will play the role of subject matter experts, change agents, and risk identifiers throughout this transformational journey.

Do not assume that all executives understand the success map: It is critical that your executives take the time to build the "success map." If they do not understand this valuable tool, there is no way they will be able to share such information with their respective teams. If it does not already exist, plan on developing a leadership team specifically around measurement.

Regularly update models: The success map may uncover some additional linkages amongst various departments (or groups) within the organization. I hence highly encourage you to go back and update the engagement and governance models that were done in lap nine—this is critical.

Your Own Map to Success

Now let's take a look at the success map we started crafting in lap five. In this lap we will work on the next two layers of the success map (see Illustration 10.1). Before getting into the project outcome layer, let's recap what we have done so far so you understand the relevance of this vital step in the process:

In the first level, namely "key success areas," you are trying to highlight the customer's perception of value as seen through the lens of your organization's vision and mission. This should remain constant over (at least) a two- to three-year time horizon.

The next layer defines the critical path to success; i.e., critical areas of improvement to achieve the goals you mention in the first layer (key success areas). These will have a significant impact on the organization's ability to execute its strategy across the entire organization. If we execute

Illustration 10.1: Example QCU Success Map

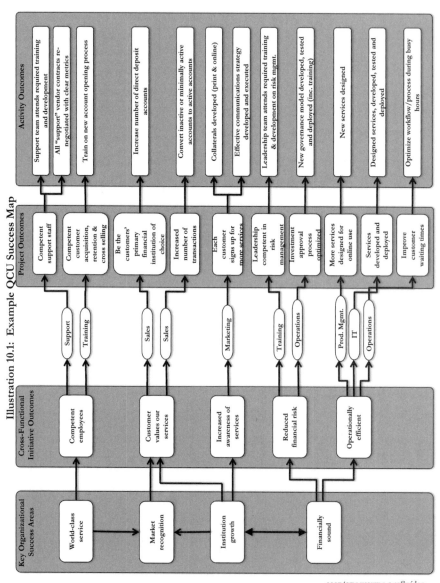

this right, they should change every twelve to eighteen months. Almost all organizations have resource constraints, and obviously there is a need for prioritizing. Leverage the work done in lap five, regarding prioritization. In other words, the most critical ones get done first and then the remaining ones get done as time and resources allow. Some initiatives may span across multiple years. That is fine. In this case, when you revisit assessing the next year's initiatives, review and add the ones that spill over. Do not forget to re-assess the measurements as well.

The next layer in this unfolding process is what I call "project-level outcomes," specifically within each of the groups (or business unit). Based on cross-functional initiative outcomes, the time horizon for these outcomes is usually one fiscal year. Again, given that almost all groups within an organization have resource constraints, there is a need for prioritization around what will (and won't) get done. In this case, as you may expect, all work efforts resulting from the cross-functional initiatives take higher priority.

Let's take a look at what the project-level outcomes are in our QCU example:

Competent employees: There were two specific areas to focus on based on SWOT and customer-survey results. This is what the management team focused on as an outcome for the next twelve months or so:

1. **Competent support staff.** It was determined that there was a need for the customer support team to improve "issue to resolution" speed as well as improve resolution quality. (QCU was currently outsourcing its customer support operations to a company in the Philippines.) This was reflected by a survey at the end of each support call. This will be a project that the support team will initiate and lead.

2. **Competent customer acquisition, retention, and cross-selling.** In this case, change was needed in the areas of customer acquisition, retention, and cross selling, based on customer needs. Since a major component of this was "training" related,

the training team would take on the project of developing the training material and training all customer-facing personnel.

Customers value our service: For this to happen we needed to, for example, be the customers' primary financial institution of choice (such as they choose us to direct deposit their salary checks, open a savings account for overdraft protection, etc.) and encourage them to actively use our services, as seen through an increased number of transactions. Both these projects were led by the sales organization.

Increased awareness of services: Based on a recent voice of the customer survey, it was found that many of QCU's customers were not aware of all the products/services the company offers. Also, internal analysis showed that 61% of customers enrolled in only one or two services, with considerable room to grow. This finding also aligned with the fact that there needed to be "increased competency of employees" at the retail center, as they did not have the right competency to up-sell and cross-sell based on customer needs. QCU wanted to monitor the average number of products enrolled by customers. This can be achieved by initiating and driving successful campaigns, a project that will be led by marketing.

Reduced financial risk: For this to be accomplished, two aspects need to be worked on: first we need to make sure the leadership is competent in managing risks and, second, we need to make sure that there are enough checks and balances in the system. We must also ensure that the investment approval process is optimized. Hence, the training group and operations group, respectively, will initiate and lead projects in these areas.

Operationally efficient: QCU has grown over the years. As a result, the number of customers coming into the retail centers has increased, despite the number of staff being the same. The company was considering leveraging and investing into technology to allow customers to do most of their transactions online. Many aspects of the operations were online already, but there were still some that were not. This led to customers driving over to the retail center. Also, the ATMs needed to be upgraded to incorporate new features. As a long-term goal, these did help improve the bottom line. Product management will initiate projects to define and design more offerings offline while IT will initiate projects to develop and deploy them.

They will also collaborate to see how they can leverage technology to design new offerings online.

Finally, the last column in Illustration 10.1 highlights the activity outcomes that, if accomplished, will help you achieve the project outcomes. As you will notice, these are day-to-day activities. The linkages to project outcomes are as shown in the figure. Keep in mind, however, to highlight the "outcome you are looking for," not just the activities themselves (which serve only the outcomes). This distinction between activities versus outcomes is critical to success.

As you can see, the purpose of the success map is to help you distill your vision and strategy into measureable outcomes and, most importantly, to help each of the groups, departments, or business units understand how they align to the overall strategy.

Linkages drive momentum, so it also helps that all outcomes or "successes" link with each other. What is great about this approach is that the efforts can be measured at multiple levels, from overall organization to groups or departments, down to individual teams, and even to the individuals themselves. The best thing about the process is that it is easy to communicate and, hence, quick to deploy.

What good are measurement systems if they are too complicated to maintain and deploy? This is my philosophy, anyway. Any measurement system that is not easy to communicate, i.e. where people do not understand how their activities contribute to the new strategy, is bound to fail. One key aspect that you may want to keep in mind is that the outcomes you expect should not be vague or too high-level. Instead, they should be more and more specific as you get into the project– and activity-outcome levels. Interdependency, or linkages, among various outcomes at different levels is good; map them. If you have a level of detail regarding each of the linkages, use them in a separate spreadsheet. It will make for a good reference document (see Illustration 10.2).

Once you have completed a map, as seen in Illustration 10.1, take the time to map secondary linkages, as shown in Illustration 10.2. These are cross-linkages that are good to know; they will help you understand the interdependency amongst the various outcomes mapped. To make sure that

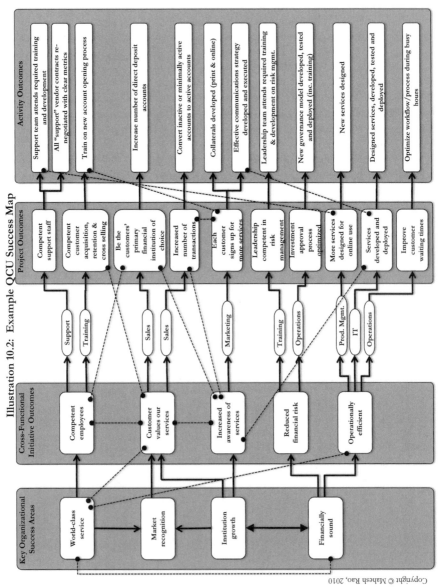

Illustration 10.2: Example QCU Success Map

you catalog all the primary and secondary links, invite the subject matter experts to come in and help draw the linkages.

Once you have the success map architected, the next step is to begin defining the measurements around it. When reaching this stage, I often ask my clients this key question: What is the difference that you are trying to create and, hence, want to monitor using the measure?

Make sure that this is something tangible. Don't make it too complicated or ethereal; simplicity is key. Making it too complicated will make the initiative difficult to communicate and, perhaps, even measure. Avoid using jargon or buzz words; even if it makes perfect sense to you and the "in crowd," it can be confusing and even misleading to the rank and file. Always keep the big picture in mind. Don't forget to test your logic to see how the metric would show up if the organization deviates from the desired result. You need to do this for each metric at each of the levels.

Sometimes you may mistake "activity" to be a measure; be aware and mindful of the difference between busy work and actual progress. What we are looking for here is the measure, not just "activity." For example: "Develop successful campaigns" is an activity—and a worthy one. However, the outcome you *really* desire is that more people sign up for multiple services. This is the level of thinking we need to have if this measure is to succeed.

Matching the Metrics

The next key step is to identify the right metric for each of the outcomes you have highlighted in Illustration 10.3. This table forces you to identify and define the measures based on your success map. If you follow across the map, you can see ample spaces to describe both the metric and its purpose.

You can then provide various linkages and detail a reporting approach to assess your progress. Doing this as a team exercise will help you hear "from other lands" and positively influence the well-roundedness of the metrics and measurements you're taking. Attendees should include: department or group leaders, subject matter experts, CFO or controller, HR representative, and measurement agents.

It is important to give "ownership" of this metric to a specific individual or group, such as "David from marketing" or, simply "Marketing Team 1."

Illustration 10.3: Table for Metrics and Measurements

Metric Level	Metric Name	Description	Purpose	Linkages	Calculation	Reporting Approach	Target	Goal	Owner	Notes
Key organizational success area measures	Metric #1									
	Metric #2									
Cross-functional initiative outcome measures	Metric #3									
	Metric #4									
Department-level project outcome measures	Metric #5									
Activity-level outcome measures										

To provide the most benefit from this measure, make sure the metrics are clearly defined and easy to understand.

The next critical step, once you have the metrics defined, is to define goals and targets. Many of my clients often get a little confused between "goals" and "targets." Let me see if I can help clarify: A "target" is the ultimate destination you want to reach or work toward, in other words, where you want to be two to three years out.

"Goals," on the other hand, are milestones that you want to reach along the way; milestones that will help you reach your target. So, in short, a specific target often has multiple goals, each of them getting you closer and closer to the final destination (i.e., to your target).

Once this is all done, facilitate a session to map the "unified execution roadmap," as shown in Illustration 10.4. This is similar to a conductor leading a symphony. In other words, here is where the single notes, players, and instruments coalesce into an audible result. So this roadmap shows you how all the critical projects tie together and support the organization's key initiatives—you can color code each of the initiatives.

You will notice how multiple groups may have a role to play in making the overall initiative successful. Each group works on its part through programs, projects, and activities. Don't forget to draw out the interdependencies amongst the various initiatives, programs, and projects.

For the purpose of the roadmap, mention only the desired outcome in each chevron. Make sure that you capture all the major project tracks that are mentioned in the department (group) plan (as discussed in lap nine). Likewise, if there are new projects/tracks that are initiated as a result of the success map they need to be added to the department/group-level plans.

At this point you have a draft. Make sure to call it as such before you share it with a wider audience. Engage the department heads, subject matter experts, "metrics ambassadors," initiative leaders, key program/project managers, finance representatives, HR representative, etc., to participate in crafting the final map. This is the best way to get them engaged and, more importantly, buy into the map and the delivery.

It is important that the hard work you've done building your strategy map, metrics, target, goals, and common execution roadmap not be enjoyed in private. For more reasons than mere publicity, communicating this

Illustration 10.4: Unified Execution Roadmap

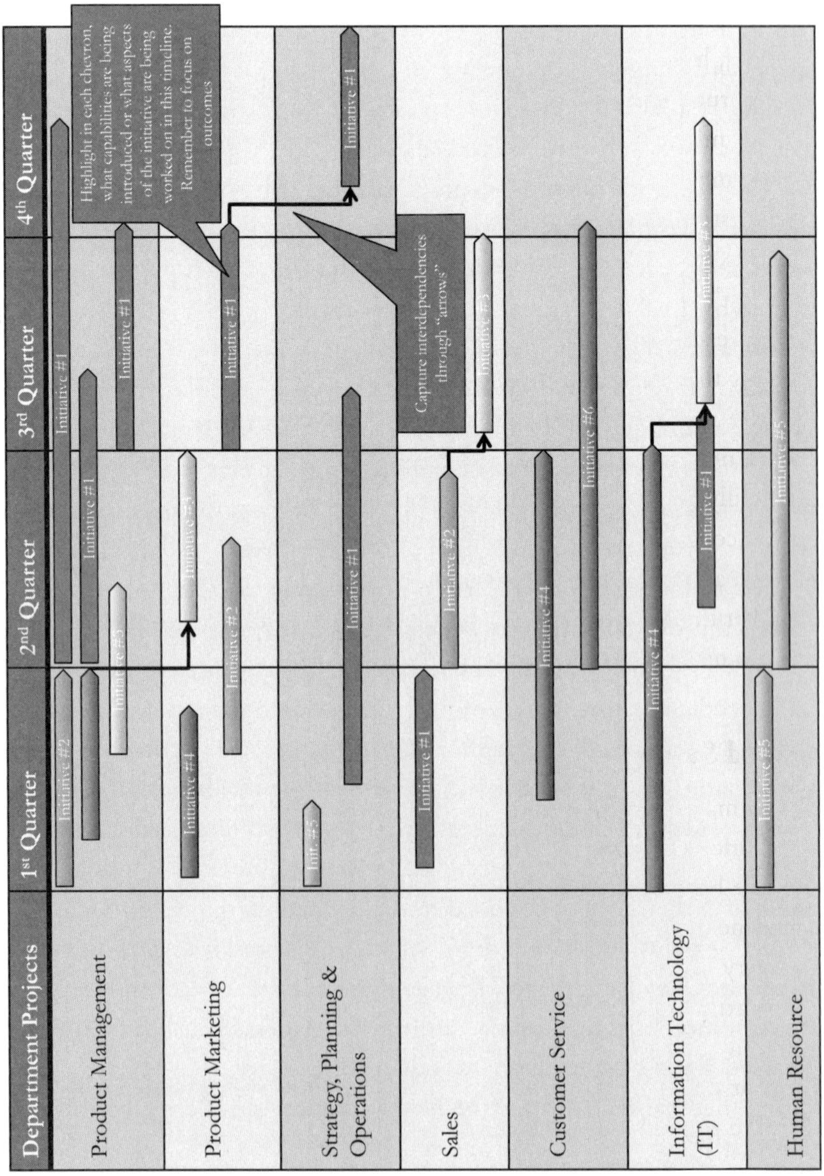

"event" to everyone in the entire organization is very important, not only to its success but yours.

Once the table is filled in, facilitate a "break the model" session with the above group (similar to the one we discussed earlier, in lap six). As a reminder, have a moderator facilitate a meeting in which several teams try to "deconstruct" the strategy map you've just built.

You might want to create small teams for this exercise. Once formed, have them play "devil's advocate." Each team should try to "break the model" by suggesting various weak points—where it might be vulnerable to various pressures, unforeseen circumstances, or climate changes. This will help you "road test" the "road map" and make it stronger as a result of this exercise.

Make sure to define a mechanism where the same team gets back again in about thirty to sixty days to take a look at the reports and further fine-tune the metrics, targets, and goals. Don't forget to have a well-defined governance structure that will help you continue to meet your goals (eventually helping you reach you final destination).

I encourage you to fine-tune the governance model you put together in lap nine, as appropriate. Department or group leaders should be on the hook to deliver the plan and should meet weekly or biweekly with their respective teams to make sure they are on course.

Reward Systems

As you may have seen from the success map exercise, it takes the entire organization's effort to make a company successful. With the help of a success map, we have been able to highlight the contribution each of the groups (departments) makes in achieving the overall vision.

Every organization has different definitions of success. In order for the organization to perform, employees need a clear view of what "success" means in their organization—in terms of the overall organization, at the group or department level, and the individual level. Employee buy-in is critical to the success of this lap.

It is important that employees understand the business strategy and how their work contributes to it. The success map (above) helps you with this. However, understanding the vision, strategy, objectives, targets, and goals is usually not enough to shape the behavior that will ultimately define success.

Even when they have been made aware of the change initiative and resulting "road map," there is no guarantee that employees will use their skills, knowledge, and capabilities for the good of the organization. How people are measured and rewarded will influence how they carry out their work each day. This fact necessitates the challenge of designing measurements and reward systems to motivate and reinforce the behaviors that add value to the organization.

Once you have defined the metrics, goals, and target(s), you need to highlight desired values and behaviors that are required to not only produce desired business results but also reflect organizational values. Then comes compensation, rewards, and recognition—these are meant to recognize a person's past contribution as well as motivate continued or improved performance. This should also include a non-monetary component that complements the compensation system to let employees know that they are valued.

Use success maps to help define these at multiple levels—hold executives accountable for achieving key success areas. The departmental (group) leads should be held accountable for the cross-functional initiatives. This can be tricky; there sometimes may be pushback from leaders, as they may hesitate signing up for something that they may not have direct control over.

It is important for the organization to hold departmental (group) leaders accountable for each other's success. This will promote the spirit of collaboration and support amongst various departments. The teams in each of the departments should be held accountable for the project outcomes, and appropriate individuals should be held accountable for the day-to-day activities.

Consider crafting MBOs (management by objectives) for all the key executives all the way down to managers. MBOs are a form of "participatory goal setting," where management and employees meet and agree upon objectives that will help reach a goal. Rather than "managing by dictating," MBOs help employees feel ownership of both the process and their responsibilities for reaching the goal. Consider designing a "bonus" reward program for those who achieve the objectives.

If this system is not already in place at your company, it may take some effort in putting this together; consult with the HR team within your organization to assist with this. If they do not have the expertise to tackle it themselves, consider bringing in a consultant to help craft this worthwhile management system.

Reward systems define expected behaviors and influence the likelihood that people will demonstrate those behaviors. They ensure that everyone is headed in the same direction. A well-aligned reward system reduces competition and the frustration of working together in a competitive environment.

Behaviors are often an overlooked component of defining and rewarding success. Behaviors do not get explicitly defined enough in most companies. By ignoring this critical aspect of success, people do not have an aligned understanding of the behaviors they are expected to exhibit. It's a little like expecting someone used to eating with their hands to know which is the salad fork and which is the fork for the main course; addressing behavior helps give employees guardrails for what's acceptable and what isn't.

Unfortunately, vision and value statements have become something of a cliché. But if you have followed lap five closely, there is a good chance you have a clearly articulated vision and values message that the company is now familiar with. The idea is to take these and translate them into a kind of "corporate compass" that guides employee behavior.

In the early 1980s, Johnson & Johnson ran into a situation where several people died due to cyanide-laced Tylenol capsules. Management made the decision to halt production and pull out every single bottle on the shelf as a precautionary measure. The employees acted in harmony without large meetings telling them how to act. Instead, they acted based on the deep-rooted values system that the company had built over the years.

In contrast, Toyota took considerable time to act upon a mechanical/electronic malfunction issue despite many reported deaths. What does this say about the deep-rooted values of the organization as a whole?

In deriving behaviors from values, the organization needs to take the time to identify the behavior that might demonstrate the value. For instance, how far are sales people allowed to go to close a sale? While taking clients to the golf course might be acceptable, is taking them to a gentleman's club equally acceptable?

A clearly held value (sell the product in a business setting) will help drive the behavior. For example, sales meetings will be held in acceptable business establishments; i.e., restaurants, coffee shops, golf courses, etc. It might help to think in terms of cause and effect as you create the values. In other words, "What behaviors will this value cause?" Other causal values and effects might include:

> **Value**: "We value our customer's safety over bottom-line profits."
>
> **Behavior**: "We will recall items immediately if anyone is hurt by one of our products."
>
> **Value**: "We value our employees and their accumulated experiences."
>
> **Behavior**: "We will make every attempt to hire from within if the candidate meets the job requirements." See Illustration 10.5 for more examples.

Do you remember the "personal development roadmap" highlighted in lap seven? This is the time to think through an overall strategy on how to reward employees who are making progress on this front, reward people who undergo the recommended training, and make strides to improve in the areas identified. Incorporate a personal development roadmap as part of the MBO (appraisal).

Here are some overall suggestions for providing reward systems in a variety of ways for a variety of employees on a variety of levels:

Make everyone in the company eligible. I recommend even long-term temps and contractors to join as well. Do not exclude executives. Why should they be excluded?

Reward high performers as well as those who are making progress. "Success" is a subjective term, and someone who is making progress succeeds in more ways than one.

Create a team-based goal. Not only will this be an exercise in team-building, but the high performers in the team will coach the others so as to reach the goal, thus promoting collaboration.

Illustration 10.5: Translating Values to Behaviors

	Behavior Externally (Customers/Partners)	Behavior Internally (Managers, Peers and Employees)
Value: Customer-focus		
Meet	Works closely with customers and takes their requests through closure. Keeps customer in the loop on progress	Assess and analyze all work from client perspective. Prioritizes all such client activities over other activities
Exceed	Proactively identifies problem areas (pattern) and takes the initiative to resolve them	Takes proactive interest in working across departmental boundaries to resolve issues. Takes them through closure. Closes loop with customers as appropriate
Value: Strong focus and commitment to success		
Meet	Having an active feedback loop from customer on how we are doing	Focus on the outcome through well thought through planning
Exceed	Developing key metrics that align with customers' needs. Monitoring and executing towards organization's targets and goals	Takes ownership for identifying the right metrics, targets and goals. Engages with the necessary entities in rallying around the common goal.

Reward all successes, big and small: Don't just pull out the stops for major accomplishments. Reward small accomplishments along the way with movie tickets or a dinner for two. Consider giving rewards for short-term, mid-term, and long-term efforts and accomplishments.

Take a vote: Make each team vote for teams that collaborated with them the best, allowing them (the larger group) to achieve their goal. Present joint awards when appropriate.

Include your customers: Consider sponsoring customers to vote for the best customer-facing team. This helps develop rapport and lets them bond with each other, allowing for further trust-building between employees and customers.

360° awards: Consider offering peer-to-peer awards, employee-to-manager awards, as well as top-down awards.

Consider rewarding successful initiatives and projects: This way, everyone on the team automatically gets recognized. This is an ideal—and quite direct—way to recognize results.

Make the reward system easy to administer. Don't bog down an otherwise worthwhile initiative with needless rules and sub-rules. Less is more when it comes to a system, not the rewards themselves.

Fair is fair: Finally, make sure that employees get the perception that reward decisions are made fairly. Playing favorites or repeatedly rewarding the same people or departments again and again sends the wrong message and can actually be counterproductive. Everyone should feel that they have a chance to win, regardless of the position or function. Rewards should be based on results and, to some degree, effort.

Change Management and Communication

If they really looked closer, most businesses would likely find that they have very weak internal communications mechanisms. Specifically, they have several employees focusing on external communications, but they pay little to no attention to internal communications. This is the weakest link in most organizations, in my opinion.

While external communications are obviously quite valuable, there are a number of factors that make internal communication equally valuable, such as making sure all employees know of change initiatives, new product rollouts, mergers and acquisitions, etc. What good does it do any company to keep employees in the dark when it is so simple—and valuable—to be transparent?

Communication is vital to the success of this process. It is important to build a communication plan around metrics and measurements; they need to be well understood by everyone. Your people should know how their work connects to the success of the company.

Regularly communicating departmental and organizational progress will ensure continued motivation among "the troops" and ensure authentic transparency throughout the transformational progress. As shared earlier, consider identifying "measurement ambassadors" who play the role of subject matter experts, change agents, and risk identifiers throughout the journey. Here, the change ambassador's job is to make sure the change sticks and is deeply embedded into the DNA of the organization they represent.

Spreading the Wealth: Town-Hall Style

It is important that the hard work you've done to build your strategy map, metrics, target, goals, and common execution roadmap is not enjoyed in private. For more reasons than mere publicity, communicating this "event" to everyone in the entire organization is very important, and not only to its success but yours.

Finally, it's time for the "big reveal" to the company as a whole. I suggest a "town hall" meeting to share the following:

- ❑ Strategy map and/or success map
- ❑ Metrics, target, and goals
- ❑ Common execution roadmap

In this case, you want to assemble the entire company; if you have satellite offices or branches this can be achieved via a Webex or Skype teleconference. This way you can share the above items, with everyone, and make it a real event. (See earlier laps for an effective way to run these meetings.)

When having these meetings, train people based on their personal development roadmaps so that they understand the vital importance of this training style. Also, "weave" the town hall meetings into your personal development style by having this type of meeting on a regular basis, perhaps every quarter or so.

Stress at the meetings that transformation should not be a one-time event. Instead, it should be embedded into the DNA of the organization. Such meetings will help you make change a habitual behavior.

To ensure that employee feedback is vital and accurate, define a mechanism for the employees to share their thoughts/ideas and contribute to the success of the organization. This mechanism can be an internal blog or "suggestion box" and/or point people, in every department, who later report to their leaders.

Finally, before, during, and after such town hall meetings, be sure to enlist one or two measurement ambassadors who can help you keep track of the metrics and measurements you are presenting. Formulas, statistics, even facts and figures can be challenging for some employees, so enlisting measurement ambassadors as point people to handle questions and concerns on an individual basis takes the pressure off of you while still managing the data effectively for 100% of your employees.

Lap 10 Key Takeaways

❑ You cannot achieve what you cannot measure. Without taking your vision and strategy to this level of granularity, you will not be able to measure it. While every lap touches on measurements, lap ten strategically pulls it all together and helps everyone understand the linkages amongst various metrics and measurements.

❑ If tracked regularly, well-defined metrics can shed valuable insights at all levels within the organization and instill business discipline.

❑ If done right, metrics help monitor processes toward goals and expose gaps or issues; it is a feedback mechanism to keep success, or failure, in check.

❑ Broadly speaking, metrics can be divided into three distinct types:

  ❑ **Strategic metrics:** Strategic metrics have a direct linkage with the vision and strategy of the overall organization.

  ❑ **Performance or process metrics:** Performance or process metrics are the next level down and measure value contributions to the strategic results desired.

  ❑ **Operational metrics:** Operational metrics measure the day-to-day tactical operations of the business.

❑ The "success map" helps you distill your vision and strategy into measureable outcomes and, most importantly, helps each of the groups, departments or business units understand how they align to the overall strategy.

❑ Any measurement system that is not easy to communicate—i.e. where people do not understand how or what their contributions do to the new strategy—is bound to fail.

❑ Avoid using jargon or buzz speak; even if it makes perfect sense to you and the "in crowd," it can be confusing and even misleading to the rank and file.

❑ It is important that the hard work you've done building your strategy map, metrics, target and goals, and common execution roadmap not be enjoyed in private. For more reasons than mere publicity, communicating this "event" to everyone in the entire organization is very important, not only to its success but yours.

❑ Every organization has different definitions of success. In order for the organization to perform, employees need a clear view of what "success" means in their organization—in terms of the overall organization, at the group's or department level, as well as at the individual level.

❑ Employee buy-in is critical to the success of this lap.

❑ Once you have defined the metrics, goals, and target, you need to highlight desired values and behaviors that are required to not only produce desired business results but also reflect organizational values.

❑ This is the time to think through an overall strategy on how to reward employees who are making progress on this front. Reward people who undergo the recommended training and make strides to make improvements in areas identified. Incorporate a personal development roadmap as part of the MBO (appraisal).

Conclusion

Congratulations!

Wherever you are on the transformational journey, be it just awareness stage that you need to transform or you have a true "sense of urgency" to change, I applaud you for beginning the process. What's more, you are to be commended for taking the initial step of investing in this book and devoting your time and careful thought to digesting its admittedly challenging content.

As you have seen throughout this book, change can be a long and challenging process; I can't solve all the "pain" of organizational change, but by now you can perhaps see that there IS a system to follow and that by closely aligning yourself with these ten steps you *will* achieve transformation in a logical and orderly fashion.

This isn't paint-by-the-numbers piecework here, so I know you will have questions along the way. That's why I established www.BeFrontRunner.com, the dedicated site specifically for readers of this book.

As someone who has already invested the time and energy to become a front runner, you will receive a discounted membership for access to the website, which provides thoughts, ideas, tools, and templates that can help you further excel at your job regardless of the industry segment or role you play in the organization.

I believe you will find this ongoing support invaluable as you begin, endure, and continue to transform. And I encourage you to send me feedback along the journey. I would love to hear how the transformation is going—good, bad, or indifferent.

Who knows? Perhaps your personal anecdote about a successful business transformation will be used as a case study in the sequel! Regardless, I believe in keeping an open line of communication, and I welcome your comments about the book, the website, or any other piece of transformational subject matter you wish to discuss.

Remember as you begin your journey that change is not something to be feared, but embraced. I know it seems easy to read that in black and white, and yet difficult to tackle here in the real world, but the fact is change is a constant in our operational success. The alternative is failure. Only by embracing change and using it to our advantage will we become front runners in an increasingly challenging and competitive race.

www.FrontRunnersBook.com

Special Access Code: XPY1982693

Glossary

"As Is" State	This is also referred to as the current state in your transformation journey. (Also see "To Be" State.)
B2B	Also known as "business-to-business," this describes commerce transaction between companies.
B2C	Also known as "business-to-consumer," this describes commerce transaction between a business and a consumer.
Business lead	This person is relatively senior in the organization (perhaps a level below the executive sponsor). While the executive sponsor will spearhead the initiative, the business lead will naturally manage the day-to-day operations of the initiative itself. This person plays the role of a strategist and has enough knowledge about the industry to perform duties at the expert level.
Change management	Change management is a structured approach to transitioning individuals, teams, and organizations from a current state to a desired future state.
Closed-loop corrective action	Take the lessons learned from completing a task or a project and feed the information back into the system so as to not make the same mistakes again next time around.

Core team	This is the team that is responsible not only for drafting your transformation charter, but for implementing it; so, naturally, choosing the right people for the right job will be mission critical to the success of this venture.
Engagement model	It is a framework that defines how each of the groups or divisions within an organization work and collaborate with each other.
Ethnography	Ethnography in an art and science that is used in observing a job performer (including customer/ potential customer) in completing his/her JTBD. Data collection is often done through participant observation, interviews, questionnaires, etc. For best results, however, you will need to hire a trained ethnographer due to the discipline associated with collecting qualitative data in the field and accurately analyzing the findings. Experts in this field are highly sought after and can help you in gathering critical data that you would have otherwise missed.
Executive sponsor	This is the person who, at the end of the day, is accountable for the transformation initiative. This individual needs to have the power and authority to be able to drive change. You must select someone who is highly respected at all levels of the organization. This person's commitment in making this initiative a success is very critical and cannot be emphasized enough. When it comes to OE, this critical team member will set the direction for the transformation efforts and will be the go-to person for any critical escalations.

Front runner	Front runner is a term to describe a leader in a race. Front runners are companies with great teams and leaders that thrive on challenge, that see opportunity in crisis and who never, ever avoid change. In fact, they welcome it! These companies are leaders in their industry and are a breed unto themselves. Great teams make great companies, not the other way around.
Functional subject matter experts	These are experts in a specific function or field.
Functional transformation	This is the transformation of a specific function within the company or organization. For example: Marketing, Sales, Product Management, etc.
Gap analysis	Gap analysis is a tool that helps a company to compare its actual performance relative to its vision. At its core are two questions: "Where are we?" and "Where do we want to be?"
Governance model	A framework that defines how decisions are made.
Group or division	It is a business unit within an overall corporate identity.
Influencers	These are people who influence "job performance" in making decisions at appropriate steps leading to accomplishing a JTBD.
Job Performer	A job performer is someone who plays a part in getting the job done (JTBD)

JTBD	Clayton Christensen, a Harvard Professor wrote about the "Job to be Done" (JTBD) concept in the *Sloan Management Review* (Spring 2007), stating, that a customer simply has a job to be done and is seeking to hire the best product or service to do it.
Management by objectives (MBO)	MBO is a process of employer and employee agreeing upon objectives within an organization that the employee is expected to deliver.
Market	Market is defined as a group of people with similar JTBD
Net present value	Net present value (NPV) is defined as the sum of the present values (PVs) of the individual cash flows. In the case of products or services this includes present value of all the cash outflow for the project along with the cash inflow generated through sales.
Opportunity matrix	This is a tool that helps you identify and analyze products versus markets.
Organization	Same as "company."
RACI tool	It is a tool that is used to articulate and clarify roles of individuals or groups in completing a task/activity.
SIPOC tool	It is a Six Sigma tool that stands for supplier, input, process, output, and customer. It helps define how you engage or collaborate among multiple groups.
Strategy	A defined path a company takes to achieve its vision.
Success metric	The metric that defines success.
SWOT analysis	SWOT analysis is a methodology used to evaluate the strengths, weaknesses, opportunities, and threats of a business entity or even a project.

"To Be" State	This is the destination or the desired state you would like to achieve at the end of your transformation journey. (See also "As Is" State.)
Transformation charter	A transformation charter is one that crisply defines the purpose, scope, approach, schedule budget, roles and accountability, engagement model (how the various teams will be engaged on this initiative), governance model (how decisions get made), etc., for the transformation initiative/project.
Voice of customer (VOC)	The "voice of the customer" (VOC) is the term to describe the stated and unstated customer needs or requirements. The voice of the customer can be captured in a variety of ways: direct discussion or interviews, surveys, focus groups, customer specifications, observation, warranty data, field reports, etc.
Voice of employees (VOE)	VOE refers to the participation of employees in influencing corporate decision-making and better understanding their perception of key issues/challenges. Employees are given a voice through informal and formal means to minimize conflict, improve communication, and encourage staff retention.
Voice of stakeholders (VOS)	VOS refers to feedback given by stakeholders of the project on a specific topic within the organization so as to influence the decision.

Resources

Buckingham, Marcus and Curt Coffman. *First, Break all the Rules: What the World's Greatest Managers Do Differently*, Simon & Schuster, May 1999.

Cagan, Marty. *Inspired: How To Create Products Customers Love*, SVPG Press, 2008.

Career One Stop. www.CareerOneStop.org, US Department of Labor, Employment and Training Administration: www.careeronestop.org/competencymodel/pyramid_definition.aspx.

Christensen, Clayton, and coauthors. "Job to be Done," *Sloan Management Review* (Spring 2007).

Christensen, Clayton. *The Innovator's Dilemma: The Revolutionary Book that Will Change the Way You Do Business*, Harper Paperbacks, January 2003.

Christensen, Clayton, Stephen P. Kaufman, and Willy C. Shih. *Innovation Killers: How Financial Tools Destroy Your Capacity to Do New Things*, Harvard Business Press, July 2010, (adapted information for Illustration 4.10 DCF).

Dun & Bradstreet survey quote, http://www.associatedcontent.com/article/2079557/top_10_reasons_why_businesses_close.html?cat=3, pg 7.

Galbraith, Jay, Diane Downey and Amy Kates. *Designing Dynamic Organizations,* AMACOM, 2002.

Halligan, Brian and Dharmesh Shah. *Inbound Marketing, Get found using Google, Social Media and Blogs,* John Wiley & Sons, 2010.

Ishikawa, Kaoru, translated by D.J. Lu. *What is Total Quality Control? The Japanese Way,* Englewood Cliffs, NJ: Prentice Hall, March1985 (Ishikawa Diagrams).

Juglar, Dr. Clement. *Business Cycle (page 307) - Des Crises Commerciales et de leur Retour Périodique en France, en Angleterre et aux États-Unis,* Nabu Press, March 2010, (originally published in 1862, and very much revised and enlarged in 1889).

Kaplan, Robert S., and David P. Norton, *The Balanced Scorecard: Translating Strategy into Action,* Harvard Business Press, 1996 (Developed the Balanced Scorecard).

Kotter, John. *A Sense Of Urgency,* Harvard Business Press, 2008

Kotter, John. *Leading Change,* Harvard Business Press, 1999.

Tim Calkins. *Breakthrough Marketing Plans,* Palgrave Macmillan, 2008.

Tucker, R.B. *Driving Growth Through Innovation,* Berrett-Koehler Publishers, October 2002, (adapted information for Illustration 8.1).

Index